Perspectives on Southern Africa

25. *The Roots of Rural Poverty in Central and Southern Africa*, edited by Robin Palmer and Neil Parsons (1977)

26. *The Soul of Mbira: Music and Traditions of the Shona People of Zimbabwe*, by Paul F. Berliner (1978)

27. *The Darker Reaches of Government: Access to Information about Public Administration in the United States, Britain, and South Africa*, by Anthony S. Mathews (1979)

28. *The Rise and Fall of the South African Peasantry*, by Colin Bundy (1979)

29. *South Africa: Time Running Out. The Report of the Study Commission on U.S. Policy Toward Southern Africa* (1981; reprinted with a new preface, 1986)

30. *The Revolt of the Hereros*, by Jon M. Bridgman (1981)

31. *The White Tribe of Africa: South Africa in Perspective*, by David Harrison (1982)

32. *The House of Phalo: A History of the Xhosa People in the Days of Their Independence*, by J. B. Peires (1982)

33. *Soldiers without Politics: Blacks in the South African Armed Forces*, by Kenneth W. Grundy (1983)

34. *Education, Race, and Social Change in South Africa*, by John A. Marcum (1982)

35. *The Land Belongs to Us: The Pedi Polity, the Boers and the British in the Nineteenth-Century Transvaal*, by Peter Delius (1984)

36. *Sol Plaatje, South African Nationalist, 1876–1932*, by Brian Willan (1984)

37. *Peasant Consciousness and Guerrilla War in Zimbabwe: A Comparative Study*, by Terence Ranger (1985)

38. *Guns and Rain: Guerrillas and Spirit Mediums in Zimbabwe*, by David Lan (1985)

39. *South Africa without Apartheid: Dismantling Racial Domination*, by Heribert Adam and Kogila Moodley (1986)

40. *Hidden Struggles in Rural South Africa: Politics and Popular Movements in the Transkei and Eastern Cape, 1890–1930*, by William Beinart and Colin Bundy (1986)

41. *Legitimating the Illegitimate: State, Markets, and Resistance in South Africa*, by Stanley B. Greenberg (1987)

42. *Freedom, State Security, and the Rule of Law: Dilemmas of the Apartheid Society*, by Anthony S. Mathews (1987)

43. *The Creation of Tribalism in Southern Africa*, edited by Leroy Vail (1988)

44. *The Rand at War, 1899–1902: The Witwatersrand and Anglo-Boer War*, by Diana Cammack (1990)

45. *State Politics in Zimbabwe*, by Jeffrey Herbst (1990)

46. *A Democratic South Africa? Constitutional Engineering in a Divided Society*, by Donald L. Horowitz (1991)

47. *A Complicated War: The Harrowing of Mozambique*, by William Finnegan (1992)

A Complicated War

A Complicated War

The Harrowing of Mozambique

William Finnegan

UNIVERSITY OF CALIFORNIA PRESS
BERKELEY LOS ANGELES LONDON

University of California Press
Berkeley and Los Angeles, California

University of California Press, Ltd.
London, England

© 1992 by
The Regents of the University of California

First Paperback Printing 1993

Library of Congress Cataloging-in-Publication Data

Finnegan, William.
   A complicated war: the harrowing of Mozambique / William Finnegan.
      p.   cm.—(Perspectives on Southern Africa; 47)
   Includes bibliographical references and index.
   ISBN 0-520-08266-4
   1. Mozambique—Politics and government—1975–   2. Finnegan.
William—Journeys—Mozambique.   I. Title.   II. Series.
DT3398.F56   1992
967.9—dc20   91-28248
                                                                                    CIP

Printed in the United States of America
1   2   3   4   5   6   7   8   9

Portions of this book originally appeared in *The New Yorker* in 1989,
in slightly different form, as "A Reporter At Large: The Emergency."

To the memory of
José Inácio De Sousa, 1955–1990

Having once been robbed by a
congregation of Christian marauders,
one is not so timorous of the heathen.
David Livingstone, March 2, 1856,
Tete, Mozambique

Contents

Preface

This book began life as a short, unsigned piece for *The New Yorker*. The piece was about the war in Mozambique, and its brisk self-assurance now makes me wince. I had never been to Mozambique, but I had written two books about South Africa and apparently believed I knew enough to write something sharp about Pretoria's destruction of its long-suffering neighbor. Like many foreign observers, I saw Mozambique through a South African lens, expecting to understand the country—and the war—more or less exclusively by way of the apartheid Cyclops next door. It was a naive expectation, and it was shattered by what I saw and heard during the time that I later spent in Mozambique. There is, incidentally, nothing in that initial column that I want to disavow except its certitude. South Africa's domination and destabilization are basic elements of Mozambique's plight. There are many other elements to the war, however, as all Mozambicans know and as I came, disorientingly, to discover.

This is not a work of scholarship, though it relies heavily on the scholarship of others. It is essentially a record of my travels in and around Mozambique, supplemented by additional reporting in Malawi, Zimbabwe, Portugal, England, and the United States. Much of this account first appeared in *The New Yorker*, where it was divided for reasons of space into two freestanding parts. Here, it finds a more natural shape for a travel narrative, with sections denominated by place. These denominations are loose. If a scene I witnessed in Sofala province seems relevant to something in the "Zambézia" section, for instance, that is where it appears. They can also be slightly perverse. For example, the most complete discussion of Frelimo's history and performance occurs in the "Beira" section. Frelimo has always had special problems in Beira. My notion in this case was to provide a critical context—a tough audience, as it were—for the story of Frelimo, which has often been told in a triumphalist key. The arrangement of sections may also seem odd—the decision, for instance, to begin the book in an obscure rural district, with Maputo, the capital city, described only toward the back of the book. My hope in this case was simply to avoid some of the hazards of looking at Mozambique primarily from Maputo, to build up some sense of the country and its particularity before taking on the comfortable, general perspective offered by the capital.

The final chapter brings the story forward to the time of writing—mid-1991—and attempts to deal more broadly and theoretically with some of the main issues raised in the book, including the doctrine of low-intensity warfare, the difficulties of nation-building in Africa, the role of the United States in Mozambique, the regional implications of the crumbling of the apartheid state, the question of social banditry, and peasant millenarianism.

Note to the paperback edition

On October 4, 1992, Joaquim Chissano, the president of Mozambique, and Afonso Dhlakama, the leader of Renamo, signed a peace treaty in Rome. The treaty called for a general ceasefire and for the creation of a new national army composed of equal numbers of rebel and government troops. While it was impossible to say whether the treaty would actually end the war, this was potentially the best news Mozambique had heard in the seventeen years since independence.

Acknowledgments

Many people helped this book come about. Robert Gottlieb, the editor of *The New Yorker*, let me go off to Mozambique. John Bennet performed editorial magic on the original manuscript—which Hal Espen, Eleanor Gould Packard, and Marcia Van Meter also improved. Some of those who helped out during the reporting and writing may now wish they hadn't—they are, of course, in no way responsible for what I've written. In the United States and Canada, I benefited especially from the kindness and expertise of Michael Clough, Robert Gersony, Gillian Gunn, Allen Isaacman, Judith Marshall, António Matonse, David Mesenbring, Bill Minter, Steve Morrison, Dan O'Meara, Stephanie Urdang, Leroy Vail, and Vivienne Walt. In London, I profited from conversations with Stephen Ellis, Joseph Hanlon, and Anthony Sampson; in Lisbon, Dr. António Dias da Cunha and Tomas Viera Mario; in Harare, Steve Askin, Carole Collins, Colin Darch, Karl Maier, Andrew Meldrum, and Mark Rule. From South Africa, Aninka Claassens gave valuable advice, as did Sylvia Vollenhoven. And Robin Hallett kindly helped me keep up with the news from Mozambique. In Mozambique itself, the list of those to whom I owe thanks is exceptionally long. For reasons which will be obvious in the pages that follow, it rightly begins with Lina Magaia and Boaventura das Dividas. I also want to thank Sam Barnes, Julian Baskin, Carlos Carvalho, Simião Cavele, Frances Christie, Iain Christie, Senhora Concenção, Rob Davies, Ann Evans, Polly Gaster, Alves Gomes, Sheila Gothmann, Harlan Hale, Luís Bernardo Honwana, Laila Ismail Khan, Iain Levine, Fernando Lima, Arlindo Lopes, Mota Lopes, Álvaro Mahumane, Mike Mispelaar, Michael Ranneberger, Prakash Ratilal, Martine Relyveld, Herbert Shore, George Tinga, and

Ambassador Melissa Wells. And then there are all the ordinary Mozambicans, some of them severely traumatized, who kindly agreed to talk to me; without their indulgence and courage, I would have had no book to write. My debt to the scholars and journalists who have written about Mozambique should be clear from the notes at the back of this book. Kaye Burnett and Harriet Barlow, of the Blue Mountain Center in upstate New York, provided a refuge when I needed it. My agent, Amanda Urban, did her usual fine job, and Richard Holway, of the University of California Press, was a sympathetic guide for a newcomer to the vagaries of academic publishing. Dorothy Conway was a superb copy editor, and Liesl Schillinger and Michael Finnegan helped out with timely translations. Finally, there was the steady emotional support of my parents, Pat and Bill Finnegan, for yet another dubious venture. And the light at the end of the tunnel was, as ever, Caroline Rule.

A Complicated War

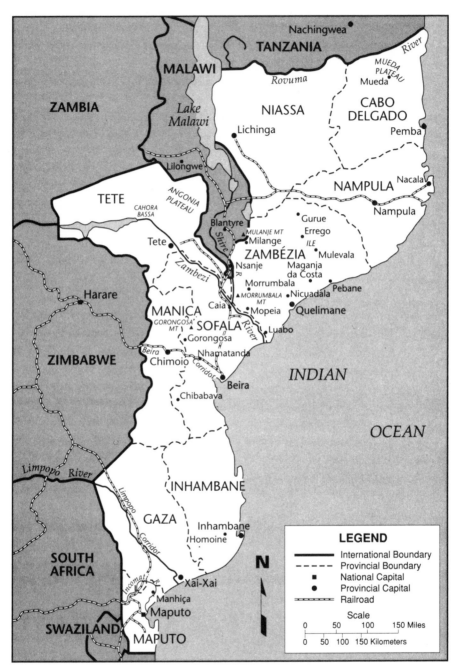

Mozambique

Part One

Zambézia

1

Morrumbala Mountain stands at the crux of the long, languid Y that Mozambique describes along the southeast coast of Africa. The mountain rises nearly 4,000 feet from the broad plains on the left bank of the Zambezi, perhaps 125 miles from the great river's mouth. In the course of two months that I spent traveling around Mozambique in 1988, Morrumbala Mountain became for me a sort of lodestar, a persistent mirage at the heart of the country. I kept seeing it from different angles—first from the west, later from the north, still later from due south. In retrospect, it seemed appropriate that I never actually reached the mountain itself, that I always had to content myself with regarding it from a distance.

The first time I saw Morrumbala Mountain, I was sitting in the remains of a tiny, octagonal waiting room—its brick walls had been reduced by bazooka fire to bench height—alongside a grass airstrip near the southwestern border of the north-central province of Zambézia. It was late afternoon, and the clouds in the west had lifted, revealing the mountain's outline. Along with a couple of hundred other people, I was waiting for a plane. All around us was rolling miombo woodland, lush with acacia, cashew, and mango trees and punctuated here and there by sheer rock outcroppings that burst out of the ground like the bluffs in Chinese ink paintings. A light rain began to fall, and a little girl standing beside me whispered, "Calamidades." She was looking at the sky to the southeast. I looked. I saw nothing.

Then other children began pointing in the same direction, all murmuring, "Calamidades." The little girl glanced at me, then looked away. Around her neck, I noticed, she wore a scrap of red felt on a string. Otherwise, she wore only a faded, shapeless piece of burlap. She was a beautiful child, but desperately thin, and she shivered in the cool rain.

"Calamidades" was Mozambican shorthand for the government's ponderously titled Department for the Prevention and Combat of Natural Calamities. The term had come to refer not only to the department itself but to the food and clothes it distributed, which were undoubtedly what those children at the airstrip were thinking of when, their senses sharpened by hunger, they spotted, or heard, the approaching plane. It was, in fact, bringing food. The natural calamities that had befallen Mozambique since the country won its independence from Portugal in 1975 included floods, cyclones, and, in the early 1980s, a prolonged drought that led to a famine in which an estimated 100,000 people starved. The list of not-so-natural calamities had to include Portuguese colonialism itself, which was of a peculiarly oppressive type, and also, paradoxically, the flight of nearly all the Portuguese colonists at independence, an abrupt decampment that left the country with a crippling shortage of skilled workers. The greatest calamity, however, and the primary cause of the extraordinary, countrywide suffering that people in Mozambique by then called simply "the emergency," was unquestionably the war being waged against the government by the Resistência Nacional Moçambicana, or Renamo.

The government and many Mozambicans called Renamo *bandidos armados*, "armed bandits," but any suggestion that Renamo's operations were mere uncoordinated banditry would have been misplaced. The war, which started in 1976 and intensified drastically after 1981, had destroyed the national economy, most of the country's transportation and communications systems, and much of rural society. A United Nations report released in October 1989 estimated that 900,000 Mozambicans had died as a result of the war.[1] As of late 1990, more than 3,000,000 had been driven from their homes, and more than 8,000,000 faced starvation or severe food shortages. Mozambique's total population, meanwhile, was estimated to be 16,300,000.[2] In 1988, a senior U.S. State Department official accused Renamo of perpetrating "one of the most brutal holocausts against ordinary human beings since World War Two."[3] Foreign news reports tended to refer to the conflict as a civil war, but the Mozambican government insisted that it was a case of external aggression, that South Africa, its powerful, white-ruled neighbor, was using Renamo as a proxy force.

Whatever it was called, it was a hard war to report on. Although people were dying in all of Mozambique's ten provinces, there was no front, and there were few pitched battles. The government released information sporadically, usually long after the events described, and the only telephone number for Renamo with which I'd ever had any success was in Washington, D.C. The only way to develop a real picture of the war, therefore, was by getting out close to it and asking questions. The collapse of the national transportation system made even that difficult. Mozambique is twice the size of California; Portugal would fit inside the province of Niassa with room to spare. Most railway lines and highways were either destroyed or frequently attacked, leaving huge parts of the country accessible only by air.

In Zambézia—the most populous province, with an estimated 3,000,000 residents—land travel was impossible except in the immediate vicinity of Quelimane, the provincial capital, and there were no intraprovincial commercial flights. Quelimane is a port city; and on my first afternoon there, I tried to talk my way onto a coastal tramp that was loading grain at the docks, but the captain refused to tell me where he was bound, or even to confirm that he was the captain. I later learned that cargo boats in that area traveled in fear of a Renamo ambush in the narrow coastal estuaries, and that I had failed to convince the captain that I was not an enemy agent.

In the end, I got around Zambézia by hitching rides in a vintage twin-engine Dakota DC-3 that was hauling food to isolated areas as part of an emergency airlift. Millions of Mozambicans were surviving only by the enervating grace of international relief. The airlift in Zambézia was being financed that month by the Swedish government. The next month, it was hoped, the Italian government would pick up the tab.

The charter company that owned and operated the Dakota was a good indication itself of the desperation of the Mozambican government. The company, which was leasing its services to the national airlines, called itself Inter-Ocean Airways; I was told it was based in Guernsey, but it was clearly South African. The pilots were Afrikaners who lived, they told me, "in the only place *to* live"—South Africa. Their names were Hennie and Ferdie, and they looked and talked like cartoon truck drivers: unshaven, overweight, profane. Hennie, who was in his thirties, flew in swim trunks, sandals, and a filthy T-shirt. Ferdie, who was older, wore aviator glasses and long sideburns. They both made no bones about their contempt for Mozambique or about their motives for working there. "We're here for the money," each of them told me. They got paid according to the amount of time they spent in the air, so they flew their old plane hard, working from dawn to dusk, seven days a week, rarely stopping for more than the few minutes it took a ground crew to heave three tons of cargo aboard or throw it out on the ground.

Hennie and Ferdie didn't care where they flew. When I turned up at the airport in Quelimane with papers from the local authorities giving me permission to fly on the *cargueiro*, they happily rearranged their schedules for the following days so that they would go in the morning to a place that interested me and return there to fetch me on the day's last flight. My being white may have had something to do with their helpfulness. I was traveling with two black Mozambicans, an interpreter and a young man from the local Calamidades office; but Hennie and Ferdie, who were quite talkative with me, never spoke a word to either of my companions. The man from Calamidades, whose name was Ismail, took to cowering around them and timidly bumming cigarettes. The interpreter, who had come up with me from Maputo, the national capital, just took their measure and laughed. His name was Boaventura das Dividas. He worked with CARE International, an aid organization that helped Calamidades distribute relief supplies, so he had seen a lot of white people in action. Dividas looked about twenty-five, but he was in his mid-thirties and was a man of wide experience. He had served in two armies; spoke at least eight languages, including excellent English, which he had learned as a refugee in Ethiopia; and owned a physical elegance that could not have contrasted more sharply with the grossness of our pilots.

Hennie and Ferdie were unreceptive to ordinary Mozambicans' pleas for passage. Because of all the uprooting, there were tens of thousands of people in Zambézia who had been separated from their families; and because land travel had become impossible, many of them collected at airstrips. The worst scene I witnessed occurred at a place that had not been reached by road for over a year. Several peasants had crowded into the back of the Dakota after it unloaded. Hennie spotted them just as he was about to take off for Quelimane. He stormed out of the cockpit and ordered the people off his plane. When they hesitated, he started picking up their bundles and throwing them out the open door. Everybody scuttled off except a rail-thin young man on crutches. He shrank back, but seemed unable to move. Hennie yelled, "Every minute we're on the ground is costing me four dollars and twenty-five cents!" Finally, Hennie grabbed the young man's crutches away from him and hurled them out the door. The young man, whose legs were withered, fell to the floor. While Hennie jogged back toward the cockpit, the young man crawled to the door, where a dozen hands reached over the threshold and lifted him from the plane.

Hennie and Ferdie were, in fact, not allowed to carry passengers without government permission, and they did carry wounded soldiers when they found them, even without permission. Still, when we got back to Quelimane that evening, Hennie seemed to feel a need to justify himself. He blamed the government for not allowing him to carry hardship cases. "There's nothing wrong with the *people* in this country," he said. "It's the *management.*" Hennie and Ferdie said they esteemed the Tanzanians who worked in the control tower at the Quelimane airport more than they did Mozambicans. "At least they speak the language," Ferdie said, meaning English. I wondered what Dividas, who was standing with us, made of that remark, but he just caught my eye, smiled wryly, and made no comment. Although both pilots had apparently been working for years in Mozambique, where the official language is Portuguese, neither seemed to speak more than a few words of it.

I was interested in exactly how long Hennie and Ferdie had been working in Mozambique, but their answers to my questions were vague. I was interested because I had heard it suggested that they might once have flown these same planes into the country illegally from South Africa, bringing supplies to Renamo. I never saw or heard any evidence of that myself, but the

South African Air Force, according to Renamo defectors, had often used Dakotas for supplying the rebels, and Hennie and Ferdie certainly seemed at home flying in a war zone. They liked to fly either very low, skimming the trees in order to surprise and thus foil potential snipers, or above five thousand feet, out of the range of small-arms fire. They hadn't figured out what to do about surface-to-air missiles, however, because the missiles' range was greater and, as Hennie explained to me, "they're heat-seeking, and these pipes"—he indicated the Dakota's exhaust pipes—"are hot. We really should put guards on them."

The Mozambican Army—usually known simply as Frelimo, for Frente de Libertação de Moçambique, the country's ruling party—had surface-to-air missiles, and the only two civilian aircraft shot down in the war had both been shot down by Frelimo.[4] Both of those incidents had been publicly regretted by the government, and stricter antiaircraft guidelines had been issued afterward. But Renamo, too, had surface-to-air missiles—I had seen a news photograph of a Renamo fighter wielding one[5]—so I was banking on the assessment of a British military journalist, who reported that they apparently didn't know how to use them.[6]

In any case, Hennie and Ferdie didn't know or care who was shooting at them. "You know what they say," Hennie told me. "Frelimo by day, Renamo by night." This little aperçu meant "They're all the same, anyway" and "The government blames everything on Renamo—including its own army's depredations," and it was, in fact, a common saying among some of the expatriates working in Mozambique.

The Dakota was a big, ponderous prewar plane that canted upward severely while on the ground. "Little Annie" was painted under the pilot's window, and Hennie and Ferdie didn't bother with a door—too much trouble to open and close. Inside, it felt like an old railroad locomotive. There were no seats outside the cockpit—just a big, filthy tarp on the floor. There was an axe, painted blue, on the back wall. My companions and I rode on fifty-kilogram sacks of yellow corn and pinto beans stamped with the message, in English, "Furnished by the People of the United States." Sometimes the sacks, which were made of rough white plastic fiber, were covered with bugs, and we would get covered with bugs, too. Hennie and Ferdie said that bullets from the ground would go through one sack but not two—they had found bullets lodged in the second sack of a pile—so we rode on top of at least two sacks whenever we could. Hennie and Ferdie put steel plates under their seats for the same purpose. Ferdie showed me where they had taken two bullets just a month before I flew with them. One had severed a brake cable, causing them to land awkwardly; the other had missed a fuel tank by three inches. Those shots had been fired near Ile, in northern Zambézia. I flew to Ile with Hennie and Ferdie, and we came in high, then made a steep descent, trying to limit our time as a target. It was their first trip into Ile since getting shot there, but Hennie reckoned that it was fairly safe now. "I've had these boys on a diet," he said, meaning that Ile had received no food deliveries for a month. "They want to see a few loads get on the ground."

In flight, the Dakota seemed to swim through the air, swerving from side to side like a rudderless barge. A warm wind roared through the open door; the green countryside of Zambézia rambled past below. Zambézia is Mozambique's most fertile province, as well as its most populous. In peacetime, it was a cash-crop cornucopia of rice, maize, coconuts, cashews, cotton, and, in the northern hills, tea; more than half of Mozambique's exports came from Zambézia. But roughly half the people in Zambézia had fled their homes since 1981, and most of the land we flew over looked deserted. Fields were overgrown, and swiftly reverting to bush. There were no herds of cattle—a stunning absence anywhere in southern Africa—and no herds of game.[7] And yet flying over Zambézia was a constant all-points assault of intense visual beauty, with Maxfield Parrish thunderheads rising around the plane like immense, glowing marble pillars and, beneath us, glinting rivers running dark-green threads through a landscape out of Isak Dinesen. It was, in its wildness, ideal country for a guerrilla army. And yet it was scarcely thinkable that a Renamo operated in such scenery.

Hennie and Ferdie banked in for landings at terrifying angles, practically clipping the treetops with the plane's lower wing. When we came to a stop, one of them would jump out, run around to the front of the plane, and stand guard there, to prevent people from running into the propellors. The danger of someone's doing so became extreme whenever a sack of food burst during unloading. I saw crowds at airstrips go wild when even a small amount of corn spilled from a sack. Children, their hunger-bright eyes rolling, would scrabble madly after it, stuffing handfuls of dried grass and turf into blackened tin cans along with the kernels. Hennie and Ferdie had had close calls— they had seen miraculous broken-field running between the props by both children and adults. "It's my nightmare that someone will run into a prop someday," Ferdie told me. "We really should just turn off the engines, but it takes too long to cool them down and restart them, and time for us is money."

2

The town of Morrumbala, which is in southwestern Zambézia, about twenty miles east of Morrumbala Mountain, had been occupied by Renamo for nineteen months. Frelimo retook the town in April 1987. This sequence of events sounded like a conventional war story, and that was one of the reasons I had wanted to visit the place. I also visited several other towns that had been occupied by Renamo, but Morrumbala was the first.

From a distance, as we came jouncing in from the airstrip, it looked idyllic. The "cement town"—a term used in Mozambique to distinguish European-style settlements, which were once occupied primarily by the Portuguese colonists, from the African settlements, or "cane towns," that invariably abut them—covered two gentle hills with fifty or sixty substantial pastel-colored buildings. Neat columns of dark-green acacias flanked wide red-earth roads. As we drew closer, though, it became clear that Morrumbala had been sacked. All the houses, for instance, had lost their roofs. And when we reached the town itself, the idea that anything like a conventional war had been fought there was quickly dispelled.

Every window, every window frame, every door, every doorframe, every piece of plumbing or wiring or flooring had been ripped out and carried away. Every piece of machinery that was well bolted down or too heavy for a man to carry—water pumps, maize mills, the generator in the power station, the pumps outside the gas station—had been axed, shot, sledge-hammered, stripped, or burned. Outside a bank, a safe, yellowing slowly in the sun, lay on its side, a gaping bazooka hole in its door. Some buildings were still identifiable from bas-relief signs carved in the masonry above their doors—PADARIA ("Bakery"), CORREIO ("Post Office"). Many buildings were scorched, and the burned wreckage of trucks, tractors, and cars littered empty lots. There were few signs of battle—only a spatter of bullet holes in walls and pillars—but a thousand relics of annihilative frenzy: each tile of a mosaic smashed, each pane of a glass-block wall painstakingly shattered. It was systematic, psychotically meticulous destruction. The only building in town with its roof untouched was the church. The only other structures intact were Morrumbala's two fountains. There was one fountain on each hill, and the northern fountain was faced with *azulejos,* blue-and-white Portuguese tiles. The scene depicted on it—painted, according to the legend, in Lisbon—showed a serene St. Anthony holding a cherubic white baby.

Morrumbala was the capital of an administrative district with a population estimated at 230,000. At the time I visited, the town itself was home to roughly 40,000 people, over 90 percent of whom were *deslocados*—displaced persons. There weren't many people around in the middle of the morning; nearly everyone was out in the fields working. Most of those I could see wore rags and looked ill fed, but they did not seem to be starving. Except during the drought and famine of 1983–84, and in a few acute local crises, the scenes of mass hunger in Mozambique did not resemble the nightmare images that emanated from Ethiopia in 1984: bare hills carpeted with skeletal bodies. Most of Mozambique is not subject to cyclical drought and famine. War generates chronic shortages, and for Mozambican peasants displacement usually meant a precarious diet of leaves, roots, caterpillars, wild berries, and, perhaps, wild game, until they could reach a food-distribution center or could plant and harvest a crop.

The most pressing needs in Morrumbala, I was told, were for maize, seeds, hoes, and clothes. Maize was coming in by air—Hennie and Ferdie brought five loads of three tons each on the day I visited—along with occasional shipments of blankets and tools. But the last road traffic to reach the district from the outside world had been a military convoy ten months earlier. Another convoy had tried to reach the area a few weeks before my visit, but it had been destroyed by Renamo on the highway in Mopeia, the next district south. Doctors from Médecins Sans Frontières and other relief organizations made flying visits, and UNICEF had brought in stocks of medicines.

I saw the UNICEF medicine stacked in a doorless room at the district hospital. For all I knew, it was getting good use, but it looked forgotten and ripe for stealing. The hospital was a rambling whitewashed building at the end of a tree-lined lane. It was getting a new roof of corrugated tin. The maternity ward, which had been burned out, was being used as a carpenter's workshop, but the rest of the hospital seemed strangely quiet. There were several male nurses, each of whom grew solemn when he saw me, but no patients except in the infirmary. The infirmary was a big, very dark room with a few mats strewn on the floor and a few people curled in the shadows. It felt like a storehouse for the doomed. In the hospital courtyard, fifty or sixty women and children were sitting in the dirt outside rudimentary grass tents. These were recently arrived *deslocados*. The children all had swollen bellies and looked seriously malnourished, but the hospital administrator assured me that they were healthy. They had been examined and vaccinated, and were now being fed. As soon as huts were ready, people would be issued cooking pots and blankets and moved to one of the eight "accommodation centers" that ringed the town.

Behind the hospital, the cane town began. Small cane-and-mud huts covered the hills, and a surprising semblance of normal life was going on. Given seeds, a hoe, and the chance to cultivate a field without being attacked, a Mozambican peasant can work wonders. Morrumbala has fertile soil and gets good rainfall, so there were glistening vegetable gardens everywhere. But a close look at some of the new huts revealed an unusual small door at the back. I asked a woman who was pounding maize in a mortar about the door. She grimaced and said that it was for escaping in the event of an attack by the *bandidos armados*.

Most of the people in Morrumbala had arrived there destitute and traumatized, but many seemed to have quickly reestablished parts of their old lives. A spirited meeting was taking

place under a tree—I was told that it was a divorce proceed-
ing—and next to a new hut I saw an "African piano": fifteen
panels of wood of graduated length lashed together and laid
over a trench of graduated depth. A tap on a panel produced a
rich, vibrating tone. Two children were giggling inside a tiny
grass tent they had built beside the road, and a lithe old man
was running a sewing machine outside a mud hut. It was the
first post-Renamo sewing machine to reach Morrumbala, he
said. It had been donated by Save the Children, a British group
that was active in Zambézia and that had also brought in quantities of cloth. As the group's officials later explained to me, they
preferred to send raw materials rather than free handouts of
finished clothes. They were starting a tailors' association in
Morrumbala and planned to send in more sewing machines.

The troops holding Morrumbala were Tanzanian; Mozambique received security assistance from several of its neighbors,
most notably Zimbabwe and Tanzania. The Tanzanian role in
the war was supposed to be strictly defensive, and I noticed that
the troops had built underground bunkers at each approach
to the town. Gardens full of chard and tomatoes flourished beside the bunkers. Unlike the Mozambican soldiers I had seen,
the Tanzanians wore complete uniforms, with pressed fatigues,
smart red berets, and reflecting sunglasses. They laughed when I
greeted them in English, and answered, "Good morning!" As in
most of the places I went in Mozambique, nobody seemed inclined to question my movements.

Dividas chatted with the soldiers in Swahili, and afterward
reported that, according to the Tanzanians, the "security zone"
in Morrumbala extended only two or three kilometers from the
center of town. In other words, any place farther out than that
was subject to attack, even in the daytime. Here was a good example of the difficulty of reporting on the war. Less than a week
later, a Reuters story, based on an interview with the governor of
a neighboring province, was headlined, in the Harare (Zimbabwe) *Herald*, "MNR BANDITS SWEPT OUT OF ZAMBÉ-
ZIA."[1] Meanwhile, I was finding that virtually every road in
Zambézia was subject to attack and that the "security zone"
around a main, Tanzanian-held center like Morrumbala was less
than four miles in diameter.

I was interested in Renamo's occupation of Morrumbala. I

first pictured it as a scene of rampaging *bandidos* shooting out the lights, swilling the contents of decent people's liquor cabinets, and sleeping in their feather beds. In fact, I was told by various people who lived through it, the town was deserted for the entire nineteen months of the occupation—Renamo commanders rightly believing that towns presented fat targets for Frelimo air strikes. On the morning Renamo arrived, everyone, including the handful of Frelimo soldiers stationed in the town, ran off. The rebels spent two days destroying whatever could not be carried away, then rounded up every able-bodied person they could find, loaded them down with plunder, and marched them off to their bases in the bush. Most of the doors, windows, and zinc roofing sheets—each porter was required to carry two sheets—ended up in Malawi, a neighboring country whose southern tip is about forty miles from Morrumbala, and were traded there for soap, salt, gasoline, flashlight batteries, and sugar. Clothes, food, furniture, radios, motorcycles, and so on, stayed at the bases. A major base was established in the Morrumbala district—I later met people who had been marched to the base from homes more than 150 miles away—but the encampment closest to the town of Morrumbala was out near the airstrip. During their occupation, the rebels allowed no one to enter the town, and people told me that the grass in the center of town grew as high as the walls of the buildings. Renamo dealt with the local population through *régulos*, petty chiefs who had once worked for the Portuguese, and *majubas*, local collaborators and enforcers. The Renamo commanders were Ndau-speakers (Ndaus are a small ethnic group from central Mozambique; they speak a dialect of Shona), and spirit mediums known as *curandeiros* or *feiticeiros* enjoyed great influence.[2] When Frelimo, backed by Zimbabweans, returned to Morrumbala, Renamo made an orderly retreat. Thousands of *majubas* and porters left along with the fighters.

Frelimo had retaken Morrumbala sixteen months before, and reconstruction of the cement town had been slow. Some houses had been reinhabited, but building materials were scarce. Reed mats covered windows and doorways, and the new roofs were all of thatch, giving the buildings they covered a disreputable look—a big cement house topped with ill-fitting thatch looks like a distinguished man reeling in drunk, his hair all flattened and sticking out sideways. But the hospital was getting its tin roof, and a new diesel pump had water flowing in the fountains again. And school was in session: all over town, we passed groups of children sitting on the ground under mango trees, some singing like robins, others listening to a teacher talk.

Much of the credit for Morrumbala's steady resumption of normal life belonged, I was told, to Alcanji Nhampinga, the district administrator. On the morning I arrived, Nhampinga was just returning to Morrumbala, by light plane. He was a tall, lanky, studious-looking man of about forty, with a constant toothy smile and an air of profound preoccupation. He had been to Maputo and wore a clean, gray, three-piece suit, but at the airstrip he clambered straight into the back of a twelve-ton truck that was waiting there. We rode into town together. The truck, Nhampinga explained, was one of only two working civilian vehicles—the other was a motorcycle—in the district. "This truck was a gift from the Japanese," he said. "It came with the last convoy. It broke down here in Morrumbala and was left behind." Nhampinga grinned guiltily. A good trick, I thought. "We repaired it, but one of its batteries is dead now, and there are no spare parts or tools. We start it by touching two wires together." The truck's health was clearly one of Nhampinga's numberless preoccupations.

When we reached his house, which was one of the bigger thatched drunks (half of it had been turned into a military command post, government administrators and their families being a favorite Renamo target), Nhampinga found a group of his assistants waiting. He seemed extremely happy to be back, and they seemed glad to see him. He made a short, quiet speech to them in Chuabo, the local language; heard a report on what had been happening in his absence; then apologized profusely to me, in Portuguese, for his inability to show me around—there were some things he just had to attend to.

It was several hours before we saw Nhampinga again. By then, his coat and vest and round-framed glasses were gone, his sleeves were rolled up, and there was a smear of red mud on one shoulder of his shirt. He was still smiling, though, still distracted, and still apologizing. His wife had given us lunch—bean soup and a chicken stew; I ate mine from a tin plate—in their dark, bare house, and Nhampinga apologized for having been absent. But he was still determined to show me at least one thing: his generator. It had been built by the best mechanic in Morrumbala, from parts cannibalized from the remains of many different machines. They hadn't been able to find a flywheel, so he had milled one out of wood. I thought the generator looked great, sitting all burly and immaculate in a cement shelter in the administrator's backyard. The wiring to the house was finished. The Nhampingas' was going to be the first house in town to get electricity in the post-Renamo period. All they needed now were two batteries. I asked when the batteries would come. Nhampinga shrugged, embarrassed. It was a question of money, he said. I recalled that a district administrator's monthly salary came to about fifty dollars. This was a fair measure of Mozambique's poverty: Nhampinga was, after all, the most powerful man in a district of 230,000 people.

But the depths of dispossession have a million levels, and in a place like Morrumbala the lowest levels are occupied by the most recently arived. In a cement-walled yard behind the ruins of a bank, under a cashew tree at the edge of a tomato patch, I found Alexandre Namanyanga, his wife, Dshassa, and their four children. They were *deslocados* who had arrived that same morning. The Namanyangas were in bad shape. All the children were extremely thin, and at least one of them seemed dangerously listless. The family had no clothes at all; they covered themselves as best they could with tree bark.[3] I couldn't imagine what they made of me, but Dividas and I sat talking with the Namanyangas for an hour or so. Mr. Namanyanga was a small, good-looking man with calm, intelligent eyes and a wispy beard. He did most of the talking. His wife was also quite alert, though she and the children were obviously frightened. The whole family shivered the whole time we talked, all having caught a chill, they explained, while walking in the bush the night before.

Mr. Namanyanga, speaking in Sena, a local language, said that he and his wife had lived as peasants near the Minduru Mission, not far from Morrumbala, until six or seven years before. Then the war came to their area, and, though they saw no violence themselves, he said, they fled. They settled in an area that he called "Tandekia." I got out my Michelin map—which, I noticed, still listed Morrumbala, somewhat surreally, as a town with an "equipped" camping site—but Mr. Namanyanga could not show me, even generally, where Tandekia was. He said he had once gone to school for two years but had since forgotten how to read. Mrs. Namanyanga said she had gone to school for four years, but she, too, had forgotten how to read. After further discussion, it turned out that Tandekia was the name of the chief in that area, and possibly not an official place-name at all. The Namanyangas were allowed to farm there, in any case, and their three younger children had been born there. The big problem in Tandekia had been lack of clothes: the Namanyangas had been wearing nothing but tree bark for the last six years. When her husband murmured this information, Mrs. Namanyanga pulled self-consciously at her rough, reddish skirt and glanced at my leather-sided running shoes.

Tandekia sounded to me like Renamo territory, but the Namanyangas, after discussing the matter, could not tell me whether Tandekia, the chief, was with Renamo or Frelimo. I suggested some ways that they might be able to tell the difference—if they ever saw, say, a Mozambican flag, or a Frelimo soldier, or a working motor vehicle in the area, that would suggest that it was government-held territory—and they seemed to want to oblige me with a definite answer. But they said they had never seen any of those things. The fact that they and their children were so thin made me wonder if armed men had been taking away the food they grew, but they said they had seen no armed men. They had started hearing shooting in the distance, however, and that was why they had fled Tandekia. They said they understood that Morrumbala was a government-held town; indeed, that was why they had come there—because they had heard the government had food. But they could not tell me, when I asked, who the president of Mozambique was. (And one of the "accommodation centers" at Morrumbala even bore his name: Joaquim Alberto Chissano.) "Mozambique" itself seemed to be a fairly hazy idea to the Namanyangas. This was not some sort of African know-nothingism, I was convinced—and Dividas agreed—but sheer lack of information. The Namanyangas had simply not heard much—if anything at all—about the modern nation-state in which they officially lived.

Among the dozens of *deslocados* I talked to in Mozambique, the Namanyangas were neither typical nor extraordinary. Many people in their situation did not know who the president of Mozambique was, while plenty of others did.[4] Those who could read and write and speak Portuguese (only a small minority of all Mozambicans) naturally tended to know more about the greater world than those who lacked these skills. Most people could say whether they had been living under a Frelimo or a Renamo administration at their last address, and some could tell me far more about their experiences than the Namanyangas did, but every "interview" of this sort was utterly problematic. The survival instincts developed by peasants being washed around in the murderous tides of a guerrilla war include, above all, the ability to sense quickly and accurately what any stronger being might want from them.[5] People might not know what to make of me, but a strange white man summoning them out of a crowd of their fellow victims was clearly more powerful than they were, even if he carried a notebook rather than a gun. What did I want from them? What did I want to hear? Such questions undoubtedly shaped much of what I did hear.

At the same time, many people seemed to figure that the safest attitude to assume with me was a hear-no-evil, see-no-evil shrug, almost as if to say "What war?" (The Namanyangas may have been doing some of this.) The nature of the war itself—a conflict in which most attacks occurred at night, neither side had a regular uniform, and Renamo's forces were reported to include many semi-independent bands (and had spawned at least one breakaway army)—only increased the difficulty of establishing precisely what had happened to anyone. Also working against people's willingness to tell me their war stories, of course, was the natural reluctance to recall traumatic events, particularly fresh traumas to one's own family or friends.

The interpreter could make a big difference. Dividas was superb at reassuring people, questioning them gently, translating quickly, and, when necessary, giving me advice. I employed other interpreters who shouted at people, and who even refused to translate what they said—"She's lying," one man in Malawi kept insisting. In Mozambique, local officials were usually willing to let me interview people privately; but if the people spoke only an obscure language, it was sometimes necessary to use a second interpreter, and the choice was again critical. Dividas would delay things for as long as it took him to find a local inter-

preter whom he reckoned our interviewees would not find intimidating. But with all these forces swirling underneath these
already stilted conversations, the facts in the narratives we elic-
ited rarely felt entirely stable.

And yet the world itself could not have felt very stable to
people like the Namanyangas. While I admired the boldly designed, undestroyed spiral staircase attached to the back wall of
the bank and tried to think of more questions, the place where
we sat seemed to me perfectly solid and secure; the world was
still on its axis. For refugees, and especially for peasants driven
off their land, however, the world is decidedly *not* on its axis.
Their homes and all that accompanies that fundamental notion—kin, society, sustenance, identity itself—have been torn
away from them by terrifying forces. To the Namanyangas, the
town of Morrumbala did not, I imagine, look the least bit secure.
I wondered if they would be willing to send their children to
school. Many *deslocados* were not, for they had learned the hard
way that it was dangerous to let their children out of their sight.
If there was an attack, they wanted to be able to grab their kids
as they ran. And who could promise the Namanyangas that the
war would not sweep across Morrumbala again at any moment?

Weeks later, across the border in Malawi, I talked to a man who
had once returned to Morrumbala too soon. He was a forty-nine-
year-old refugee named Orlando Passanjezi Galave. Mr. Galave
was a *mutilado:* his left hand, his right ear, his lips, and his nose
had been hacked off. I first noticed him—he was hard to miss—
while I was walking through a dusty yard where several dozen
newly arrived refugees were waiting for food and medical attention, and several hundred others, also Mozambican refugees but
of longer standing, were intrepidly gathering for a bus trip back
to parts of Mozambique that they had been assured were now
secure. The two groups seemed to be ignoring each other, perhaps understandably. I stopped and asked Galave, who was
there greeting the new arrivals, where he came from, and when
he said "Morrumbala," slurring the words around his permanently bared teeth, I asked if he would mind telling me his story.
He considered me silently for a moment—he was a short, wiry,
bright-eyed man—and then began to speak in rapid Portuguese.

He had been a successful peasant farmer, he said, the owner

of a motorcycle, two bicycles, and a good patch of land near the town of Morrumbala. In January 1983, a group of *bandidos* accosted him in his fields. They said the government must have given him the bicycle he had with him, to help him spy on Renamo. They bound his hands behind him, marched him to their camp, and presented him and his bicycle to their commander. He was left on the ground overnight, with his hands still tied behind him. In the morning, when he refused to confess to being a government spy, the Renamo commander hacked off his right ear with a knife, stuffed the ear in Galave's mouth, and then forced him to chew and swallow it. Galave was blindfolded—the blindfold was red, he recalled—and was told that there was more mutilation in store for him. Galave murmured that he had placed his fate in the hands of God. "Do you know God?" his captors demanded. No, Galave admitted, he did not know Him. His captors proceeded to chop off his nose, his lips, and his left hand. They had trouble severing the ligaments in his wrist, but managed eventually. They then slit his throat—Galave showed me a ten-inch-long scar I had not noticed—and carried him out to the road, "so that Frelimo might find me."

Galave, bleeding heavily, fainted. When he awoke, he saw that there was no one around, and crawled into the bushes, where he fainted again. The next time he awoke, he could hear the *bandidos*, who had returned, searching for him. Galave lay still, and eventually heard them give him up for dead. That evening, he found some mud with which to staunch the bleeding at his wrist and throat. The next day, he got up and tried to walk, but he was lost, and every time he saw people, they fled at the sight of him. Just when he thought he must be at the point of death, he came upon a ripe watermelon in the bush. "This watermelon was a gift from God," Galave told me solemnly. He broke it open with his foot, ate it all, and, with renewed energy, resumed his trek. He eventually found his way back to his farm. It was deserted—his family had fled at the news that Renamo was near—but Galave waited there, and he was on hand when his family returned to collect their belongings. His family carried him into town, and a plane was called from Quelimane, but the pilot, fearing sniper fire, refused to come. Finally, a military plane carrying wounded soldiers out of Morrumbala took Galave to Quelimane.

Galave spent the next two years in hospitals in Quelimane, Maputo, and Beira (the second-largest city in Mozambique). A Swiss specialist took skin grafts from his thigh to close his wrist. Surgeons in Maputo tried to rebuild his lips—"but that was a failure," Galave said, pointing to his exposed gums. There was nothing to be done about his nose or his ear. Since he could not go back to farming with only one hand, he and his wife decided to settle in Quelimane. In 1985, they returned to Morrumbala to collect their belongings. It was the worst time they could have picked. Renamo launched an offensive, and the Galaves were trapped. They had to flee Morrumbala on foot. They eventually made their way to Malawi, and at the time I met Mr. Galave they had been there two years, living on handouts from international relief organizations. Some of the people sitting in the dust around us, he said, were old neighbors of his from Morrumbala. Until their escape last week, they had been living with Renamo.

I told Galave that I had been in Morrumbala and Quelimane, and that they were both in government hands. He stared at me awhile, then said he thought he would wait until the war was over before trying to return.

3

The cruelty of Renamo mesmerized everyone in Mozambique, from the peasant whose own head sank before its scythe to the members of the many foreign delegations that came to survey the wreckage. Westerners groped numbly through their own history for precedents and analogies. When Orlando Galave told me that his captors asked him if he knew God, I remembered a story I had heard a few days before on the BBC's Africa Service about a medieval Catholic crusade against the Albigensian heresy. One day in 1209, the story went, the crusaders were busy slaughtering 7,000 people in Béziers, in southern France. Activities included burning a church that was full of people. A lieutenant pointed out to his commander that there were some good Catholics in among the heretics. The commander's reply: "Kill them all. God will know his own."

The European Middle Ages were, in fact, a favorite metaphor, among some observers, for what was happening in Mozambique. One British newspaper even quoted a Mozambican official saying, "This is a war from the Middle Ages."[1] In the sense that tribal and feudal arrangements still dominated rural Mozambique—much as they did, say, medieval Germany centuries before the consolidation of the modern nation-state—the metaphor was useful. But the butchery occurring in Mozambique was not really so foreign to modern warfare. One common Renamo practice was to throw people, usually after killing them, down wells; American soldiers did the same thing in Vietnam.

American soldiers in Vietnam also practiced mutilation—they even turned it into a drinking game, "Ears for Beers"—and, in their creative use of modern weaponry, our troops often out-warped any medieval imagination.

Renamo's ferocity did have unique aspects. In 1985, the United Nations sponsored a vaccination campaign for children in south-central Mozambique. The country's under-five mortality rate had risen horrifyingly as a result of the war—to 375 deaths per 1,000 live births,[2] perhaps the highest in the world—and many thousands of children were dying each year from preventable diseases like measles. In a vast area with no newspapers (and few literate people), radio was the obvious choice for announcing the campaign. But it was feared that announcements would provoke Renamo attacks. So the vaccination campaign was conducted clandestinely. Small teams went out to schools and villages to proselytize about the importance of vaccinations, with nothing said about dates. Weeks or months later, word would suddenly go out through the Frelimo Party structures, down to the level of the ten-family cell: the vaccination team is coming tomorrow. People would be assembled, vaccinated, and dispersed as quickly as possible. Although some of those who were vaccinated were *later* attacked by Renamo, the campaign was, on the whole, a success. But the United Nations health workers I spoke with said that the campaign's security problems had been unprecedented in their experience. The American makers of the film *Apocalypse Now* once imagined a scene in which the Vietcong cut off the arms of children vaccinated by American doctors. Nothing like that ever happened in Vietnam, though.

By the end of 1988, Renamo had destroyed, looted, or forced to close 978 clinics and rural health posts—46 percent of the country's primary health-care network. The rebels had killed at least 40 health workers and kidnapped 43 more.[3] In Zambézia, where sixteen of seventeen districts had ambulances in 1983, only five ambulances were running by mid-1986.[4] In July 1987, a Renamo attack on the town of Homoine—where, according to the government, 424 civilians were killed—included a rampage through a hospital, in which patients, even pregnant women and newborn babies, were killed in their beds.[5] Along with health centers, prime Renamo targets included schools, relief convoys, and relief workers. By 1989, more than 3,000 schools had been destroyed or forced to close, with some 400 teachers killed and an unknown number kidnapped or mutilated.[6] Relief convoys were being attacked regularly: CARE International's inventory list for its trucks was studded with the notations "ambushed," "burned," and "mined," often with an accompanying "killed" for its drivers. Captured Renamo documents showed that international-aid workers were indeed considered valid, even important, military targets.[7]

According to the Southern African Catholic Bishops Conference, Renamo had boiled children alive in front of their parents and had used the decapitated heads of old people as seats.[8] *Newsweek* quoted a peasant saying that Renamo was eating children.[9] The British *Guardian* reported that Renamo was crushing skulls, disemboweling people, and nailing them to trees.[10] In April 1988, the United States Department of State issued a major report, based on interviews with nearly 200 Mozambican refugees, that included in its catalogue of Renamo's violence against civilians "shooting executions, knife/axe/bayonet killings, burning alive, beating to death, forced asphyxiation, forced starvation, forced drownings, and random shooting at civilians in villages during attacks."[11] The State Department's report, which estimated that 100,000 civilians may have been murdered by Renamo, had a powerful impact on the debates in the United States over American policy toward Mozambique. It had a powerful impact on me, too. Among other things, it reinforced an unexamined assumption that Renamo came from Hell.

Several months after the release of the State Department's report, I met, in Maputo, an American psychologist who was working with war-damaged children. He told me some of the worst Renamo stories I heard. He described a six-year-old boy who had been forced to light the match with which Renamo burned down his family's hut, and who was then forced to watch while his family ran outside, were hacked to death, and burned. He described a ten-year-old boy who had seen his best friend decapitated by Renamo, and who was then forced to carry his friend's head on top of his own head back to the Renamo camp. The psychologist had worked with child soldiers from the Khmer Rouge in Cambodia, and he said he thought that Renamo's behavior toward the children it abducted was "more insidious than what the Khmer did, from a psychological point of view." Renamo's ultraviolence was linked somehow to the psychology of South African apartheid, he said. Beyond that, he couldn't explain it. This, to me, was another way of saying that Renamo came from Hell.

But the time I spent in Mozambique undid that idea for me. I never forgot that Renamo was linked in a multitude of ways to South Africa, and I never doubted that Renamo had murdered civilians by every method mentioned in the State Department's report, and probably forty others. But Renamo did not come from Hell. Renamo came from Mozambique.[12]

4

The fact that some people scarcely realize they live in a country called Mozambique is, in light of the region's colonial experience, unsurprising. Portugal, which declared the place an administrative unit to begin with, never had the wherewithal to turn it into anything of the kind. The first Portuguese arrived in 1498, but it was not until the twentieth century that Lisbon even gained control of the entire colony.[1] There was competition from Swahili traders for commercial supremacy along the coast. Inland, two African empires and numerous independent chieftancies frustrated the attempts of the Portuguese to extend their rule. In the seventeenth century, Portuguese merchants did lucrative business with the great gold mines of the Muenemutapa empire, in what is now west-central Mozambique and eastern Zimbabwe, but in 1693 an African army drove the Europeans back to the coast. In the eighteenth century, the major international trade was in ivory. In the nineteenth century, it was in slaves. Powerful slave-raiding states grew up, and the entire northern half of Mozambique was impoverished and almost depopulated as more than a million people were captured, sold, and shipped to Brazil, the United States, and the Caribbean islands. Still, in 1885, when the European powers were dividing up Africa at the Berlin Conference, the effective rule of Portugal in Mozambique was confined to a few coastal settlements. The area that the Europeans called Mozambique contained people speaking at least nine languages and dozens of dialects. It embraced the Yao, Makonde, Makua, Maravi, and other matrilineal societies in the north; the Shangaan, Ronga, Chopi, and other patrilineal societies in the south; and, in the center, the Manyika, Ndau, and other Shona-speaking descendants of the Muenemutapa empire.

The sudden appearance of large-scale mining in South Africa and Southern Rhodesia, in the late nineteenth and early twentieth centuries, created demands for migrant labor and the development of Mozambique's ports. These changes, in combination with Portugal's weakness, shaped Mozambique's economy decisively. In Lourenço Marques (now Maputo), according to Allen and Barbara Isaacman, "only 27 percent of the investments in 1900 consisted of Portuguese capital. The city's electrical system, trolley system, and first modern wharf complex were all financed by foreign, primarily British, capital—a situation not unlike that in Lisbon itself."[2] Even the concessionary companies licensed to develop agriculture and industry in Mozambique were largely British-owned. On the plantations that were started, labor conditions were frightful and agricultural practices backward.[3] The slave trade persisted, in one form or another, into the twentieth century, and forced labor was not abolished until 1961. Hundreds of thousands of Mozambicans fled their homes for the higher wages and marginally less murderous colonial systems in neighboring states. The journey, usually made on foot, was long and hazardous, and the effects of this exodus were profound: at independence, less than 10 percent of the land was under cultivation. (In 1988, because of the war, the figure was only 4 percent.)[4]

Although Mozambique runs north-south, nearly all development in the country was along east-west lines. Railroads, highways, and ports were built to serve Rhodesia and South Africa as outlets to the sea. (Mozambique has more than 1,500 miles of coastline.) The South Africans agreed to pay part of the wages of Mozambican mineworkers directly to the Portuguese in gold. Since an average of more than 80,000 Mozambicans were working legally in the mines after 1910, these remittances became the mainstay of the colonial government's budget, and southern Mozambique was effectively integrated into the expanding South African industrial economy.[5] António Salazar, the dictator who came to power in Portugal in 1932, struggled to assert the metropole's control over its colonies, and in the late 1940s Portugal did finally manage to account for more than half of Mozambique's external trade.[6]

Under Salazar, Portuguese emigration to Mozambique increased sharply. The European population of the colony was 27,000 in 1940;[7] in 1970, it was over 200,000. The Salazar regime was trying to export some of its social and political problems, such as unemployment and landlessness. It was also trying to develop Portuguese industry, concentrating on textiles—a traditional first phase of industrialization—by increasing cotton production in the colonies. Mozambican peasants were forced to grow cotton and sell it to the state at fixed prices, an arrangement that required brutal enforcement and, in the 1940s, led to a series of famines. Most of the Portuguese who went to Mozambique were peasants—a 1955 census showed that only one-third of them could read and write[8]—but racial discrimination guaranteed them a level of security and comfort that few had known in Europe. Blacks were barred from most jobs; even the bus drivers and the movie ushers were white. Local industry grew, and in the 1960s actually boomed. By 1975, Mozambique was the eighth-largest industrial producer in Africa.[9] But a ban on trade by Africans meant that the country still had no indigenous business class. As Joseph Hanlon, correspondent for the BBC and the *Guardian* from 1979 to 1984, wrote, "Mozambique is one of the poorest countries in Africa not because it lacks natural resources, nor because Portugal left it undeveloped, but rather because Portugal actively underdeveloped it."[10]

Among the many features of their own repressive political machinery that the Portuguese brought to Mozambique was a fearsome secret police. In the decades following World War II, when other African countries were gaining their independence, the Portuguese were crushing every hint of resistance to colonial rule in Mozambique, Angola, and Guinea-Bissau. Nationalist groups were harassed, outlawed, and driven into exile, their leaders jailed, tortured, and murdered. In 1960, a group of Mozambican peasants gathered in the northern town of Mueda for a peaceful protest, and colonial troops opened fire, reportedly killing 600.[11] Finally, in 1962, three outlawed nationalist groups met in Dar es Salaam, in the newly independent Tanganyika (now Tanzania), to found the Frente de Libertação de

Moçambique. Frelimo's first president was Eduardo Mondlane, an American-educated anthropologist (and Mozambique's first Ph.D.). Frelimo's armed struggle against Portuguese colonialism began in 1964.

The war lasted ten years. Eduardo Mondlane was assassinated in 1969. His successor was Samora Machel, a former nurse and a gifted commander. Frelimo received support from China and the Soviet Union. Its main rear bases were in Tanzania; and, despite Portugal's vast military superiority, Frelimo, waging guerrilla warfare with light weapons, steadily expanded its "liberated zones" until they covered the northern fourth of the country. Frelimo also had cells among intellectuals and workers in all the major towns. Portugal was fighting grueling wars in Angola and Guinea-Bissau at the same time, and in April 1974 a leftist coup in Lisbon, led by military officers, toppled the government. A year later, Samora Machel became Mozambique's first president.

The war had radicalized the Frelimo leadership. In 1977, the liberation movement became a Marxist-Leninist vanguard party and signed long-term assistance pacts with the Soviet Union and Cuba. By that time, more than 90 percent of the Portuguese in Mozambique had departed. Frelimo was nonracial—its leadership contained whites, Asians, and people of mixed race as well as blacks—but the end of legal racial privilege was clearly intolerable to many whites. The new government guaranteed that private wealth would be protected, but postindependence nationalizations of land ownership, rental property, and social services, including education, medicine, and law, sped the flight of the former rulers. Most went to South Africa or back to Portugal, abandoning their farms and factories and, in many cases, destroying the cattle, tractors, and machinery they could not take with them.

Frelimo was left to run an effectively bankrupt country with virtually no trained people. The illiteracy rate was over 90 percent. There were six economists, two agronomists, not a single geologist, and fewer than a thousand black high school graduates in all of Mozambique. Of 350 railroad engineers working in 1975, just one was black (and he was an agent of the Portuguese secret police).[12] A vast expansion of the educational system was undertaken, along with a crash program to provide health care in the rural areas, where 85 percent of Mozambicans live. An ambitious plan to modernize and socialize agriculture and industry was drawn up. As the victor over the Portuguese, Frelimo was hugely popular, but the basic task facing the new government was still nation-building. The colonial regime had violently discouraged all forms of national consciousness, and millions of isolated peasants still had to be persuaded that they belonged to something called Mozambique.

The gravest threat to the fledgling country was, however, external. While the victory of the liberation movements in the Portuguese colonies was an inspiration to the black majorities struggling for freedom in South Africa and Rhodesia, it was regarded with alarm by their white rulers, who had been allies of the Portuguese. The liberation war in Rhodesia was intensifying, and Frelimo, which had a close relationship with the Zimbabwe African National Union, the larger of the two movements fighting white-minority rule there, began providing rear bases to the ZANU guerrillas. Frelimo also began applying the trade sanctions against Rhodesia which had been ordered by the United Nations, and which the colonial regime had flouted (and South Africa continued to flout), although the cost to Mozambique was staggering. The Rhodesians, on their side, launched raids into Mozambique. They bombed bridges, dams, railway lines, and oil-storage facilities. In August 1976, they massacred more than 600 people at a refugee camp.[13] They also assembled a gang of former Portuguese soldiers and secret police, Frelimo deserters, and escaped prisoners who had fled Mozambique, and created what its mastermind, a Rhodesian military-intelligence chief named Ken Flower, called a "pseudo-terrorist" movement: Renamo.[14]

Renamo was originally meant to be a Fifth Column, its task to spy on ZANU guerrillas in Mozambique.[15] Later, its assignment was expanded to include the destruction of infrastructure, seeking to raise the cost to Frelimo of supporting ZANU. Many Renamo fighters, including the group's first leader, André Matsangaíssa, and his deputy, Afonso Dhlakama, had escaped from "reeducation" camps—rural prisons established by Frelimo after independence. Matsangaíssa was a former Frelimo soldier who had been convicted of stealing a Mercedes-Benz; Dhlakama, who fought with the Portuguese colonial army and later joined Frelimo, had also been cashiered for theft. Matsangaíssa was killed in battle in 1979 and was replaced by Dhlakama. By 1980 Renamo had succeeded, primarily through raids on re-education camps, in raising a force of between 1,000 and 2,000 men. Operations were still confined to the center of the country, however, near the Rhodesian border. And then the Rhodesian war ended. In March 1980, with independence coming to Zimbabwe, Renamo looked like a spent force. But on the eve of Zimbabwean independence, South Africa sent a fleet of military transport planes to ferry the remnants of Renamo south.

Pretoria had been helping Rhodesia run Renamo for some time. It had also been putting great economic pressure on Mozambique, decreasing its traffic through Maputo port until, in 1983, it was barely one-fourth what it had been a decade before; reducing the number of Mozambican migrant workers in South African mines by over 60 percent; and ending the practice of paying part of the miners' wages to the Mozambican government in gold.[16] These blows were caresses, though, compared with the damage that South Africa began to inflict once it had taken over Renamo. Recruiting was stepped up, training was expanded and upgraded, and in late 1980 the infiltration of large Renamo contingents into Mozambique by air, land, and sea began. Fronts were opened in the south, near the South African border, and in the north, with transit routes through Malawi (whose government had a long association with Pretoria). By mid-1981, nine of Mozambique's ten provinces were under attack. Schools, clinics, communal villages, highways, railways, bridges, factories, large farms, and ports were the primary targets, and the ferocity and the scale of the onslaught clearly caught Frelimo unprepared. Ken Flower himself later wrote, "I began to wonder whether we had created a monster that was now beyond control."[17]

South Africa had several objectives in unleashing its monster on Mozambique. One was to stop Frelimo's support for the African National Congress, the leading liberation movement in South Africa. The ANC, which was then outlawed in South Africa, was using Mozambican territory to infiltrate guerrillas into the country. A second, broader objective was to increase the economic dependence on South Africa of all the neighboring countries. In 1980, coinciding with the declaration of Zimbabwe's independence, nine of South Africa's neighbors formed the Southern African Development Coordination Conference (SADCC), whose main purpose was to *reduce* the region's dependence on South Africa. That meant developing the regional transportaton system, which, in turn, meant using the short, convenient routes to the sea through Mozambique. Renamo therefore concentrated on disrupting those transport routes, and by 1984 three of the four rail lines running from SADCC countries through Mozambique to the coast had been cut and the fourth was being attacked regularly.[18] Landlocked countries like Zimbabwe, Botswana, Zambia, and Malawi were left with no alternative but to import and export goods through South Africa. A third objective in South Africa's campaign against Mozambique (and its neighbors) was, finally, symbolic: because the fundamental justification for apartheid was that majority rule in Africa was a disaster, Pretoria was determined to ensure that it always turned out that way.

Pretoria's destablization campaign was not limited to Mozambique. South Africa recruited, trained, or gave support to armed dissidents in Angola, Zimbabwe, and Lesotho as well, and between 1980 and 1988 the South African military itself staged bloody raids into no fewer than six nearby countries. South Africa occupied large parts of southern Angola for seven years, toppled the government of Lesotho in 1986, and in 1981 tried to assassinate the prime minister of Zimbabwe. In Mozambique, there were air raids, commando attacks, sophisticated sabotage, and assassinations of prominent ANC members: Ruth First, a sociologist, was killed by a parcel bomb in Maputo in 1982; Albie Sachs, a distinguished legal scholar, lost an arm to a car bomb in April 1988.

While Renamo remained the blunt main instrument of South African policy toward Mozambique, Pretoria was not Renamo's only source of external support. Portuguese ex-colonials living in South Africa, Portugal, Malawi, and Brazil, including wealthy businessmen who had lost property when independence came to Mozambique, contributed heavily.[19] Pretoria sent Afonso Dhlakama to Europe in November 1980, on the first of a series of trips to meet with right-wing groups in Portugal, West Germany, and France, seeking their support. Saudi Arabia and

Oman, ostensibly concerned about Frelimo's treatment of Muslims, began sending supplies to Renamo. Delegates started turning up at the meetings of the World Anti-Communist League with shopping lists of weapons.[20] Right-wing groups in the United States eventually became important backers, and some of the more dedicated proponents of the "Reagan Doctrine" (the idea that the United States should support insurgencies in any and all countries with "Marxist" governments) in Congress, in the administration, and in the Central Intelligence Agency began to push for direct American support for Renamo. This push gained strength after the United States started sending weapons to the União Nacional para a Independência Total de Angola (Unita), the South African–backed rebels in Angola, in 1985. The State Department opposed aid to Renamo, but the State Department had also opposed aid to Unita.[21]

By 1983, Mozambique was in desperate shape. The national economy had essentially collapsed, all ambitious socialist-development plans were off, and Frelimo was suing for peace. In March 1984, a "nonaggression pact" known as the Nkomati Accord was signed. South Africa agreed to end its support for Renamo; Mozambique agreed to evict the ANC. By all accounts, Mozambique kept its end of the bargain. South Africa did not. Renamo attacks continued, and in August 1985 diaries were discovered at an overrun Renamo headquarters on Gorongosa Mountain, in central Mozambique, that contained clear evidence of continuing South African support. Top South African officials, including the commander-in-chief of the army and the deputy foreign minister, had actually visited the Renamo camp only weeks before it was overrun. The diaries showed a split inside the South African leadership over support for Renamo, and Pretoria's foreign minister, who apparently opposed continuing aid, was clearly annoyed to read in the diaries that the army's commander-in-chief had told Renamo that he, the foreign minister, was "treacherous." The foreign minister was forced to admit that his government had been violating the Nkomati Accord. But no disciplinary measures were taken against those officials responsible for the violations. Indeed, some of them were promoted.

Evidence that South Africa—or, at least, elements of the South African military—was still supporting Renamo continued to surface, though none of it was as clear-cut as the Gorongosa diaries.[22] Renamo's chances for official American aid dimmed in 1987, after several major massacres were attributed to its forces, and then seemed to disappear altogether in April 1988, when the State Department, delivering the coup de grâce in its long battle with the Republican right on the issue, released the report that accused Renamo of murdering 100,000 civilians. No government could now be publicly associated with Renamo. Even the South African–backed rebels in Angola had refused to let Renamo representatives visit their camps, saying, "They have no nationalist credentials."[23] By the time I visited Mozambique, governments from every point on the political spectrum were all but tripping over one another in their rush to assist the government. The Soviet Union was still Frelimo's main military supplier, but Margaret Thatcher's Britain was providing much-needed radios and training, and even the Reagan administration had proposed sending a consignment of nonlethal military aid. (It was not approved by Congress.) Mozambique was the largest single recipient of Italian foreign aid. (The United States was the largest donor of emergency aid.) In the previous five years, Mozambique had turned to Western financial institutions for help, joining the World Bank and the International Monetary Fund, encouraging investment by foreign multinational corporations, and making a serious effort to revive a domestic private sector—all somehow without alienating its East-bloc allies.

So Renamo had lost the propaganda war. And yet the war war went on. In 1986, a major Renamo offensive in Zambézia, driving from Malawi down to the coast, had nearly succeeded in cutting Mozambique in two. Samora Machel's death, in October 1986, in an airplane crash inside South Africa, had stunned Frelimo, and the international press had reported in December that the fall of Quelimane was imminent. If Renamo had succeeded in taking Quelimane, its plans called for the declaration of an independent republic in the northern half of the country. That offensive fell short, finally, and a joint Mozambican-Zimbabwean counteroffensive in 1987 succeeded in driving Renamo from the main towns (such as Morrumbala). But hundreds of thousands of refugees continued to pour out of Mozambique in 1988, and Renamo still moved freely in the countryside, attacking and pillaging at an undiminished pace in all ten provinces. Foreign support undoubtedly still reached Renamo, but it couldn't begin to account for the destruction being wreaked.

Externally, Renamo seemed to be in shambles. The movement's main international spokesman, a Portuguese lawyer of Goanese descent named Evo Fernandes, had been murdered in April 1988 near Lisbon.[24] When I went to Lisbon to talk to Renamo, I was told that its new spokesman was a law student whose office was the law school cafeteria at lunchtime. I never managed to catch him there. Instead, I found the spokesman for a breakaway group, the União Nacional de Moçambique (Unamo). Renamo's office in London turned out to be a mailing address where no one recognized the name on the Renamo literature that supposedly originated there. Renamo's office in Washington, D.C., turned out to be space borrowed from a right-wing foundation called Free The Eagle. Its representatives there denounced their brethren in Lisbon.

And yet the war went on.

5

The population of Quelimane, which was 60,000 before the war got to Zambézia, had more than doubled by the time I visited. (The only reason it was not several times larger was that the government did not distribute free food in the cities.) As in every Mozambican city, most of the people lived on the outskirts, in the cane town. The cement town down on the waterfront was quiet, almost deserted; dogs slept in the middle of the main street at noon. Quelimane was once the busiest slave port in Mozambique—in the 1820s, 12,000 to 15,000 slaves a year passed through[1]—and a number of ancient, thick-walled homes and crumbling, whitewashed warehouses from its heyday survived. An eighteenth-century church stood with its back to the quay, which faced onto a wide, steamy, mangrove-edged bend in the Cua-Cua River, fifteen miles from the sea. A few garish new buildings—the Banco de Moçambique, with its two-story lobby and bright abstract mosaics; the Hotel Chuabo, seven floors of glass, steel, wood paneling, and ersatz marble—evoked the short boom of the 1960s. But most of the storefronts were empty or had little in their salt-smeared windows beyond a scatter of cheap, sun-ruined goods.

At the airport in Maputo, a young Indian man had approached Dividas and me, asking us to carry two parcels to his family in Quelimane. He stressed that they contained no merchandise, only food—eggs and apples and cheese. He said he had been sending his family food this way for years. At times, he said, it had been a matter of their survival. We took the parcels, but I began to wonder if they were entirely noncommercial when, over the hours we spent waiting for our flight, I kept seeing the same young Indian darting around the airport, looking as if he had many more things on his mind than the daily diet of the Zambézia branch of his family. My doubts deepened when he paused at one point in his rounds to confide to me, "Ninety-nine percent of the Mozambique people have not respect for time. 'Time is money'—no, they don't believe that. They think next week to do something is as good as today."

Food wouldn't be a problem for us in Quelimane, I had been told, as long as we had foreign currency. Traveler's checks were no good in the north, however; nobody knew what they were. Since the banks in Maputo were themselves short of foreign currency, I ended up having to buy a series of small items—Cadbury's chocolate bars, mostly—with large-denomination checks in the diplomats' supermarket, and thus accumulate some hard currency in change. I wanted dollars, but all that was available was South African rands. Nobody seemed to find it strange that South Africa's currency was essential for traveling in a country whose destruction had been financed by South Africa. Mozambicans are accustomed to such ironies.

As things turned out, I did need the rands for a hotel and meals in Quelimane, but meticais, the Mozambican currency, were also in use. Food was, at that moment, not scarce in Quelimane. The central market had fish, vegetables, and fruit, and even the city's single supermarket was open intermittently. I went to the supermarket for supplies, hoping to find bottled water or anything potable, for the long days out in the districts. Instead, I found dim aisles sparsely stocked with South African detergent and cooking oil. I had to settle for Portuguese table wine and what looked like strawberry soda (it was strawberry concentrate and quite unpotable—as I discovered one thirsty afternoon—without water to add). The value of the metical was such that, to pay for these items, I had to count out seven large piles of bills, and when one fifty-metical note disintegrated in my hand, the cashier calmly swept the remains onto the floor.

Cash seemed to have a gloriously weak hold on the Mozambican imagination. At the Ministry of Information in Maputo, I once came upon two American hundred-dollar bills lying on a desk in an empty office. I was flabbergasted. Per capita income in Mozambique was less than one hundred dollars a year, and this was *hard currency*. The ministry's offices were unlocked— indeed, nearly every doorknob I ever touched there came off in my hand—and saw an endless traffic of clerks, messengers, and reporters. But when the young official who sat at the desk in question showed up, and I pointed out the money, he shrugged, said something about a foreign correspondent wanting hotel reservations, and pushed the bills aside. I pursued the subject, pointing out that in most places cash had an aura, a little nimbus of emotion that grew according to the sum printed on the bills.

"But here in Mozambique, money means very little," the official said. "You could put this in the street, and the children would pick it up, then throw it down. It's such a new thing, people don't know what it means. I could leave this money on my desk for two days. No one would take it. If I left this shirt, O.K., someone would take it right away." He indicated the ordinary South African soccer shirt he wore. It had "Charles" (not his name) written on the breast. His own salary, I knew, was about fifteen dollars a week.

The official was right, no doubt, about what it was safe to leave on his desk. But money was less a new thing in Mozambique than it was a debased thing. In the countryside, it had lost value with the collapse, after independence, of the rural trading network. The Portuguese had abandoned the shops where peasants bought manufactured goods. Frelimo's attempts to keep the shops going failed, and peasants soon found themselves with piles of cash, which they earned from selling their surplus produce but now had nowhere to spend. Eventually, they stopped marketing their surplus. That meant food shortages in the cities, which helped create a giant black market. By the early 1980s, even schools, state farms, and the army were forced to buy their food, at grossly inflated prices, on the black market. Renamo attacks also prevented produce from reaching the cities. And since cashews and cotton, export crops produced primarily by peasants, were main sources of Mozambique's foreign exchange, the lack of peasant production meant, too, that the hard currency available for imported consumer goods dried up. With the disappearance of both agricultural produce and imports, the pickings in urban shops grew increasingly scarce. By 1983, money was worth little more in the cities than it was in the country-side. A fierce economic-recovery program, backed by the International Monetary Fund and implemented in 1987, had succeeded in filling urban shops with goods again by 1988, but, after a series of devaluations of the metical, so few Mozambicans could afford to buy anything that, for the ordinary worker, money still meant far less than access to a vegetable plot did. Meanwhile, in rural areas—where Renamo had destroyed or looted some nine hundred shops[2]—there was less to buy than ever.

About the value of clothing, the information officer was certainly right. In Maputo, where a laborer's monthly salary was about the same as the price of a shirt, I was told that the primary responsibility of the guards posted before every middle-class residence was to protect the clothesline from laundry thieves. The journalist Philip Van Niekerk has written about being in a movie house in Lichinga, in the northern province of Niassa, and watching a Soviet film about "a truck driver who rapes and murders two young girls and deposits their naked bodies on a garden dump. As he shoves their clothes into a furnace, the audience rises in protest: it is hard to imagine a worse crime in Lichinga than burning clothes."[3] In Quelimane, young women were continually calling out to Dividas on the street, asking him if he wouldn't like to give them his hat or his shirt. Even at a distance, he explained, the women recognized that the things were not locally made. His shirt, which had a catamaran silkscreened on the breast, came from Swaziland, where his sister had bought it. Swaziland is a tiny, conservative kingdom, wedged between South Africa and Mozambique, where casinos cater to South African tourists. It was widely envied in Mozambique for its well-stocked shops and had become the setting for many a bittersweet joke. Here's one told to me by a government employee: A Mozambican goes to Swaziland to buy a shirt. When the shopkeeper asks him what style, size, color, quality, material, and type of sleeves he wants, the Mozambican is overwhelmed by all the choices. He just wants a *shirt*. The same thing happens in a bakery, where he goes looking for bread. The baker offers him brown, white, rye, French, sliced, or rolls, and the Mozambican is again rendered speechless. Finally, he visits a car dealership, where the salesman reels off all the makes and models available, and the Mozambican is once again bowled over. When he returns home, a friend asks how he liked Swaziland. "It's all right," he says. "But it's very backward. It's just like Mozambique before independence."

Actually, in the cities in Mozambique, a tide of new prosperity appeared to be rising. Late-model Land Rovers were a common sight on streets that, until recently, had not seen a new vehicle since 1975. But the only growth industry in Mozambique was foreign aid, and all the new hardware belonged, in fact, to international organizations. More than one hundred organizations, including governments, religious groups, United Nations agencies, and nongovernmental relief and development outfits, had projects going in Mozambique.[4] Their employees numbered in the thousands; aid spending totaled about a billion dollars a year.[5] The East-bloc countries also had thousands of teachers, advisers, and technicians in Mozambique. Foreign aid represented, of course, more than false prosperity; it was also crucial to the survival of millions of Mozambicans. And Renamo recognized its importance. The documents discovered at the rebels' headquarters on Gorongosa Mountain in 1985 gave, as noted, high priority to stopping "the activities of foreigners because they are the most dangerous in the recovery of the economy."[6] Dozens of foreigners—most of them Portuguese or Soviets—had been kidnapped by Renamo; dozens had been killed.[7] By 1988 the war confined most foreigners to the cities.

In Quelimane at the time I visited, the nonprofit foreign organizations on hand included, besides CARE International, Save the Children, Oxfam Britain, Oxfam Canada, Médecins Sans Frontières, the International Red Cross, the Mozambican Red Cross, Action Aid, World Vision, Air Serv (a missionary aviation service), International Volunteer Service (a left-wing British development group), and three or four other nongovernmental organizations I never got to know. There were also a slew of United Nations agencies, bilateral aid projects, and religious orders. Inevitably, there was jostling among these groups, but I was most struck by the tone of professional respect with which one American aid worker acknowledged, gazing at a map of Zambézia, that Action Aid, a newcomer to the province, had gone to the right place at the right time when it started operations in the district of Pebane. "They're drumming up a lot of business out there," the aid worker said. What was meant was that people in Pebane were starving. The district had just reported the highest rate of child malnutrition in Zambézia, and people were actually dying of starvation in the camps. The boat on which I had tried to book passage on my first afternoon in Quelimane had been bound for Pebane. Its arrival, loaded with maize, had reportedly started a riot. Soldiers had to beat the crowd back. And then the soldiers had taken the maize for themselves. It seemed they were starving, too. There really was a lot of business in Pebane. (Two years later, there was even more. With its *deslocado* population grown to 170,000, Pebane had become the largest camp for displaced persons in Mozambique, and starving soldiers were still battling starving civilians for the maize off the boats from Quelimane.)[8]

The expatriates in Quelimane ran the gamut from tireless saints to bumblers and cynical time-servers. Everyone, good and bad, contended with numbing frustration. Quantities of food seemed to be constantly rotting in the truck parks while convoys waited in Quelimane for military escort vehicles that awaited spare parts from Maputo that awaited a barge to return from Pemba. One of the best approaches that I encountered belonged to a mechanic for British Leyland, a big friendly lad from Liverpool named Steve. Mozambique was the first country Steve had seen outside England, and he was utterly charmed. "These people have nowt, and they're still happy," he liked to say. Steve flew to Morrumbala to see if some of the damaged vehicles there could be salvaged or if the local tinsmiths should be allowed to turn them into buckets, machetes, and hoe blades. He returned to Quelimane shaking his head. He hadn't found a single salvageable vehicle, and he didn't think there was much left even for the tinsmiths. Later, Steve told me that he loved American football. His favorite team, he said, was the Cleveland Browns. "They don't win very often, *but they try so hard.*"

Some other expatriates seemed terminally incapable of getting on the local wavelength. One UNICEF official I met took an especially formalistic approach. She was from the Middle East and, though she had been in Mozambique for two years, still spoke very little Portuguese. One day, in a district administrator's house in Zambézia, she turned to Dividas and asked, in English, "Do you think it would be all right if we ate these biscuits now, from a cultural point of view?" It was the only time I ever saw him at a loss for words.

While we were in Quelimane, Dividas and I stayed at the Hotel Chuabo. It was a big, hideous, modern place, run by a Portuguese woman known as Dona Amélia. Dona Amélia "kept up standards" with a vengeance. The Chuabo was said to be the best hotel in Mozambique outside Maputo, and she was said to be the second most feared person in the country—after Afonso Dhlakama. She was a stolid, imposing woman in her forties, plainly but impeccably dressed, with a stiff back, large jowls, large earrings, and a large beehive of brown hair. Her husband was much older than she was, and every evening, at a well-set table in a corner of the seventh-floor dining room, they ate supper with the same companion, a dissipated-looking Portuguese with a scraggly mustache and a cigarette hanging permanently from his lip. The three of them represented a significant share of the Portuguese population remaining in Quelimane. After supper, Dona Amélia did her accounts, sitting ramrod-straight on a barstool, while her terrified staff lurked in the background. Her waiters and bellhops all seemed to have been lobotomized. They tiptoed around in white jackets in a sort of sullen trance, dull-witted and invariably hostile to any guest they encountered. Samora Machel had once visited the Chuabo, it was said, and a deputation of the hotel's workers had approached the president to protest Dona Amélia's treatment. It was worse than the plantations in colonial days, they said. Machel had been torn. He had long preached the need for black Mozambicans to decolonize their minds as well as their country, but he also had a military man's love of order and efficiency—and the Hotel Chuabo, by God, *worked*. Dona Amélia survived that revolt, and she also survived a crisis, it was said, after her son, who was working as a shipping clerk in Beira, was discovered to be a Renamo agent. She even arranged somehow for him to be deported to Portugal long before his prison sentence was served out.

The Hotel Chuabo's reputation seemed to be based partly on the general terror of Dona Amélia and partly on her ability to procure, perhaps through the same channels that she used to spring her son from prison, light bulbs. There was, and had been for years, an acute light bulb shortage in Mozambique, but much of the Chuabo was illuminated for much of the evening, and every room had at least one working bulb.

The hotel's reputation was certainly not based on the service. Guests were the enemy at the Chuabo, never to be pleased and certainly never indulged. The dining room had coffee in its stocks, but Dona Amélia decided, while we were staying there, to serve it only in the evenings. My pleas to have mine served in the mornings—I promised to forgo my rations in the evenings—were rejected with contempt.

Though the war seemed far away from Quelimane, it wasn't. One day we drove out to Nicuadala, the nearest district capital and one of the few places in the province that could be reached by road. Nicuadala was little more than a few dilapidated buildings, but unlike Quelimane it had free food distribution and, as a result, more than 50,000 *deslocados*, most of them living in wretched conditions in camps that were frequently attacked. The Nicuadala administrator's house was full of bullet holes from a Renamo attack four months earlier, and a former teacher-training college, now a Tanzanian Army barracks, had been attacked only two months before. The fields alongside the road to Nicuadala were lush with banana, papaya, cassava, sweet potato, rice, cashew, mango, and coconut, and the shoulders of the road were full of people walking, carrying baskets and bottles and babies and tools. But the shops and gas stations and roadhouses were all abandoned, shot up, and reverting rapidly to bush. We interviewed eight or ten *deslocados* in Nicuadala, including an old woman, Delfina Muita, of Morrumbala, who had just heard that morning that her son had been killed by Renamo.

6

In the evenings in Quelimane, I asked Dividas about himself.

"I was born in Beira, in 1951," he said. "My father was a nurse. That was one of the best jobs an African could have in those days. We lived in a cement house and always had a servant. My father was one of the big men in the community, so the men used to come to our house to talk. I liked to listen to them, but they never let me stay when they talked about politics. I liked to listen to Radio Frelimo, but I had to do it in secret, because my father wouldn't allow it. He said it was dangerous, because someone standing outside the window might hear it and tell the PIDE"—the Polícia Internacional e de Defesa do Estado, the colonial secret police. "My father and his friends wanted the Portuguese to leave our country, but they were afraid.

"I went to a Catholic boarding school near Caia. My father wanted to send me on to high school in Beira, but I wanted to stay where I was. In those days, I only wanted to study, and there were too many distractions in the city—sports, girls, different things to do. My father and I could not agree about anything. I didn't know why. Finally, I came back to Beira, but I stopped going to school. On Radio Frelimo at that time, they were always calling for young boys to join Frelimo. They said they had scholarships. Anybody could become a doctor or an engineer. I didn't really care about politics, but I wanted very much an education. So I decided to join Frelimo then. The problem was how to leave the country. There had been some priests who helped boys to leave, but they had been caught by the PIDE.

"When I was nineteen, I joined the Portuguese Army. My father was very unhappy about it, but he would have been even more unhappy if he knew my real plan, which was to desert to Frelimo. I was trained as a paratrooper, then sent to Tete"—a northwestern province where the anticolonial war was intense after 1968. "Because I could speak the language there, they made me an interpreter. I went on patrols, and I helped with interrogations. I tried to interpret what people said so that the interrogators heard what they wanted to hear, and in the night I would go to the prisoners and explain to them that they must always tell the same story, no matter what happened, because as soon as they changed their story, they would have even bigger trouble. Many people were killed anyway. The worst torturer was a very big black guy named Chico Nyaka. *Nyaka* means 'snake.'" Dividas laughed quietly, shaking his head. "Chico, Chico, Chico," he said. "Hey, Chico." Dividas pronounced it "sheik-o" and sounded as if he were calling, very gently, to a mad child. "When independence came, the people in Tete found Chico, and before Frelimo could stop them, they tore him apart and chopped him into small pieces with machetes.

"My chance to desert came one day when I had to deliver a group of Frelimo sympathizers to the PIDE. I asked the sympathizers to take me to Frelimo. At first, they refused. I said, 'O.K. Then you will suffer.' Finally, they took a chance, and they led me into the bush. We walked for eight hours. They took away my pistol and my uniform. At last, we came to a Frelimo camp. I was very surprised to find some people I knew there. These were people that the Portuguese had interrogated, but I had *believed* them when they said they knew nothing about Frelimo. The camp commander believed my story, because those people told him that I was a good man and had not hurt them when they were prisoners.

"The next morning, a Frelimo soldier who had been following us came into the camp. He had been very frightened when he saw me on the trail, and he said I was a spy. They tied me up, and then they beat me and kicked me. When I said I wanted to fight with Frelimo, they said, 'We are not your brothers! Where are your brothers here?' They sentenced me to death, and the women and children were sent away from the camp. Then there was a meeting to decide how to report the execution. While the meeting was going on, a Frelimo political commissar arrived. He saw me there. When he heard that I had not been captured but had come to the camp myself, he told them to untie me. He told me that it was all a mistake, and he welcomed me to Frelimo.

"I was sent to Zambia by foot, and then to Tanzania by truck. In Tanzania, I received training in antiaircraft and rocket artillery. I was at Nachingwea, in southern Tanzania, waiting to go back into Mozambique, but my orders never came. People started saying that deserters from the Portuguese were not trusted, and that was why I was not sent. Then my commander told me that they wanted to send me overseas to study. That was what I really wanted. But the scholarship never came, either. I was in Nachingwea for nearly a year. Finally, people started saying that because most of our leaders were from the south of Mozambique the scholarships were going to other people from the south, and because I was from Beira I would never receive one. That was when I deserted from Frelimo.

"I hitchhiked to the Kenyan border, walked across at night, and went on to Nairobi. I was very hungry, so I went to the police station. The police arrested me and said they would deport me. But after two days, they sent me to a government office in charge of refugees. There I heard some people speaking Portuguese. I discovered they were Mozambicans. They took me home with them, fed me, gave me a bed to sleep in, and even washed my clothes. A few days later, they took me back to the refugee office. The Kenyans told me that I had to be out of the country in forty-eight hours. I was shocked. I didn't know what to do. That was when the Mozambicans I was staying with told me they belonged to Coremo"—the Comitê Revolucionário de Moçambique, a guerrilla faction that had broken away from Frelimo. "They said I should go to Zambia to join Coremo. I discovered later that those people often waited at the refugee office for Mozambicans in my situation, and that they worked with the Kenyans to gain recruits. I think the people at Nachingwea who told me I would never get a scholarship because I was not from the south may have also been Coremo.

"I didn't want to join Coremo, so I went to the United Nations high commissioner for refugees in Nairobi. After some weeks, they sent me to Addis Ababa and gave me a scholarship. I studied six years in Ethiopia, in English, and I graduated high school there. I married an Ethiopian girl, and we had a daughter. I was afraid to contact my family, because I was sure the PIDE would be watching them, hoping to find out where I was. But after the coup in Lisbon in 1974, I wrote to my sister. She wrote back to me that our father had traveled to Tete to look for me after he heard that I had disappeared. But now he didn't believe it was me, writing from Ethiopia. Even after I sent her another letter, he didn't believe it was me. Then, in 1976, when my daughter was born, I sent a photograph of myself with her. My sister told me that our father carried the photograph around with him, and that he would show it to people, especially after a few drinks: his son and his granddaughter in Ethiopia. I think I was his favorite child, even though I disobeyed him. He never wrote to me himself, though. There was still a security risk. Frelimo was in power, and they hated me for deserting, just as the Portuguese had. Then, in 1977, my father died.

"My family started writing letters begging me to come home. They said they were suffering. Luís Bernardo Honwana, who is now the minister of culture, came to Addis Ababa and talked to the Mozambicans there, telling us we should come back. I told him I had never seen him at Nachingwea, and I asked how he could prove that Frelimo would not kill us, and he said he would ask Samora himself to protect me. My wife did not want to go to Mozambique, but when my older brother, who had joined Frelimo, wrote to me that our mother was really suffering, I decided to come back. I was detained at the airport in Maputo, but Honwana and Samora did protect me, and after a few hours I was allowed to go. I found that my family was not suffering— they had just wanted me to come home. My daughter later came from Ethiopia, but I have not seen my wife again. I have a Mozambican wife now, and two more children, and my daughter from Ethiopia also lives with us."

Dividas settled in Maputo and began working for international organizations. He got one warning from Frelimo. "Armando Guebuza, who is now the minister of transport, called a meeting for people in my position. He said the government would be watching us very closely, and we should know it. I've never had any trouble with the government, but if you write something about me, perhaps you could say I deserted from Frelimo because of 'political immaturity.'"

Dividas laughed lightly. If he had stayed with Frelimo, I thought, he would have been in a high-ranking job in the government or the army by now. Many top Frelimo officials are surprisingly young, and Frelimo, unlike many ruling parties in Africa, is known for rewarding competence.

7

Like many places in Mozambique, the Ile district, in northern Zambézia, was beautiful in the piercing way of imperiled things. Errego, the district capital, is built on a ridge, with tremendous rocks, hundreds of feet high, rising all around it. A park and a playground fill the center of the town, and a wide esplanade lined with trees—eucalyptus, palms, acacias, flamboyants—runs from the pink, tile-roofed hospital, which looks like a miniature Italian palace, to the administrator's house, a grand structure that was roofless and gutted by the time I visited. Renamo had overrun and briefly occupied Errego three times in the previous two years, burning down most of the buildings, kidnapping more than 200 people, and destroying three tea factories, several schools, and all the machinery at a local coal mine. Ours was the first airplane Ile had seen in a month, and there had been a number of Renamo attacks during that month. No road traffic had reached the area in more than a year. Food and clothes were scarce. There were 300,000 people in the Ile district; Errego alone had more than 23,000 *deslocados*.

Dividas and I spent most of our day in Ile interviewing *deslocados*. Those we talked with ranged from former tea-factory managers to the wildest-looking person I saw anywhere in Mozambique—a very tall, very black young man who wore nothing but a burlap loincloth, spoke only a few words of Lomwe, looked about twenty, had no teeth, and moved with the power, wariness, and grace of a panther. Just as we had started talking with a doughty young mother named Elena Adriano, a boy came running up, saying that the *cargueiro* was at the airstrip. The airstrip was six miles away. Our instructions from Hennie and Ferdie had been to rush to the strip as soon as we heard the plane returning, but we hadn't heard the plane. I doubted we could have missed it. But it was midafternoon. I ran for the administrator's Land Rover. Dividas was reluctant to abandon Elena—his wife is named Elena, and the coincidence delighted him. As we tore out of the camp, he called, "Ciao, Elena!" And he was still grinning a minute later when one of our fellow passengers spotted a DC-3 high in the sky, headed south.

We pulled over. It was definitely Little Annie, droning through the puffball clouds. I jumped out and started waving my arms. The eight or ten local people who had been riding with us were hugely amused. I asked one of them to take off his shirt, which was white, and I waved it. The Dakota did not change course. We watched it recede until there was no doubt left. The others tried to stifle their laughter. Even Dividas seemed amused. He shrugged. "They'll come back," he said. "They'll make a special trip."

Our host that day was an unassuming, serious young man named Januario Romão. He was not the district administrator, but a substitute—most of the local officials I met in Mozambique were substitutes; the *chefes* always seemed to be away in the provincial capital, or Maputo, or overseas, attending a meeting or taking a course. When I asked Romão about the fate of the hundreds of people from Errego kidnapped by Renamo—they included the town's postmaster—he said that he could be certain only about what befell them during the first few weeks, because after that his own wife and children had escaped, and few others had returned in the two years since. But, he said quietly, his wife and children had told some terrible stories.

Romão had been overjoyed to see the food we brought to Ile. He was going to send it immediately to a place called Mulevala, he said, which had been liberated by Frelimo less than two weeks before. The people there were starving. But Mulevala was more than one hundred kilometers away, and local men were going to be carrying the food there on their heads, so first they would have to tear each of the big, fifty-kilogram sacks in half, then sew each half closed. Transport was the big problem in Ile,

Romão said. Could I, when I got back to Quelimane, ask Calamidades to send him a helicopter? I said I would try. Of course,
when Hennie and Ferdie left Ile without us, I began to wonder
just when I would see Quelimane again.

Since the road back to Errego was uphill, and fuel was more
precious than gold-backed currency in Ile—Dividas and I had
brought a drum of diesel from Quelimane, which had gone
straight into the district's two working vehicles—we proceeded
to the airstrip. It was down on a wide plateau surrounded by
dark, brushy hills. Hundreds of people were there, still milling
excitedly after the departure of the Dakota. The district's one
truck was already loaded with the latest delivery. But Romão
was nonplussed to hear that the sacks contained maize. The only
thing Ile did not need, he said, was maize. He had sent that message to Calamidades in Quelimane every chance he got. There
was a white face among the airstrip crowd—an Italian priest.
He was close-mouthed, deeply tanned, and wore his hair in a
homemade crewcut. He told Romão that the Dakota's pilots had
indicated that they would return for us.

We had several hours, at least, to wait. Ismail, the young man
from Calamidades who accompanied me everywhere in Zambézia, drifted away, looking for food. I had noticed that, on trips
to the districts, Ismail always came away with a box full of fresh
produce. From Morrumbala, he had taken tomatoes and onions.
In Ile, he gathered tomatoes, bananas, sugar, and corn. When I
asked someone in Ile about it, they murmured that Ismail was
leading a "provincial delegation" and that the gifts were a sign
of respect. Ismail was a strange kid. He was thin, but his lean
and hungry look was more spiritual than physical. He was, in
fact, the only Mozambican I ever met whom one could describe
as grabby. And in this case he was grabbing from people who
were starving. When I asked him about it, he looked nervous and
said he only took things that could not be found in Quelimane.
That was not true, and I said so, and Ismail whined that the
prices were too high in Quelimane. In the end, I told his boss at
Calamidades about his levies, and Ismail was fired. (Months
later, I got a letter from an aid worker in Quelimane saying that
Ismail had been rehired.)[1]

There was a thatch-roofed lean-to at the edge of the airstrip,
which turned out to be, on closer inspection, a school. Of the five
hundred schools still functioning in Zambézia, most, according

to the provincial director of education, had no materials whatever; they consisted of a teacher and students, who typically met under a tree.[2] The school at the airstrip in Ile had a roof and some rudimentary benches, but no blackboard and no walls. Class was out when we arrived, but some children were shyly studying Dividas and me from across the road. We sat down on a grassy bank, they drew closer, and Dividas asked them their names.

There were Luísa Sábado and Victoria Viegas and Zeca Vidro. All but the smallest children spoke some Portuguese. They learned it in school, they said. Dividas asked who among them was the best student. They giggled and squirmed, and Zeca, a thin boy with huge eyes, was finally nominated. Dividas asked who the best soccer player was. More giggling, more squirming, and another boy was pointed out. Dividas asked to see the school exercise book that Luísa, an angel-faced thirteen-year-old, was carrying. With painful reluctance, she handed it over. It was a geography workbook, tattered from what looked like use by several predecessors. It had scenes of karate fighting drawn on the cover in a childish hand, with the caption "The Five Masters of Xao-Lin." "The Five Masters of Xao-Lin," Luísa mumbled, studying her bare feet desperately, was a movie she had seen in Gurue. Gurue, the capital of a prosperous tea-growing district, was about fifty miles north of Ile. She had traveled there by bus, Luísa said, long ago, when the roads were open. It was the farthest she had ever been from Ile. Yes, she would love to see Quelimane someday. And Maputo. She wanted to go to secondary school. Dividas asked when she planned to marry, and Luísa said, "When I am nineteen." She tried to suppress a smile, but that looked difficult to do—her lips had two or three extra flutings, for maximum expressiveness. Their expression in repose was a gentle, precocious irony. Dividas asked Luísa if she had heard of America, and she whispered, "No." None of the children had.

Did the children want to hear a story? They did. By this time, a number of people had collected around the edges of our group, including a noisy older man—"drunk from *aguardente*," Victoria Viegas whispered to me—who sat nearby and tried to get the children to listen to *him* rather than to this stranger in the clean white cap. But the children listened to Dividas. His first story was called "How the Pig Got a Flat Nose." It was a variation on the Icarus myth. The pig had always wanted to fly, so his friend the eagle made him a pair of wings out of wax. After ignoring the eagle's advice and flying too close to the sun and losing one of his wings, the pig careered through the sky with his remaining wing, out of control, for several minutes, thrilling the children of Ile, before he finally lost it, too, and crashed to earth nose first.

Next, Dividas told "Why the Crocodile Eats People." It was a much sadder story. While Crocodilo was living peacefully on the riverbank, some people suddenly came and took three of her *crianças* (babies). She went to the village the next day to find them. The villagers were having a big party. To her horror, Crocodilo saw that the people had baked one of her *crianças* and were eating it. She could not see her other *crianças*, and she could not approach, because of the party. She enlisted the help of a hen, and the hen reported that the others were still alive. The next day, Crocodilo returned, hoping to rescue them, but now the hen told her that her two remaining children had also been killed. Crocodilo went back to the riverbank heartbroken and enraged. Her revenge, she vowed, would be to eat the next person she saw.

While Dividas was telling these stories, I noticed an infant whose mother had drawn close to listen. Although the mother looked healthy, the baby was clearly suffering from severe malnutrition. It was extremely scrawny, with lots of loose, grayish skin and a frightening, monkeylike look. It was a look that I had seen on a number of infants in Zambézia. The baby was clinging to its mother's breast, but it was obviously finding no nourishment there. Its chances of surviving another year were, I guessed, poor to nil. The mother noticed me watching her and looked alarmed. I turned away and studied the children sitting on the ground around us. Most of them were painfully thin. Victoria's wrists were tiny. Several of the children had the potbellies that meant either malnutrition or parasites, and one boy was missing an eye. But none of them was starving, as far as I could tell. All of them had probably lost friends or neighbors or family members to hunger or the war; but as they listened to Dividas, they looked so lovely, so unbrutalized, so oblivious to everything else, including the spectral infant sucking frantically behind them, that I found I had, at least temporarily, lost all interest in discovering the details of their hard times.

As Dividas came to the end of "Why the Crocodile Eats People," a teenage girl dressed in a loud, new turquoise dress and white platform shoes walked past, laughing raucously. Her clothes were wildly out of place in Ile, and Dividas asked Luísa if the girl was, by any chance, "a friend of the director of Calamidades." Luísa laughed. She was indeed, Luísa said. Luísa herself wore shapeless gray rags full of holes through which her breasts, despite her best efforts, kept falling. Some of the younger children wore nothing but scraps of burlap.

Dividas and I dug through our bags and came up with half a dozen ballpoint pens. We started handing them out. Each child who received one would pull off the cap and slide out the cartridge to check the ink level, while the others cheered or hooted, depending on what was revealed. Luísa got the last pen, and she let the tension build as she slowly withdrew the cartridge. It turned out to be full to the brim. The other children screamed with glee and envy, and Luísa whispered, with devastating irony, "God is great."

Hennie and Ferdie returned, dangerously late in the day, bringing yet another load of unneeded maize. The children of Ile ran out to the plane with their tin cans, and the last I saw of them, they were darting under the district's truck to snatch the stray kernels that fell from the sacks.

That evening I asked Dividas about the prospects of a Luísa Sábado. Would she really be able to go to secondary school? "If this war ends, yes," he said. "But she must be able to leave that area. Even just to go to Gurue. She doesn't like the clothes she has. You can see that. She wants a new dress. She says she doesn't want to marry until she is nineteen, but if some boy just a little bit clever, who perhaps works at the hospital, offers her a new dress, she may go with him. Then, if she gets pregnant, the parents will get involved, a marriage will be arranged, and her education will be finished. Or if she gets a new dress from Calamidades, some soldier might notice her and start to give her little things. And if she gets pregnant with him, he may not marry her. Luísa's world is small now, because of the war. She is too isolated. Many people in this country are too isolated. It's all because of the military situation."

8

The war had reached a stalemate. Frelimo launched seasonal offensives but, as a Western military attaché in Maputo put it, "Renamo just moves away, like mercury when you try to catch it on the end of your pencil." The Mozambican armed forces were small—fewer than thirty thousand men[1]—and unimposing. When Frelimo came to power, its leaders had declined to admit soldiers who had fought with the Portuguese into the new national army—a grievous mistake, according to a young, British-trained Frelimo officer I spoke to. After independence, the new government, anticipating a South African invasion, turned the liberation army into a conventional force, relying on Soviet training and heavy weaponry. The South Africans had, after all, invaded Angola in 1975 on a grand scale. But no invasion came, and when Renamo's guerrilla-style attacks spread, Frelimo's tanks, artillery, and interceptor aircraft were of little use. Many former guerrilla commanders, the *antiguos combatentes* from the liberation war, were recalled to service in 1983 and 1984, on the theory that it takes a bush fighter to beat a bush fighter. But they proved ineffectual, too, and by 1988 they were being retired again.

Special commandos trained by the Soviet Union and Great Britain in counterinsurgency were the main hope of the army, but they represented only a small fraction of a small military in a large country.[2] Most of the Mozambican Army was under-trained, underequipped, underpaid, and underfed. The collapse of the national transportation system, together with the general lack of administrative skills, disrupted military logistics just as thoroughly as they did civilian life. Troops in the field often did not receive pay, uniforms, ammunition, or rations. Morale suffered, and when soldiers were forced to find food any way they could, the army's reputation suffered. Tales of military haplessness abounded. When I was in Maputo, it was rumored that a battalion had suddenly appeared in Gaza province. Nobody knew where it had come from. It had been left there for months, apparently, without orders or supplies, simply forgotten. Draft evasion was widespread, especially in the cities, and provincial commanders, who seemed to be given a free hand in the raising of forces, resorted to rough-and-ready conscription, which further tarnished the army's image.

Renamo spokesmen claimed that Frelimo would face defeat if it were not for the support of "foreign mercenaries," and the assistance of Tanzania and, especially, Zimbabwe had in fact been crucial to the government's survival. Zimbabwe had as many as twenty thousand troops in Mozambique, most of them concentrated around the Beira Corridor—a highway, railway, and oil pipeline that connect Zimbabwe to the port at Beira.[3] The Zimbabwe government owed its own existence partly to Frelimo's steadfast support during the liberation war in Rhodesia, so the military assistance helped repay a historic debt. It was also essential to the Zimbabwean economy to keep the Beira Corridor open. (The railway from southern Zimbabwe to Maputo, known as the Limpopo Corridor, had been closed for several years by Renamo sabotage. It was actually a more economic route for some goods, and an international consortium was working to repair it. Zimbabwean troops were also posted along the Limpopo Corridor.) The financial drain in the meantime was serious, however;[4] and Renamo, seeking to scare off Robert Mugabe's government, had conducted brutal raids into Zimbabwe, kidnapping, mutilating, and murdering villagers and students.[5]

Unlike Mozambique, Zimbabwe was able to transform a guerrilla army into a professional military force after independence (largely by integrating it with the Rhodesian armed forces, its erstwhile enemy), and Zimbabwean participation had been the key to some of Frelimo's few successes in the war. The alliance was not without friction, though. After the Renamo

headquarters at Gorongosa was overrun by a joint Zimbab-
wean-Mozambican force in August 1985, the Zimbabweans,
having secured the area, withdrew. Within months, Renamo had
retaken the base from Frelimo. The Zimbabweans returned in
their helicopter gunships, took the base again, and thereafter defended the area themselves. The Zimbabweans, it was said,
sometimes refused to engage in joint operations with Frelimo.[6]

Renamo's military prowess was difficult to assess, since its
main targets were civilians and infrastructure. Its record of destruction was, of course, prodigious. Renamo had little, if any,
heavy artillery and virtually no mechanized transport. Its communications system, however, was superior to Frelimo's. Captured radiomen described a comprehensive system, linking all
areas of the country with a shifting headquarters in central
Mozambique. The headquarters was linked, in turn, with a base
in South Africa by an advanced British Racal system, which
shifted frequency sixteen times a minute to avoid monitoring.[7]
Renamo had been consistently able to mass large numbers of
small units for major attacks and disperse them rapidly for strategic retreats. Some Renamo commanders, according to reports, communicated on solar-powered radios through laptop
computers.[8]

The notion, advanced by many observers, that Renamo violence was just "wanton barbarism" (Bob Geldof, on a heavily
publicized four-day visit to Mozambique in 1987)[9] was belied by
the military facts. Even when Renamo adopted a strategy of
mass terror in the mid-1980s, most of its brutalities had discern-
ible motives. Someone was suspected of withholding information, or a village was suspected of withholding food, and the
bandidos wanted to make sure the neighbors got the message.
Homoine, the scene of the worst single massacre of civilians,
was that rarity in Mozambique, a thriving town, and as such
was widely seen as an advertisement for the government. That,
according to many Mozambicans, was what provoked the
slaughter. A survivor told the *New York Times* that the *bandidos*,
during their rampage through the hospital, shouted, "We want
to finish off the people of Samora Machel!"[10] Predictably,
Frelimo-created "communal villages," which were originally intended to be the centerpiece of rural development but had often

been used simply to keep peasants away from Renamo, became major Renamo targets.[11]

Frelimo's declared strategy for winning the war relied heavily on an amnesty program launched in December 1987 (and discontinued in December 1989). The government claimed that four thousand Renamo fighters had turned themselves in under the amnesty, which stipulated that they should not be punished for their actions while with Renamo, but the program had had no visible effect on the war. Militarily, Frelimo's declared strategy involved cutting off supplies to Renamo from outside the country—this interdiction seemed to have met with little success—and also cutting off Renamo's food supply. Communal villages played an important role in the effort to deny food to Renamo, and so did the "accommodation centers" for *deslocados*, as I learned first from a peasant named Augusto Mainyoa.

I interviewed Mainyoa amid the ruins of the electrical power plant in Morrumbala. He was a small, thin, sad-eyed man dressed in ragged shorts and a filthy yellow sweater vest. He could not name the president of Mozambique but, given four names to choose from, he chose the correct one. He said he could read and write, and he could speak Portuguese. He came from a place he called Codzombe—that was the name of the chief there. Mainyoa said he had never seen any *bandidos*, though he had heard about them. He had arrived in Morrumbala just a few days before. He said he had left Codzombe simply because he was tired of living there. I didn't believe that. Mainyoa had a large bandage around his head and a dogged, shattered look. Moreover, when I started talking with him, a local official of some kind—a stocky young man, also dressed in rags, who was helping to register *deslocados*—had approached us and, muttering uncomfortably, told me that there had apparently been some misunderstanding with this man.

Mainyoa eventually told me the story. He had actually been accosted in his fields by Frelimo soldiers. They had demanded to know what he was doing living there in the bush. Where were the bandits? Was he not collaborating with them? When Mainyoa could not answer, but said that he did not want to leave his land, the soldiers attacked him. They stabbed him with bayonets and smashed his head. Mainyoa showed me a number of fresh stab wounds on his neck and stomach. After he fainted, the soldiers took his wife and children away. Relatives found Mainyoa and treated his wounds with traditional medicines. After three weeks, he felt well enough to travel, and came to Morrumbala. He had found his family there, safe and well, and got his head bandaged at the hospital, but he was still suffering from dizziness.

There was a group of Frelimo soldiers standing near the power station. I pointed them out to Mainyoa, who confirmed that it was their comrades who had attacked him. I asked if he wasn't afraid to tell me his story. He said he was not. With his bandaged head and basset hound eyes, Mainyoa looked as though he had trudged out of the pages of Tolstoy: the violated, heartbreakingly honest peasant.

But the attack on him had not been a misunderstanding. It was, rather, part of a pattern. In some areas of the countryside, Frelimo troops seemed to suspect every resident of collaborating with Renamo. The suspicion was not, perhaps, unfounded: there were rural areas where it was apparently impossible to live *without* collaborating with Renamo. In such areas, Frelimo was therefore simply bringing everyone it could find into the district capitals—a rough-hewn policy, to say the least.

Hundreds of miles south of Morrumbala, in a town called Chibabava, in the province of Sofala, I talked to a widow who said she had six children. But she had only one child—her youngest—with her. She had been "captured by Frelimo," as she put it, while working in her fields with her baby on her back.[12] She had told the soldiers about her other children, but they had refused to allow her to fetch them. Her home was at least forty miles away from Chibabava. It had been nine months since she was seized. The government was feeding her and her baby, but she had no idea what had become of her five older children.

Chibabava felt like the front. It was a Wild West town: hot, dusty, rundown, with boys driving skinny, longhorned cattle down the red-dirt main street. When I arrived, there were soldiers manhandling a rowdy, shirtless, drunken teenager across the main square. Stern, bearded officers in orange berets went bouncing past in jeeps. Crude murals of Frelimo troops killing Renamo bandits were splashed on the crumbling walls, along with "VIVA MARXISMO-LENINISMO." Soviet helicopters came and went from the airstrip, dumping huge piles of cheap new Russian combat boots on the ground. (I had hitched a ride to Chibabava in a cargo plane carrying emergency food. The pilot, a former member of the Portuguese Air Force—and a close spiritual cousin of Hennie and Ferdie—clearly considered it a combat zone. He gave new meaning to the term *treetop flying*, sticking so close to the terrain for the first ten miles out of Chibabava that in every dip and gully the view through the airplane's windshield became a solid wall of trees.) Renamo controlled the countryside around Chibabava, and had done so for at least seven years. No road traffic had reached the town for more than five years. And yet Chibabava had never changed hands. The town had been attacked many times, according to the local administrator—the last attack had been just three months before—but it had never been overrun. Chibabava was not the front. It was just another example of the war's deep stalemate.[13]

9

Renamo's leaders claimed that they controlled more than 80 percent of Mozambique.[1] The claim was absurd, if only because Mozambique is far too large and undeveloped for any small group to "control" much of it. That includes the government, of course, which itself "controlled" little outside the towns and cities. What fraction of the armed men roaming the countryside owed allegiance to any organization was not known, and neither was the proportion of those that called themselves Renamo who actually took commands from Afonso Dhlakama. A wild guess on both questions might have been half. In many areas, Renamo did not practice anything resembling standard guerrilla warfare; that is, it did not take and hold territory and try to provide some form of alternative administration. Instead, it engaged in hit-and-run attacks, usually on nonmilitary targets, pursuing a strategy of maximum destruction and mass terror. In some areas, however, and particularly in central Mozambique, Renamo had held territory, sometimes for years at a stretch, and hundreds of thousands—possibly millions—of Mozambicans lived under some form of Renamo administration.

As I traveled around Mozambique, I became obsessed with developing an accurate picture of life with Renamo. It was an ambition sure to be frustrated, because there were countless versions of the thing, many of them contradictory, many of them purely local. Viewed through the stories of those who had survived it, life with the rebels—or *matsangas*, as they were called, after the first Renamo leader, André Matsangaíssa—became a kind of African shadow play, with a large cast of arcane and traditional characters. I imagine that *matsanga* stories will eventually be adapted to local oral literary traditions and become formalized, but in 1988 most of them were raw and unpredictable. Politically, they were already bitterly contested terrain. Pro-Frelimo researchers returned with horrifying tales of slavery, starvation, and mass murder. Pro-Renamo observers found "liberated zones" of well-fed peasants happy to be rid of communism.[2] Many of the stories told by both sides were true, I believe, but so was a great deal else.

The standard Renamo practice after entering an area was to loot it and kill any suspected Frelimo members or sympathizers. Usually, if plans did not call for long-term occupation, houses were burned and people marched off to Renamo bases, where they were used as farmers or porters; or, if the plan was to stick around, the rebels reinstalled the local *régulos*, or *muenes*—the petty chiefs who once worked, basically as tax collectors, for the Portuguese, and whom Frelimo systematically deposed at independence. I heard about *régulos* who brought their colonial uniforms out of storage, dusting off the epaulets. Others brought their old enforcers, the African policemen known as *sipais*, out of retirement. Village elders, called *mambos*, also found themselves rehabilitated and working for the *matsangas*.

Even more important to Renamo administration than the *régulos* were traditional religious authorities. The Portuguese were not energetic missionaries in Mozambique; during nearly five hundred years of nominal occupation, they succeeded in converting less than 15 percent of the population to Catholicism. At independence, the country had at least as many Muslims—most of them living along the northern coast—as Catholics. But the majority of Mozambicans are what census takers call "animists"—a term that covers a great range of beliefs and practices. Because the Portuguese were not energetic anthropologists, either, there has been little formal study of the subject, but religious life in rural Mozambique, like religious life everywhere in rural Africa, is definitely complex and intense. Traditional religious figures—known as *curandeiros* (healers), or *feiticeiros* (witch doctors), or *profetas* (prophets), or *espiritistas* (spirit mediums)—retain great authority and prestige.[3] Their functions range freely across modern categories: medical, political, religious, psychiatric. They are weathermen, family counselors, insurance adjusters, priests. Some are knowledgeable herbalists; others are pure fetishists. Apprenticeships are long and costly, and are often limited to persons who have survived serious illnesses themselves. *Curandeiros* were subject to less repression and manipulation under colonialism than chiefs were, so their standing with their flocks actually rose while that of the *régulos* fell.[4] There were urban *curandeiros*, and famous *curandeiros*, some of whom charged high fees for their services and became quite rich. After independence, some *curandeiros* went into government training programs and became village health workers, but Frelimo gave them no special recognition and officially scorned traditional beliefs as *obscurantismo*. Like the *régulos*, most *curandeiros* were merely pushed aside by the new government.

Renamo used *curandeiros* both to gain the respect of peasants and to give its fighters courage. I heard stories of Renamo being led into battle by a *curandeiro* waving a goat's tail and of rites meant to make warriors invisible to their enemies.[5] Belief in magic apparently extended even to the "President of Free Mozambique," as Afonso Dhlakama styled himself. Documents found at a captured Renamo base showed Dhlakama's adjutant filing straightfaced accounts of battlefield "miracles," in which helpful spirits caused Frelimo troops to shoot at one another.[6] And Renamo's alliance with the supernatural also seemed to be accepted at face value by many ordinary Mozambicans. In every part of the country I visited, I heard people say that the *matsangas* were "bulletproof," that they were "immortal."

Some of this belief was related to the awe in which Ndau-speaking people were held. The Ndaus are one of the smaller ethnic groups in Mozambique, accounting for less than 2 percent of the total population, but they seemed to have a big reputation for magic and bellicosity. The Ndaus are a subgroup of the Shona, the majority ethnic group in Zimbabwe, and their homeland is a narrow belt across the waist of Mozambique, south of the Beira Corridor, from the highlands of southeastern Zimbabwe to the sea. Their political and religious traditions, within which chiefs and spirit mediums share power, had survived domination by the Gaza state, which ruled the area for most of the nineteenth century, and then by the British and Portuguese colonial empires, which divided the Ndau territory between them.[7] In the twentieth century, Ndau chiefs unhappy with Portuguese rule often fled across the border to live with their kin in Rhodesia. When Rhodesian military intelligence went about creating Renamo, it used Ndau networks to find recruits. (British colonialism was always stronger in ethnography than its Portuguese cousin—this in spite of the greater Portuguese willingness to cohabit and, in some cases, intermarry with *indígenas*.)[8] Frelimo never really made it to Ndau country, either before or after independence, so it was a natural base for Renamo's early operations. Ndau-speakers dominated the Renamo military leadership from the start. Afonso Dhlakama was the son of an important Ndau chief, and he had been quoted as saying of Frelimo, "They wanted to do away with our traditions—something not even the colonialists did."[9]

I went to Chibabava, which is in Ndau country (it is, in fact, Afonso Dhlakama's home district), partly in hopes of learning more about Ndau culture and religion. On that score, the trip was a bust. The local people I interviewed looked at me as if I were slow. Yes, they went to the *curandeiro*—if they were sick, and if they could afford it. Yes, the *matsangas* no doubt went to the *curandeiro* as well. But that was their business, wasn't it. As for the *feiticeiro*—well, his trade was in spells, a subject which only a fool would discuss. And the ancestral spirits would undoubtedly prefer that we left them out of it, too. On the differences between Ndau beliefs and other people's beliefs, the Ndaus had little to say: they didn't *know* any other types of people. The *deslocados* in Chibabava were, in fact, among the most isolated Mozambicans I met. None of them had been to school. None of them knew how old they were. I asked one woman if there had been any whites in the area she came from. She told the interpreter, "The first time in my life I saw a white person is today. I am very surprised." She said that her husband had gone away to "Joni"—Johannesburg—"for clothes." I asked if she meant money. She said she meant clothes. Nobody knew who the president of Mozambique was. One woman said that she remembered "independence" because she had heard about a big party in town. She hadn't gone to the party, but she knew that it was a Frelimo victory being celebrated. She wasn't sure who Frelimo had defeated, though. Later, a Frelimo man had come to the district briefly with a maize-grinding machine. After he left, the *matsangas* came, and she heard nothing from Frelimo for many years.

The anti-Ndau feeling that I expected to find elsewhere in Mozambique I never found. The loyalty of Ndau-speakers was not an issue even in the army, I was told. That some Ndaus were *bandidos* did not reflect badly on the others. The Ndaus happened to live where the Rhodesians went to recruit. Other ethnic groups were also involved. In fact, the *curandeiros* working with Renamo were often not Ndau. *Curandeiros* were powerful in every region of Mozambique, and the war, by generating so much anxiety and grief, clearly increased the demand for the solace and guidance of their magic.

And it was not only illiterate peasants who believed. I heard stories about the spirits from schoolteachers and from air-traffic controllers. It was a teacher, in fact, who first told me the legend surrounding the death of André Matsangaíssa. Matsangaíssa was killed during an attack on a government position near Gorongosa, in central Mozambique. According to the legend, Matsangaíssa was first shot, point-blank, with an automatic rifle, *but he was not harmed.* Then he was shot with a bazooka. That killed him, but the man who fired the bazooka later went mad, the victim of a Renamo witch's spell. The teacher who told me this story came from Milange, a hill town in Zambézia on the Malawi border. He had been taken by Renamo to the base near Morrumbala, eighty miles from Milange, and there had seen *curandeiros* washing the bodies of Renamo fighters with herbs before battles. One of the ways Renamo sought to preserve its reputation for being bulletproof, he said, was by going to great lengths after battles to drag away its dead and bury them secretly. Of course, Frelimo soldiers, most of whom were peasants themselves, also believed in magic, and in March 1988, in a notorious case, two local officials in a Beira shantytown killed two old women who were accused of casting spells.

Renamo's entente with traditional structures was sometimes mistaken for the restoration of a precolonial order, a "cashless society," to the Mozambican countryside. The war had even been characterized, here and there, as a crusade by African traditionalists against a modern state. In truth, the uprooting of millions of peasants by Renamo had sown only profound disorder. In its early years, Renamo's external wing proudly published the number of villages it had destroyed—in 1981 it claimed to have destroyed 803; in 1982, 607.[10] Eventually, someone thought better of releasing such figures, but the destruction continued. Some peasants were permitted to stay on their land—and obliged to turn over a portion of their crop to Renamo—and some villages were not burned, but the decisive factors in Renamo's dealings with civilians were always the rebels' military aims, not the health and welfare of the peasants. And the alliances with *régulos* and *curandeiros* were the same. When disputes arose between Renamo and local authorities—as they always will where large numbers of unproductive men are living among people with little to spare—they were settled, inevitably, by the guns of the armed party. Indeed, the death of André Matsangaíssa was popularly attributed to the bad advice of a famous wizard, who, disgruntled with Renamo's depredations among his people, told Matsangaíssa that the government position at Gorongosa was undefended.[11]

In the stories of those who had lived with Renamo—*recuperados*, they were called, "the recuperated"—the collaborators known as *majubas* actually figured more prominently than Renamo fighters themselves. The duties of *majubas*, who were usually armed with machetes, axes, and knives rather than guns, and were often local people, included guarding captives, organizing work parties, and collecting food and clothes for the fighters. The layout of the larger Renamo bases, in which peasants were settled in concentric rings around the base and only *majubas* were allowed to enter it, ensured that peasants had little contact with the fighters—also, that they bore the brunt of any Frelimo attack. I thought that former captives spoke about the *majubas* with amazing mildness. They often pointed out that the *majubas* had little choice; that they were just ordinary peasants themselves, compelled to do the dirty work of the *matsangas* to survive. Of course, when they talked about *majubas*, they were often talking about members of their own families. And when Renamo left an area, the *majubas*, perhaps feeling too compromised to remain, often left with them.

Estimates of the number of full-time Renamo soldiers ranged from 8,000 to 25,000.[12] A handful had been fighting for twenty years or more, since the early days of the war for independence. These included veterans of the Portuguese colonial army as well as Frelimo deserters. (In Zambézia, I heard of *antiguos combatentes* who, although now fighting with the *matsangas*, liked to reminisce in camp about the good old days with Samora in Tanzania!) Many fighters were recruited in South Africa, most of them Mozambicans who were working there, got arrested, and were given the unhappy choice of prison or military training. Renamo did a great deal of press-ganging itself, taking men and boys from among its captives for military training. Former Renamo soldiers, such as the boys with whom the American psychologist in Maputo worked, reported a ritual brutalization in which they were first accustomed to gunfire by having guns shot off next to their ears, then were forced to kill an animal in a group, then to kill an animal alone, then to kill a human being in a group, and finally to kill a human being alone. By the end of this "training," they were not only deadened to many normal emotions but were convinced that they could never be readmitted to civil society, a belief which naturally bound them to their new peer group: Renamo.[13]

The fear that Frelimo would kill them if they were captured was apparently widespread among Renamo fighters. The tone of the amnesty offer that Radio Mozambique started broadcasting in 1988 could not have reassured them. "The armed bandit is criminal, murderous, genocidal," the announcement said. "He kills the innocent, massacres the people, steals, burns everything. Armed bandit means monster, means terror. The Mozambican people say to the armed bandit, 'Don't be a lackey of the racists, lackey of apartheid. Abandon armed banditry. Hand yourself over to be pardoned. Contact your family, the authorities, the [army], the party, and return to work on your land as a free man. But if you stick to armed banditry, you will be eliminated.'" This invitation was later replaced with less off-putting ones, but the *matsanga's* fear of abuse if he fell into Frelimo's hands was not altogether misplaced. And the same went for *majubas*. In Zambézia, there had been reliable reports of the summary execution of *majubas* by a Frelimo commander.[14]

What percentage of Renamo fighters were volunteers? Renamo's spokesmen said they all were, naturally. In 1989, William Minter, an American researcher, concluded, on the basis of thirty-two interviews with amnestied and captured fighters, that over 90 percent of Renamo's soldiers were forcibly recruited.[15] A high-level Renamo defector—Paulo Oliveira, who ran a Renamo radio station in South Africa until 1984 and defected to Frelimo in 1988—said that *all* of his black colleagues there had been kidnapped. As Minter acknowledged, however, his interviews were arranged through the Frelimo Central Committee, and the defector was under Frelimo's protection. Both the defector and the amnestied and captured fighters knew, without necessarily having to be told, that the government preferred the kidnapping version of the Renamo recruitment story. A later amnesty announcement on Radio Mozambique said, "You who were kidnapped and are involved in armed banditry, hand yourself over to benefit from the Amnesty Law. The people are able to pardon you for the crimes you were forced to commit." A Mozambican researcher who was himself close to the Frelimo Central Committee told me that he believed that the majority of Renamo soldiers were volunteers. And it did defy common sense that an army of captives should fight as fiercely as Renamo was often reported to do. In October 1989, President Chissano seemed to acknowledge the commitment that many *matsangas* felt to their cause when he urged a crowd in Zambézia to try to persuade the bandits to leave Renamo, saying, "We have to explain that they have been deceived."[16]

Mozambique had a vast population of the absolutely marginalized—people with no skills, education, jobs, homes, or future. They were a fertile field for Renamo recruitment, constantly watered by the government's inability to help them. Since the war was the main cause of the collapse of the economy, the war ended up reproducing itself. An economy of pillage had developed alongside the ordinary economy of production, and the opportunities in the former were, for some people, simply greater than in the latter.[17] Also, quite apart from the war, many Mozambicans blamed the government for the economy's decline. And Frelimo's mistakes had certainly made Renamo's work easier. One such mistake was Operation Production, in which 50,000 unemployed city dwellers were summarily shipped to the countryside in 1983 and told to start farming. Mozambicans immediately dubbed Operation Production "a recruiting program for the bandits," and it did seem to have been effective as exactly that. Many of those expelled from Maputo were, moreover, migrant mineworkers thrown out of work by South Africa's cutbacks in its Mozambican labor force—a group that apparently proved particularly susceptible to the blandishments of the *bandidos*.

Besides the *régulos* and *curandeiros*, there were many peasants, businessmen, clans, even whole age groups who felt that they had lost out somewhere in the various redistributions of power and wealth since independence. The Frelimo deserters to Renamo included people who, like André Matsangaíssa and Afonso Dhlakama, believed after independence that they were entitled to more spoils of war than their superiors would allow them (some clearly expected to become warlords in their home districts, owing only vassalage to the central government), and others bearing more recent grudges. Some of the losers in local elections to the national assembly, for instance, had gone off and joined Renamo.[18] Peasants who lost property or power in Frelimo's drive to develop "communal villages" were often amenable to Renamo's arrival, especially in areas where forced villagization had occurred.[19] I once asked a Mozambican agronomist about why people joined Renamo. He replied, "What happens if you have a cat, and you kick the cat, and starve it, and throw hot water at it?" Then he answered his own question. "The cat goes away, and he lives in the bush. But he comes back at night to steal food and, if he gets a chance, to bite you. That is what has happened here."

Many new governments in Africa have alienated large parts of their own populations. Few have had the bad luck to live next door to a powerful foe ready to exploit their every misstep. From its origins as a puppet group, Renamo evolved into a broad, violent collection of Frelimo's enemies.

But perhaps the commonest reason for joining Renamo—and certainly the commonest reason for joining the many independent groups of *real* bandits—was hunger: with a gun in hand, one's chances of eating in rural Mozambique were clearly better than they were without it. "A gun is your money; it's a system," as one Mozambican explained it to me. Indeed, the army and the government's popular militia sometimes had to rely on the same allure to fill their ranks. Guns also had abundant local cachet. "The gun in a country that was liberated by the gun is a symbol of status," a Mozambican journalist told me. "It's on the flag. It's everywhere." Guns were useful, too, in the pursuit of local feuds. I heard about an area where the pattern of allegiances was a checkerboard: each clan chose to work with the side that its nearest neighbor and traditional rival had not chosen, so as to be armed against that rival. Larger regional and ethnic rivalries inevitably came into play, as did smaller intrafamily disputes, and this escalating spiral of strife only swelled Renamo's ranks.

Finally, there was one of the dirty secrets of the war: the suspicion that being a *bandido* might be fun. I heard about an Angolan mechanic who was captured by Renamo and spent many months repairing the rebels' motorcycles. After he escaped, he reported that the *matsangas* he had lived with were having themselves a hell of a time. They stole motorcycles, used the oil to fashion natty dreadlocks, got high on marijuana and drunk on traditional beer, and spent their days roaring around homemade racetracks in the bush. When they smashed up the bikes, he was made to fix them. These were illiterate country boys who, if they had not joined Renamo, were probably looking at a career behind a hoe, a life of tedium and deprivation perhaps relieved only by long, dangerous stints in the army, where the fun quotient was reported to be nil. (Frelimo strongly disapproved of marijuana, while Renamo tolerated and even institutionalized its use.)[20] Another story I heard came from the survivors of an attack—twenty-one people died in it—on a town near Maputo. When the rebels swept into the town in the middle of the night, they caught everybody off guard except a large contingent of local teenage boys, who greeted the invaders enthusiastically, joined in the looting of their neighbors' homes, and, richer by many radios and bicycles, retreated to the bush with Renamo.

But the nature of the war was so different from region to region that it may be misleading to write about "Renamo." In Zambézia, for instance, the level of military organization was high. The rebels operated at battalion strength, built major bases, and held towns for long periods; many of the fighters there had extensive training, usually received in South Africa. A history of heavy colonization, a porous border with Malawi, good forest cover, and the local political weakness of Frelimo relative to the rest of the country—all made Zambézia ideal for large-scale rebel operations.[21] In Zambézia, too, there was a long tradition of independent armies, ranging from the armed forces of the old *prazos*, the huge Portuguese Crown estates that dominated the Zambezi Valley for more than three hundred years, to the Renamo breakaway group, Unamo, which was cutting a swath through the Zambézian countryside in 1988.[22] Meanwhile, in other areas of Mozambique, Renamo was represented by small, roving bands whose relationship to any central command was distant at best.

Major massacres all seemed to happen in the south of the country, a pattern often attributed to the fact that Renamo got its start in the center of Mozambique and still derived strength from popular resentment of the fact that southerners dominated the top jobs in government. The idea was that men would commit mass murder more readily among strangers, especially strangers whom they resented, and who didn't speak their language, than among people like themselves. Many of the participants in the major massacres in the south, however, had apparently been local men. I asked people in the south how anyone could kill his own kin, and they usually sighed heavily and said something about hallucinogenic drugs.[23] In any event, people in the center and the north consistently denied that Renamo committed massacres there. Many who had lived with Renamo claimed never to have seen any violence against civilians.

But a distinction needs to be made between military operations and administration. The same people who saw little or no violence while living with Renamo had sometimes been kidnapped in bloody ambushes. A health worker in northern Zambézia, for instance, told me about being accosted by a Renamo unit on a trail. He was walking with six militiamen, who, after some discussion of methods, were all executed on the spot by rifle shots. He survived only by managing to convince the *matsangas* that he was a lay minister—he actually worked for the Mozambican Red Cross, which Renamo considered a Frelimo organization.[24] He was abducted and spent a year with Renamo. The only violence he saw in that time, besides the beating of a captive who attempted to escape, he said, was the severe punishment given to Renamo soldiers. For mistakes in battle or for attempts to desert, he said (and I heard this from a number of other people as well), Renamo soldiers were often executed. The regional variations in military discipline were, as in everything else, great. In some areas, the punishment for raping a local woman was reportedly death. In other areas, Renamo troops clearly practiced rape without fear of punishment, and they were widely blamed for an increased spread of AIDS and venereal disease. The health worker, whose recollections of life with Renamo were unusually thorough, was an *amnistiado*. He said he had never carried a gun and had escaped from Renamo at the first opportunity, so I could not understand why he had had to be amnestied. After the interview, Dividas laughed at me. "Of course he carried a gun," he said.

10

Renamo was first and foremost a military organization. Its political structure, where it existed at all, was minimal. In a few areas, Renamo had gained local support by killing unpopular administrators or managers, but once it gained control of an area, it apparently delivered few, if any, services. Some former captives recalled attending compulsory political meetings, at which opposition to Frelimo and its works was the sole theme, but none that I spoke with—or heard of—reported any effort to build a consensus, or to consult with ordinary people, on any issue. The movement was authoritarian to an extreme degree. Its founders and leaders all had military and police backgrounds;[1] and the modern political understanding of both fighters and *majubas*, the great majority of whom were illiterate, apparently hovered near zero. The Renamo flag looked as if it had been concocted in some politico-military chamber of horrors in Pretoria: five downward-pointing arrows over the slogan "War and Death to the Enemies of the Fatherland." Renamo's connection to South Africa seemed to be widely understood in the south of Mozambique, but as one moved north that understanding faded steadily. Outside the cities, few people in northern Mozambique even knew South Africa existed, and fewer still had heard of something called apartheid. Those who had heard of South Africa seemed to associate it with, above all, material wealth. There was no equivalent in Mozambique of the minstrels who ride the trains and buses in North Africa singing for their supper about the suffering of the Palestinians.

Renamo, through its European and American spokesmen, claimed to run schools and clinics in the areas it controlled. In Caia, a district in northern Sofala where the rebels claimed to be operating dozens of schools, I asked people who had lived with Renamo about the schools. They stared at me in disbelief. I did find one place, farther north, where Renamo soldiers had urged the teachers among their captives to start classes again. They had no materials and no classrooms—they were living near a base deep in the bush—but the teachers I interviewed said the Renamo soldiers used to come and sit at a respectful distance from the classes they convened under the trees. The soldiers were illiterate, in awe of education, and did not speak Portuguese, so they apparently never realized that the teachers had resumed their work with the hated Frelimo curriculum.

Looking for clues to Renamo's foreign support, I always asked people who had been living with the rebels if they had seen any white men around. At Casa Banana, a former Renamo headquarters that had been turned into a camp for *deslocados*, I found men who had helped unload cargo planes—probably South African Dakotas—and had seen the Renamo high command, including Afonso Dhlakama, but they could not remember seeing the pilots of the planes. One man in northern Zambézia said that he had definitely seen a white man at a Renamo base and that he had actually talked to the white man himself. My pulse increased. The white man, he said, was a British journalist. My pulse returned to normal. Many journalists had accompanied Renamo into Mozambique.[2] One Italian reporter was even killed in a Renamo attack on a Frelimo-held town.[3] None of their stories had told me much; Renamo's control over their movements and interviews was absolute. The journalists saw an African Potemkin village, and most of their stories, even those that struggled to be more than Renamo propaganda, ended up in the press packet issued by the external wing in Washington. Although the man in Zambézia who had been interviewed by the Englishman spoke perfect Portuguese, his captors, he told me, insisted that he answer the journalist's questions in Lomwe, a local language, so that a Renamo interpreter could censor his answers during the translation. Speaking Portuguese was actually a problem throughout his year with the rebels, he said. Only two officers in the battalion he lived with understood it themselves, and the fighters and *majubas* resented the education he displayed when he spoke it.

The violent hostility of Renamo toward such symbols of modernity as schools, hospitals, and machinery encouraged the idea that the movement was traditionalist, or simply antiurban. It was a bent that would make sense in much of Africa, where ancient and modern worlds collide daily, and the ancient usually gets the worst of it, and where the cities, the government's crucial constituency, prey voraciously on the countryside. One explanation for the rebels' hostility toward clinics and hospitals might be that the *curandeiros* working with Renamo regarded modern medicine as competition, cutting into their business as traditional healers. But the truth was that when the *matsangas* looted clinics, they always took the medicine for their own use; and when they kidnapped health workers, they always put them to work behind Renamo lines teaching others the mysteries of their craft. And Renamo soldiers were not averse to modern technology. They relied on a sophisticated radio system. When they destroyed the sugar refineries at Luabo, an Italian priest who was kidnapped there told me, they used the bulldozers they found to clear new roads back to their camps and trucks to transport their loot.

Although *curandeiros* might also be expected to feel some rivalry with Christianity, Renamo's treatment of priests and missionaries had usually been gentle.[4] In many destroyed towns, the only building left unscathed had been the church. In some instances, Catholic priests had remained under Renamo, conducting business as usual, and a number of intrepid Protestant missionaries, including some Americans, were apparently working in Renamo territory. A young Australian Pentecostal, Ian Grey, who was captured by Frelimo in 1987, confessed to spying for Renamo and was sentenced to ten and a half years in prison. (He was released in August 1989.)

What was so hateful about schools and clinics, from Renamo's point of view, was that they were identified with Frelimo. They were, in fact, among the main sources of the government's popularity. That was why they had to be destroyed. As Renamo's spokesman in Europe explained it, "In the villages we must destroy the presence of the party and the state."[5] The destruction of machinery was less symbolic, but the intent was the same: to make the Frelimo-run society less desirable. It was a maximalist strategy, and a pure equation: that whatever weakened Frelimo strengthened Renamo. Afonso Dhlakama had said that his strategy was merely to "make problems for the enemy."[6] The enemy, of course, was everywhere. Dhlakama told the *Washington Times*, "The Beira Corridor provides the Maputo government with customs duties and Zimbabwe with goods, so it helps keep the Marxists in power. But since it passes through Renamo's liberated area, we will make sure that it does not function."[7] The Beira Corridor was functioning, but Renamo's constant attacks on trains, buses, cars, trucks, and the transportation infrastructure itself had succeeded in stopping most long-distance ground travel. This slaughter certainly had not enhanced Renamo's popularity, but it did make the point that the government could not protect people. That might in turn reduce the chances that people would, say, inform the army of Renamo movements.

"Freedom of religion" was a Renamo slogan, and the diversity of faiths operating behind Renamo lines was sometimes offered as an example of the good life to be had in Free Mozambique. But the Catholic Church and some of the evangelical Protestant sects had often been unhappy with Frelimo, which after independence closed religious schools and hospitals and even confiscated church property.[8] Like its alliances with *régulos* and *curandeiros*, Renamo's warm relations with certain priests and missionaries were often more convenient than immutable. Renamo's external spokesmen hawked their movement's commitment to "free enterprise," but the *matsangas* attacked privately owned factories and farms just as readily as they attacked publicly owned property.

Identifying Renamo's ideology was not, in fact, a task for the fainthearted. The movement was often tagged "right-wing rebels" in the international press. The editors of the *Times* of London called it "pro-Western," while the editors of the *Wall Street Journal* called it "the anti-communist resistance."[9] But few of the illiterate peasants who fought with Renamo were likely to think of themselves as right-wing, any more than the *deslocados* who told me they adored Frelimo could tell me what

Marxismo-Leninismo was. And those good Londoners who believed that Renamo was pro-Western needed to glance through the literature coming out of Renamo's London office, which took Western multinational corporations (at least, those investing in Mozambique) to task in terms as blistering as any Frelimo ever mustered. The same literature pledged to "support all progressive forces within Mozambique" and, for good measure, railed against "apartheid oppression" in "racist South Africa," while condemning what it had the brass to call "Frelimo's alliance with Pretoria."[10] In truth, there was little or no evidence of any sustained political discussion, or any line of ideological development, within Renamo. The few intellectuals associated with the movement tended to be right-wing foreigners.[11] The contrast with Frelimo's tradition, both as a liberation movement and as a ruling party, of fierce internal ideological debate could scarcely have been sharper.

Renamo was often compared, at least in the West, to Pol Pot's Khmer Rouge. The State Department's influential 1988 report made the comparison, and *Newsweek* dubbed Renamo "southern Africa's blood-curdling answer to the Khmer Rouge."[12] Although both groups were barefoot armies of great brutality, the analogy was worse than useless. The Khmer Rouge was founded by French-educated children of the Cambodian elite, who sought to create a pure communism, purged of all feudal, bourgeois, and foreign elements; they nationalized the fruit on the trees and the fish in the streams and were antireligious in the extreme. Renamo apologists actually liked to compare *Frelimo* to the Khmer Rouge—an unsurprising but equally uninformative comparison. A truer parallel between the two countries was simply that both Mozambique and Cambodia had suffered, and continued to suffer, tragedies of staggering magnitude. The Khmer Rouge sought to take Cambodia out of the twentieth century. Mozambique, which was a poorer country to start with, had seen its extreme underdevelopment turn into conditions that in 1987 caused the Population Crisis Committee in Washington, D.C., to rank it first in the world on a comprehensive index of human suffering.

What did Renamo want? Afonso Dhlakama: "Democratic government, freedom of movement, freedom of religion, and the freedom to eat."[13] Dhlakama had often predicted imminent military victory, but Renamo had never actually been close to winning the war—to taking Maputo and Beira—if only because its lack of air defenses would have made holding the cities impossible. Paulo Oliveira, the Renamo defector, whom I interviewed in Maputo, was told by a South African colonel in 1983 that Pretoria had no wish to change the government of Mozambique, but simply to "put Machel on his knees." According to Oliveira, Renamo leaders who understood that Pretoria's plans gave them no chance of winning the war, and who began trying to cultivate new backers in Washington and Paris by promising to break with Pretoria, developed a habit of dying violently— "destabilization" might be a game with limited objectives, but Pretoria played it seriously.[14] Renamo's handlers were in a position to know, in any case, that the rebels would be incapable of governing the country. As it was, the war in Mozambique was inexpensive, at whatever level South Africa still funded it, while a counterinsurgency war—thousands of Frelimo guerrillas would undoubtedly go back to the bush if the government were overthrown—could quickly become South Africa's Vietnam.

In an interview in 1988, Dhlakama shifted position. "Our aim is not to win the war militarily," he said, "but to force Frelimo to accept negotiations for a democratically elected government."[15] The government derided Dhlakama as a powerless puppet, and the rebel chief was, in truth, no one's idea of a charismatic politician. He was poorly educated—he had attended a rural Catholic mission school[16]—and unworldly. He referred to his South African patrons as "my parents"[17] and boasted to Portuguese journalists that he had been made a colonel in the South African Defense Force and had been told by the South African minister of defense that "your army is now part of the S.A.D.F."[18] Roland Hunter, a South African corporal who worked as an aide to Renamo's chief sponsor in the SADF, described taking Dhlakama and his delegation on a clothes-shopping spree in Pretoria before they made a trip to West Germany in 1983.[19] In 1988, *Africa Confidential* reported that Dhlakama was again being prepared by his handlers for a European publicity tour and commented, "South African secret servicemen teaching Dhlakama to be articulate and televisual have an uphill job since he is no genius."[20] Dhlakama's skills, such as they existed, seemed to be entirely military.

What did Renamo's various foreign backers want? It was a question with too many answers, most of them contradictory—hence the homicidal disarray of the movement's external leadership. The Portuguese revanchists wanted their property and power back; the American extremists wanted to roll back the red tide of communism and harvest millions of African souls; the pertinent elements of the South African military wanted to keep their black-ruled neighbors weak and weary. Meanwhile, several Western intelligence services reportedly retained strong contacts with Renamo, including the West Germans,[21] the Israelis, and, in apparent defiance of official United States policy, elements of the CIA and of American military intelligence.[22]

What did the rebels themselves want? Because Renamo had no real prospects of taking power nationally, the thousands of *matsangas* had thousands of different, more immediate agendas. This deep political incoherence undermined Renamo's claims to be a nationalist movement just as seriously as the group's puppet beginnings and continuing shady international connections did. It also strengthened the government's argument that the conflict in Mozambique was not a civil war.

What about "the people," the hapless millions caught, as they say in Africa, between the snakes and the lion? They were, after all, the ostensible judges—or, in another view, the prizes—of the contest. Everywhere I went in Mozambique, I heard, "All the peasants really want is to be left alone." I also heard that, in the areas it controlled, Renamo gained popular support by running a "minimalist administration"—in contrast to Frelimo's revolutionary activism. But the State Department's report, based on refugees' accounts, made Renamo administration sound, at least in what its author described as "control areas," extraordinarily repressive. "The only reciprocity the captives appear to receive or to expect is the opportunity to remain alive," the report laconically concluded.[23] My own interviews with people who had lived with Renamo also evoked a brutal, arbitrary system, but the State Department's tone, which conjured up great slave camps, seemed wrong. The tone of the stories I heard was more modest, more African. Someone's father was kidnapped. The family knew where he was being held, and they knew the ransom would be two shirts. While the family were trying to find the shirts, he was moved farther away. Now they didn't know where he was. All those who had lived with Renamo talked about hunger, but usually that was why they had left Renamo territory. The International Committee of the Red Cross started flying into Renamo areas in 1988, and its teams found that the greatest needs in the areas they visited were for seeds and medicine. Food was not an immediate problem.

The cruel truth was that most of Mozambique's peasants had never been left alone. Armed invaders, autocratic chiefs and kings, slave traders, tax collectors, plantation owners, ten-family party cells, and now Renamo had all seen to that. The history of Mozambique's peasantry was one of bottomless pain and sorrow, and its great store of brutalized rage was now being used, cynically and savagely, to destroy the country's future.

Part Two

Beira

11

There were few Mozambicans who had not been personally affected by the war. And yet *afetado* had a specific meaning in Mozambique. In the west-central town of Chimoio, I was talking to a young man whose job was to count *deslocados* and *afetados*—affected persons. I asked him, in passing, where he came from. He said he came from Luabo. I knew that Luabo, which is a sugar-refining center on the Zambezi River, had been overrun in 1985 by Renamo, so I asked about that. The young man said that he and his brothers had managed to flee, but their father, who was sixty years old, had been kidnapped by the rebels. For a while, he said, they heard news of their father from friends who had been kidnapped and had escaped. He was apparently being held at a base somewhere north of Luabo and, because he was a mechanic by trade, had been put to work on the rebels' rickety fleet of motorbikes. But then he was moved, and now they had heard nothing for two years. The young man's expression was unreadable. I asked, somewhat lamely, if he considered himself an *afetado*. He said, "Of course not." I had been thinking that if *my* father were being held prisoner by the rebels I would probably consider myself affected by the war, but he had a place to live, a job, enough to eat—he was not an *afetado*.

Chimoio had an abundance of real *afetados* and *deslocados*. The town is in the Beira Corridor, the strategic transportation route that cuts across the narrow waist of Mozambique, connecting Zimbabwe and other landlocked countries to the Indian

Ocean port of Beira. The Corridor, which contains a highway, a railway, and an oil pipeline, is strategic because—unlike most of the other routes from those countries to the sea—it does not pass through South Africa, and it was the only route that had not been closed by Renamo attacks and sabotage. Renamo did attack the Beira Corridor, but a heavy deployment of Zimbabwean troops had helped to keep the line open, and traffic and oil—although frequently interrupted—continued to flow through it. Many thousands of Mozambican peasants—*deslocados* and *afetados*—had flocked to the Corridor, looking for security from the troops stationed along it.

I first rode through the Corridor in September 1988, in a truck hauling Zimbabwean steel to Beira. The driver, who picked me up at the border post, was a Zimbabwean named Peter Nyamupenza. He said that I was the only non-African hitchhiker he had ever seen in Mozambique. It was a wet, misty day in the mountains that surround the border; spectral soldiers loomed at the edge of the road. There was almost no traffic. Nyamupenza, who drove the route regularly, said he had never been ambushed. "I only drive in the daytime," he said. "You cannot drive at night. But most of the goods go by rail. And the railway, it gets attacked sometimes." Nyamupenza said he had been held up by armed members of Mozambique's popular militia, who stopped him at a roadblock and demanded some of the maize he was carrying. The maize was part of an international relief shipment; so the first time it happened, Nyamupenza refused, and the militiamen eventually let him pass. The next time they stopped him, he relented. "These people are so hungry," he said. Depot robbery was a more serious problem, in any case. "Renamo watches where we unload food—at Dondo, Nhamatanda, Chimoio, Gondola. Then they come at night, and attack and steal the food." Nobody would bother us today, he said, because we were carrying steel.

Nyamupenza said he preferred driving in Mozambique, despite the dangers, to driving in some other countries. In Zaire, he said, the police demanded outrageous bribes. In Malawi, officials were nicer, but they also wanted bribes. In Mozambique, nobody wanted money, because money here was worthless—there was nothing to buy. People wanted soap, cigarettes, matches, food.

It is 195 miles from the border to Beira. Nyamupenza was in a hurry because it was a Saturday morning and he wanted to unload before the workers in Beira knocked off for the weekend, but the condition of the road made progress slow. There were a million potholes (made even more unpleasant by the knowledge that potholes were a site of choice for Renamo land mines), and one stretch of at least ten miles had been washed out by floods. We took that at walking speed. Nyamupenza drove very gently—the truck, a 1983 Scania cabover, was in immaculate condition—and never seemed to let the obstacles bother him. He was a cool, lanky fellow, about thirty years old, and he played a great selection of African pop and American country and western on his tape deck. He had also picked up two Mozambican schoolgirls at the border post, and he chatted and joked with them so easily that I was surprised to learn, after we dropped them in Dondo, that he had never met them before. It's something one sees often in Africa, and if one's home is New York City, it takes some getting used to. Nyamupenza and the girls had been speaking Shona, the first language of most Zimbabweans and of most people in central Mozambique.

Compared to conditions in the rest of Mozambique, the economy along the Corridor seemed to be thriving. There were shops open in the little towns we passed through, tractors in some of the fields, and even small family-sized herds of cattle grazing near the road. The buildings all had the unpainted, crumbling, deserted look that was standard throughout Mozambique, and yet some of the timber mills, citrus plantations, and factories were operating. In a country where industrial production had fallen by more than 50 percent between 1981 and 1986, this sort of activity was unusual.[1] There was even a little factory in a hill town called Vila Manica that was still turning out bottled spring water. Whether any of this dogged production affected the lives of the thousands of people living alongside the road in reed huts was difficult to say. For their survival, they were clearly relying on the small family plots, or *machambas*, which have always sustained the great majority of Mozambicans and which blanketed the land on both sides of the road.

The guarantors of this strange, linear city—the soldiers—mostly blended in with the rainy-day masses, trudging along the road carrying a sack of rice, squatting under a tree cooking

lunch over a fire. Most were Zimbabweans. They had camouflage-patterned uniforms. The Mozambican soldiers had partial
uniforms, of undue variety, and the popular militia had nothing
but guns, sometimes not even shoes. We were stopped at a number of roadblocks but had no trouble. Nyamupenza was impressed when a Zimbabwean soldier tried to sell us his rations.
It was another positive economic indicator: it meant there was
something around to buy with meticais. Usually they just wanted
to bum cigarettes, or barter. It was officially forbidden to leave
the Corridor on any of the north-south roads that cross it, but I
had been told that the Zimbabweans would look the other way
for two cigarettes.

On the flatlands near Beira, we came upon the scene of a fresh
attack on the oil pipeline. A fierce orange fireball was raging out
of the ground in the middle of a green field, sending up thick
bursts of rich black smoke. A few soldiers watched it unex-
citedly. We asked a soldier at the next roadblock about the attack. He shrugged. "Renamo," he said. It never made even the
local news. Little of the war did.

As we approached the city at last, a young Mozambican appeared out of the truck's bed. He had apparently been riding on
the steel in the rain all the way from Zimbabwe, and he had a
tape he wanted to hear. It was a Bob Marley concert tape, and it
did provide a perfect sound track for our arrival in Beira. We
crawled down a wide, deeply rutted road through the middle of
a vast shantytown with the sun coming out and a cluster of sky-
scrapers shining in the distance and Saturday-afternoon crowds
swirling all around the great mud-splashed truck, calling to the
driver and double-taking to see a white face in the cab—and
"No Woman, No Cry" absolutely soaring on the tape deck.

It was the high point of the week I spent in Beira.

I stayed at the Hotel Dom Carlos, a ponderous, six-story establishment that had seen better years but was still the premier
hotel in Beira. It was situated across the street from the beach, a
few miles north of downtown, but was unaccountably construed
to a medieval theme. Suits of armor lined the dark, dank lobby,
along with huge oil paintings in preposterous perspective of ancient armies locked in battle. Attached to the wall above the bed
in my room was a large, fly-specked, cardboard crown, which
held the musty shreds of what had once been a mosquito net.

The reign of more recent princes was suggested, somehow, by the phone (now disconnected) on the wall next to the toilet (now lacking a seat). I found a telephone directory in my room, dated 1972. Leafing through it was like entering another world: the beauty parlors and driving schools and electrical equipment suppliers maintained not only in Beira but in the northern towns of Pemba and Nampula and Vila Cabral (now Lichinga), by Senhores Ribeiro and Da Silva and Da Costa.

The Dom Carlos, like every enterprise in Mozambique, was plagued by shortages. My room had one light bulb, which I was invited by the staff to shift around between the six or seven light sockets. The dining room never had more than two items to offer, and they were always the same two, boiled pork or boiled fish. During the week I was there, the beverage stocks ran out. There was nothing left in the hotel to drink—no beer, no wine, no fruit juice, no Coca-Cola. The hard-currency store in the city had beer, I was told, but it was miles away and transport was a problem. There were no taxis in Beira, a city of 400,000, and no cars to rent. Perhaps there was a bus.

But the most serious shortage at the Dom Carlos, as far as I was concerned, was of quiet in the early mornings. The hotel had an intercom system that, at 6 o'clock each morning, would suddenly begin to blare hideous Soviet pop music. This, I was told, was the preferred reveille for the Soviet helicopter pilots who occupied the entire second floor. Perhaps the fact that the Soviet Union was Mozambique's largest military supplier gave the pilots special rights. Most of them were young, sturdy, slightly awkward fellows who reminded me of American GIs circa World War II.

The Soviets weren't the only pilots living at the Dom Carlos. There were Portuguese cargo pilots, flying for the Mozambican national airlines, and a group of Christian missionaries—including Americans, Canadians, and Australians—who had come to help with the emergency food airlift. Hennie and Ferdie were also at the Dom Carlos. It had been a month or so since I first flew with them in Zambézia. When Hennie saw me passing the open door of his room, he laughed and called out, "Hey, still trying to get the goods on the racist regime down south?" He offered me a marvelously cold German beer. Hennie and Ferdie and the Portuguese went to great lengths, it seemed, to stock their suites at the Dom Carlos with Western goods and comforts, mostly brought in from South Africa, that could not be had in Beira. While I savored the beer, they told me about a close call they had just had in Zambézia. They had been heading into Maganja da Costa, the district just south of Ile, they said, when a flare from the ground alerted them that something was wrong. They decided not to land, and as they flew past, they saw that a major battle was raging in Maganja da Costa. If they had landed, they might have taxied right into Renamo's hands.

The most serious shortage in Beira was of power. Because Renamo delighted in destroying the transmission lines that carried electricity to the city, Beira had been forced to go without power for boggling amounts of time. As of September, when I visited Beira, it had had power for an average of only five days a month in 1988. That was even worse than 1987, when the city had had power for an average of thirteen days a month. The cumulative effects of the cutoffs were devastating. Little of the city's business could be conducted without electricity, of course. And when the power was off, the water was also off, because the pumps needed electricity. The city had a generator, which could provide a small fraction of the power the pumps needed, but whenever it was announced that the water would be turned on for, say, a one-hour period, all the toilets in Beira would be flushed, and the strain on the system would burst pipes all over the city. People who had outdoor latrines used them; many were forced to use the streets. The water table in Beira, which is built on a swamp, is high, so the latrines were polluting the groundwater. Since most Beirans, deprived of running water, were relying on well water, the pollution was a serious health hazard. Water for cooking and drinking had to be boiled long and hard. Because stoves weren't working and kerosene was in short supply, large amounts of firewood were required for boiling the water; and because of the huge demand, firewood had become extremely scarce. Wood gatherers were having to go ever farther into the countryside, where the danger of a Renamo attack grew with every mile. So the price of firewood had skyrocketed. Few working people could afford it, and they were starting to burn pieces of their houses or apartments—doors, shutters, windowsills, doorframes. They were even tearing up wooden floors. All the open fires had left a heavy stench of soot in every building in

Beira. They had also scorched and blackened the walls. The city looked both besieged and already sacked.

A giant Swedish generator was said to be coming to the city's rescue, but Beirans didn't seem to believe it. In 1987, I was told, a Finnish generator had been on its way. It never arrived. Something about an unusually cold winter in Finland. The Hotel Dom Carlos had its own generator, but that failed sometimes, too. In the elevator, the thick glass panels on the doors had been smashed from the inside at every floor by desperate passengers trapped by power failures. When I mentioned this eerie sight to a Beiran, he said I was crazy to get in an elevator anywhere in the city. Even aging asthmatics who worked on the tenth floor in one of the downtown high rises that still had a working elevator used the stairs.

Beira had seen much better days: a vast modern train station and a cluster of downtown high rises were hallmarks of the brief boom of the 1960s. Thick-walled old tropical mansions and, in the business district, colorful sprays of the fancy prewar neon signs that still adorn Lisbon cafés and dry cleaners recalled an earlier prime. In 1988, the neon hung from the façades in sad, unilluminated tangles, and old British-style pillar post-boxes stood unapproachable among heaps of garbage. And yet there were still graceful, palm-lined *avenidas,* and Beirans still sat in the tile-walled cafés, on eternal watch for the return of coffee. Beira's prosperity had come mostly from Rhodesia, in the form of port and rail revenues and tourism. When Mozambique gained its independence, however, and the new government began to honor the trade sanctions ordered by the United Nations against the Ian Smith regime—sanctions that Portugal had ignored—the border had been closed. The cost to Mozambique of this noble gesture was appalling, and Beira paid most of it. The hotels and holiday camps were suddenly empty. So were the port and the rail yards. The city's wealth vanished. In 1980, when Rhodesia became Zimbabwe, the sanctions were lifted, but the recovery of Beira had hardly started before Renamo began to close in, strangling the city again. The beach bungalows of the old holiday camps out past the Dom Carlos became shanty-towns full of refugees fleeing the war in the countryside.

The only glint of economic hope in Beira in 1988 was flickering around a multilateral attempt to revive the Beira Corridor.

Because the effort would not only help Mozambique but would also help reduce regional dependence on South Africa, it had become an internationally fashionable project: sixteen foreign governments and five international financial institutions were funding the rehabilitation of the port, railway, highway, and oil pipeline. Italy was the largest single contributor. The United States was working on the locomotive fleet. Rui Fonseca, the executive director of the government's Beira Corridor Authority, told me that business at the port was booming and attacks on the rail line were a thing of the past. "We are not an alternative," he said. "We are *the route*. The natural pattern of shipping in central southern Africa has been distorted by South Africa through the armed aggression against our country, and through economic aggression." Fonseca, a big, bearded man with bright blue eyes, was persuasive, but a few days later I went back up the Corridor with a young regional planner for the government, and I saw a place quite different both from the place I had seen before and from Rui Fonseca's Beira Corridor.

12

That trip was actually postponed once when the planner, whom I shall call Gimo, realized the date. It was September 7, the anniversary of the day that the Portuguese government agreed, in 1974, to hand over power to Frelimo. Gimo had told me that the Corridor was totally safe in the daytime, but here was an exception. "Renamo likes to make a statement on Frelimo holidays," he said, and we went to the beach instead.

We left town in Gimo's government-issue pickup truck early the next morning. Gimo had just completed a year-long study of the people living along the Corridor. Over half of them, he had learned, had no household possessions whatsoever. Not a bed, chair, table, lantern, radio, anything. This was partly from sheer destitution and partly because of the size of their huts, which averaged less than one square meter per resident. Nearly all the people living in the Corridor were, as I had thought, totally dependent on their *machambas*, but productivity, even when the rains came, was low. "That's because everybody has to walk so far from their house to their *machamba*," Gimo said, indicating the throngs walking along the road carrying hoes and buckets. "The average is between one and a half and two hours each way. Why so far? Because they can't sleep near their *machambas*. They have to sleep near the soldiers' camps. Why? *Bandidos armados*, of course."

Gimo suddenly pulled off the road. "These people shouldn't be here," he said, pointing to a group of new-looking huts in a field. While he got out and started talking to an old man sitting under a tree, I studied the flotsam drying in the sun on the roof of a hut: tobacco leaves, a big frog, many small fish and river prawns. Gimo returned, shaking his head. "I can't believe it," he said. He seemed distressed. "These people came from Masasegueça, that village over there, across the road. The report I just submitted says that Masasegueça is a good place for resettling more people. It has the river on one side, the road on the other, and the Zimbabweans there guarding the bridge, and it's always been very secure. It can also feed a lot of people because the river here is full of fish. Now this old man tells me that the village was attacked twice last week. Many people were killed, and many kidnapped—he doesn't know how many. But that's why these people have come here, to be closer to the Zimbabweans at the bridge. It's impossible to prepare a reliable report on the situation along here. Whatever you write is obsolete the next week."

We headed down the road to a resettlement camp. It was a small place, but it was scheduled, Gimo said, to receive seventy-five thousand *deslocados* over the next few months—mostly people who would be returning from Malawi, where there were more than six hundred thousand Mozambican refugees. (Altogether, there were more than a million Mozambican refugees living in neighboring countries.)[1] At the resettlement camp, which was clearly unable to accommodate seventy-five thousand more people, hundreds of huts were going up in more or less regular rows. While Gimo was measuring plots, I noticed two rudimentary benches under a cashew tree, with a hunk of iron hanging from a branch. This, I was told, was a school. The iron was the schoolbell. I asked where the children were. "This is the *adult* school," our guide said, as if I should have known. "Classes start at two. The children's school is over there." The sound of children singing wafted from that direction.

Our guide around the camp was an exuberant Zimbabwean woman named Emily. She said she had come to Mozambique as a refugee during the war in Rhodesia. (Mozambique sheltered two hundred thousand refugees during the period between its own independence and Zimbabwe's. In a grim historical irony, some of the old Zimbabwean refugee camps—and even some of the old Zimbabwean guerrilla camps—were now being used to hold

Mozambican *deslocados*.) Emily had worked for many years as a typist for a freight-forwarding company in Beira. She and her husband seemed to be world-class stragglers—most of the Zimbabwean refugees had left in 1980—but they were now finally ready to go home, she said. While they were waiting for their passports, Emily was working for the Organização das Mulheres de Moçambique, the semiofficial Mozambican women's organization, in the resettlement camps. She spoke good but heavily accented English. When she pointed out some English rape growing in a garden, and said it was a "manumeca," I thought that must be the Portuguese name for the vegetable, and noted it down. When she said it again later, I realized that she was just calling it a "moneymaker."

Gimo was confused about the triple-sized plot allotted to one man, and it took several minutes of conversation in several languages before he realized that the man was building three houses, one for each of his wives. He asked another man why he was building a mud bank up against the outside walls of his reed hut, and the man demonstrated: when the *bandidos armados* attacked, he and his family just lay flat on the ground inside their hut, like this. The banks, which were two or three feet high, stopped bullets quite well.

As we left the resettlement camp, Gimo asked me, "Do you know why the adult school starts at two? Because people want to be back from their *machambas* by the early afternoon, because it starts getting dangerous after that. It's also dangerous early in the morning. That's another reason that productivity is low."

The Beira Corridor was, for all its appearance of security, a free-fire zone. As we traveled through it at Gimo's pace, stopping often, bullet holes were suddenly visible in every cement wall, along with bazooka holes the size of dinner plates. That intact timber mill I had seen farther up the Corridor? It stood on a peninsula near the confluence of two rivers; with such a natural moat, the mill was easily defended, and that was the only reason it was still operating. "You know, it's physically impossible for the army to guard this country," Gimo said. "You can figure it out. They say that it takes twelve soldiers to guard one kilometer of infrastructure, on average. Mozambique has something like a hundred thousand kilometers of infrastructure that needs guarding. That would require over a million men just for defense, and that's not to mention going out and *fighting*. Meanwhile, Mozambique's army has thirty thousand men! The IMF says that's all the economy can afford, and I'm sure they're right. In the Corridor here, we have the Zimbabweans, and they are a big help. They make it possible for traffic to move in the daytime. But they can't really protect the people, and they can't really fight the war." The Zimbabwean troops, while superior to the Mozambican armed forces, had a morale problem in Mozambique, I was often told. They did not, understandably, want to die in someone else's war, and therefore tended to travel in large groups, stick to the roads, stay in their camps at night, and rely overmuch on their helicopter gunships—all ineffective tactics in a counterinsurgency war.

Gimo wanted to show me a large cotton farm a few miles off the Corridor. It was a joint venture between the government and Lonrho, the British multinational corporation and the largest single foreign investment in agriculture in Mozambique. We picked up two soldiers on the way out there, whether for their convenience or our protection, I wasn't sure. The cotton farm was vast, the red fields running off to the horizon, and the headquarters was a fortress. Great triple stacks of concertina wire ran for at least a mile around the place. Huge watchtowers stood on tall embankments at each corner of the compound, and a Soviet tank was parked outside, its cannon trained across the fields to the north. Gimo pointed out the bullet holes in the managers' houses inside the compound. For several years, there had been no attacks on the farm. Everyone assumed that Lonrho had made a deal with Renamo outside the country. If so, the deal had fallen through earlier in the year. All these fortifications were new. One morning, Gimo said, he had driven out here and come upon a horrific scene. The bodies of Renamo fighters were strewn all around the entrance to the farm. "There had been an attack the night before," Gimo said. "The bodies of the soldiers and militiamen who had died were already taken away, but the farm's guards seemed to be trying to make a statement by leaving the dead *bandidos* around for a while." It was unclear exactly who was in charge of the farm's security. Lonrho is a secretive firm. When I later called the head office in London and asked about the ownership of the tank, the company's spokesman first denied that there was a tank, and then denied that I had ever been in Mozambique. (Four months after our visit, the Lonrho farm's defenses were tested again. Five people were killed in the attack, five wounded, two shops were sacked, and 119 houses were burned.)[2]

Gimo also wanted to show me a school near the cotton farm. We headed off down progressively smaller dirt roads. The soldiers abandoned us at a river crossing where they could fill their canteens. Finally we found the school. It had been burned to the ground. Knowing that Renamo had destroyed thousands of schools throughout Mozambique did not ease the starkness of the sight—the charred timbers, the scattered chunks of exploded clay. Gimo started trying to turn the pickup around. He mentioned that it wasn't too far from here that a group of foreign missionaries, including one American, had been kidnapped by Renamo. They had been marched around in the bush for three months and finally released, somewhat the worse for wear, over the border in Malawi.[3] Gimo got the pickup stuck under a bank. The boundary of Gorongosa National Park, once a world-famous area for hunting big game and now Renamo Central, was just a few miles from where we were. Gimo finally got the truck turned around, the afternoon stopped shimmering strangely, and we drove back down to the highway.

We were about halfway up the Corridor, near the point where the coastal plain starts to rise into the great African escarpment. We rendezvoused with a colleague of Gimo's who needed a ride back to Beira, and the two of them began to talk about recent attacks. There had been a number of raids on villages and settlements at the Beira end of the Corridor, and a spate of land-mine explosions. "The *bandidos* like to scatter little antipersonnel mines around on paths in the villages at night, so the first person to come along in the morning steps on one," Gimo's colleague said. "The person usually loses a foot or a leg or a hand or an eye. It's often a child. That's Renamo's way of telling the *povo* that Frelimo cannot protect them."

And the raids near Beira?

"Social banditry," the man said. "Among us. Not Renamo."

I asked who the attackers would be.

"Probably popular militia." He shrugged. "Maybe soldiers. Guys from farther up the Corridor. They're so poor, and bored, and hopeless, and they have these guns. Some of them just decide to head toward the city and take whatever they can find there."

The outskirts of Beira itself were subject to attack. On our way to the beach, Gimo had shown me outlying suburbs that were totally deserted. The beach itself was a festive scene. People sat on the dunes mending fishing nets, radios played, and women and children ran down the dunes to meet the skiffs and dugout canoes as they landed, heavy with sand shark and smelt; but in the middle of the afternoon, we, and everyone else, left the beach. "This is a very bad area at night," Gimo said. The beach was near the approach to the Beira airport, and a missile emplacement was somewhere around. There were crude barracks in among the dunes, and soldiers everywhere. "Renamo hits this area every night," Gimo said. "When the wind blows north, you can hear the shooting in town."

Before we headed back down the Corridor to the city, we stopped at a bar in a settlement called Muda. The bar, which was a tiny place, set back from the road, had Manica, the local beer, on tap, which struck me as a great luxury. A glass of beer cost less than a dime. There was an adjoining shop, well stocked with biscuits, machetes, *capulanas* (a square of colorful cloth, the all-purpose women's garment in rural Mozambique), cooking oil, and long bars of brown soap, from which a block could be sawed off as needed. These goods were, for many people, just as strong a reason to pick up and move to the Corridor as any dream of safety. Behind the shop, there was a broken Foosball machine sitting amid a gaggle of red-faced ducks. The ducks, Gimo said, were for customers—the bar also had a kitchen. Several soldiers and militiamen were hanging around the bar, nursing beers. They were all very young, and they wore a complete range of headgear: a straw cowboy hat, a billed khaki forage cap, a big round khaki cap with a drawstring, a camouflage-patterned topee à la the French Foreign Legion, and a high-crowned hat that looked as though it had once belonged to the Royal Canadian Mounted Police. The erstwhile Mountie, who could not have been more than fifteen, had a radio playing and a small, live tortoise hanging from a thong on his wrist. I suddenly remembered a photograph of a Renamo band in a British newspaper. The Renamo fighters also wore an absurd collection of hats. One had a Soviet airman's cap with long, fur-lined ear-flaps, another a forage cap with wraparound side panels. Beside the photograph was the headline "RENAMO'S HARD MEN RULE OVER THE BUSH." The memory made me shudder.

We had eight or ten people, including several soldiers, in the pickup's bed on our way back to Beira, and again I was struck by the way that the soldiers blended in with the civilians. They carried cooking pots, empty bottles, bags of cassava. One even had a baby on his hip. Fear of the boys with the guns, if it existed, was invisible to me. At one roadblock, an old peasant woman started berating a soldier for some shortcoming (the performance was in Sena, a local language, so I got none of it), drawing peals of laughter from bystanders while the soldier scuffed the dirt with his bare foot, clutched his Soviet assault rifle, and looked sheepish. The scene reinforced my impression that nearly everywhere in Mozambique the level of social peace, of trust between strangers, was extraordinarily high. It was hard to understand how such a savage war, and mass starvation, could be raging in the same country. At another roadblock, a man threw a raft of bananas into the pickup, saying that it should be given to his uncle at the roadblock near Nhamatanda. When the woman who caught the bananas protested that she did not know the man's uncle, he said, "Just shout for António. He is expecting bananas."

Back at the Dom Carlos, one of the Portuguese pilots, a small, trim, balding man with blue eyes and a Pancho Villa mustache, confided to me that he had lived in Mozambique before independence—he had, in fact, flown against Frelimo for the Portuguese Air Force—and had only recently returned. He was absolutely appalled, he said, by the condition of the country. "There is no civilization left anywhere," he said.

I could not have agreed less.

But a certain ruefulness about the joys of independence was, in truth, unavoidable in a place like Beira. Nothing had been painted "since independence." So many things had gone to hell "since independence." And the struggle to put together again what had broken into a thousand pieces could often seem hopeless. At the port, a great new contraption for transferring coal from railcars to ships had been installed, with an overhead conveyor belt that seemed to run for half a mile. The contraption had never been used because the railway that brings coal down from Tete, the northwestern province where it is mined, had been closed by Renamo sabotage. And now the conveyor belt was unusable. It seemed that a number of local people had decided that their shoes needed resoling more than the port needed an idle conveyor belt.

Of course, Mozambique under Portuguese rule was never anyone's idea of efficient. Portuguese businesses were, as a rule, badly undercapitalized, and much of the machinery used in Mozambique was secondhand or thirdhand when it arrived. By independence, it was already antique. Most of the cranes at the port in Beira dated from 1929. And the decay, after independence, of the "cement city" was actually not of crucial importance to most people, since they had never had anything to do with the modern city. The same might be said for the disappearance of services that the African masses had never had any use for, and the disappearance from the shops of what had to be considered in Mozambique luxury goods. The import bill for consumer goods for the Portuguese settlers had, in fact, badly distorted the colonial economy, contributing to underdevelopment.

Some of the alienation of black people from the modern city ended at independence. Not only was there now a government ruling in *their* names but, with the mass exodus of the Portuguese settlers, most of the nicer homes in Beira suddenly stood empty. When rental property was nationalized by Frelimo, government employees got first crack at the newly available housing. Since rents were pegged to income, city gardeners and street sweepers were able to move into spacious modern houses and apartments. Of course, many of the new tenants had no experience with electricity or indoor plumbing, and no funds to maintain the places they occupied, hastening the deterioration of the city's housing.

And by the time I visited Beira, the housing party was over. Earlier in 1988, the government, under pressure from the International Monetary Fund, had reversed its longstanding policy. Rents were now being pegged far more closely to property values. All over Beira, people were receiving notices of huge rent hikes. Many were moving out of the dilapidated mansions they could no longer afford. Others were simply moving more people into their places, creating ever greater squalor, in hopes of making the increased rents. The new housing policy was part of a general retreat by Frelimo from socialist programs, but in Beira it was also seen as part of the effort to please the international consortium working to rehabilitate the Corridor. As such, it was sharply resented.

Cynics were calling Beira "the new Saudi Arabia." That overstated the case, but there were hundreds of foreign workers in town, most of them Scandinavian, most of them generically described as "engineers," and they were in Mozambique for the money, which was reported to include "hardship pay," and they were clearly beneficiaries of the new housing policy. Foreign companies and organizations were snapping up the luxury homes that were being emptied, as well as prime office space downtown. The same sort of thing was occurring all over Mozambique. In Beira, as in other towns, the only new vehicles to be seen belonged to foreign organizations. Indeed, Mozambicans sometimes called the foreigners "the new colonialists"; and they called the Mozambican clerks, drivers, translators, liaisons, and trainees who worked for the foreigners and were paid partly in hard currency—thus escaping much of the privation that afflicted their compatriots—"the new *assimilados.*" (Under the Portuguese system *assimilados* were a handful of Mozambicans who, by virtue of their education and their adoption of European customs, qualified for a specially designed second-class Portuguese citizenship.)

Prostitutes had even begun to reappear along the Beira waterfront. Prostitution had thrived in colonial times, when white Rhodesians and South Africans came to Mozambique in droves to escape the laws that restricted their access to black women at home. To Beirans, prostitution had become a symbol of their own debasement, and its resurrection was cause for alarm. The foreigners were the main customers, which did not increase their popularity. Neither did the fact that some of the international organizations were building colonial-style "compounds" for their employees, complete with generators, on prime beachfront property given them by the government at concessionary rates.

The most that could be said for the popularity of the Westerners tooling around Beira in their new Land Rovers was that it was greater than that of the Russians. All over Mozambique, the

Soviets seemed to be deeply disliked. They were variously described to me as arrogant, second rate, and racist. They did not mix socially with Mozambicans, and they rarely learned Portuguese. Soviet instructors tried to teach mathematics through local interpreters, who themselves knew nothing about mathematics—a hopeless arrangement, if you think about it. The director of a Beira technical institute told me, in disgust, that the iron cables sent to Mozambique from the Soviet Union were inferior to the cables Mozambique produced itself. He, like many other people, said the Soviets were a spent wave in Mozambique. The future was with *Sweden*. This new generator would clinch the deal.

The power was actually on in Beira the week I was there. By the time I left, it had been on for nearly three weeks straight, and people were delirious. It was the longest stretch of continuous power all year. The consensus analysis was that the *bandidos* had decided to take it easy on the Pope. Pope John Paul II was going to be visiting Beira later in the month, and apparently even Renamo didn't want to see the Pontiff sloshing through streets full of raw sewage. Some Renamo fighters, it was said, actually wanted to attend the outdoor Mass that the Pope would be celebrating in Beira, and were supposedly already slipping into town.

It was a stunning idea. (Even more stunning than the news that the Beira golf course was being mowed, in honor of the Pope, for the first time in fourteen years.) I wished there were some way to know if it was true. Wouldn't the bandits be recognized and turned over to the police?

The Beiran to whom I put this question said, "Not necessarily. The police are not popular here."

Were the bandits popular, then?

"Not necessarily."

The police in Beira were in fact notorious for their brutality and corruption.[4] The city's administration as a whole had always been plagued by incompetence and dishonesty. That had been true under the Portuguese, and it had remained true after independence. Frelimo had been popular in Beira at the time of independence, but its reputation had suffered when the old abuses of power began to reappear. Frelimo's leadership was aware of its Beira problem and took it seriously. Samora Machel, in a 1980 speech in the Beira football stadium, admitted that, in the transition to independence, local agents of the Portuguese secret police had "infiltrated government structures, enterprises, factories, infiltrated everywhere and took the reins. And up till now we have not removed them."[5] The president vowed to clean house. In the early 1980s, Frelimo sent members of its Political Bureau, the top decision-making body in the country, to act as governors of Sofala, the province of which Beira is the capital. It was an unusual move, since provincial governors were not normally drawn from the party's top ranks;[6] and, from what I could tell, it had not worked. All that people in Beira seemed to be able to recall of the two-year reign of Marcelino dos Santos, one of the most powerful men in the country, was that he had raised troops for the army high-handedly, sending his men to grab youths out of movie houses. Many Beirans seemed to see the local party as an organization for the ambitious, for opportunists, and not much more.

Machel, in his speech at the football stadium, had also characterized Beira as a city plagued by "tribalism, racism and regionalism, and a population filled with complexes."[7] The president was no doubt referring to the widespread resentment in central and northern Mozambique of the fact that southerners like him dominated the Frelimo leadership. Frelimo's first three presidents were all, in fact, Shangaan-speakers from the southern province of Gaza. Among the "complexes" that the population of Beira itself could be said to labor under, I gathered, was a serious case of second-city rivalry. As far as Beirans were concerned, the high-powered governors had been sent from Maputo to force Beira back into line. All important decisions were made in Maputo. All talented young people went off to Maputo. All the top jobs and perks went to people from Maputo. Why was Maputo the capital anyway, since it was in the extreme south of a very long country? The city had been built for the convenience of South Africa, and for no other reason. Meanwhile, Beira was in the center of the country. The city was always being overlooked when it came to allocating resources, unless those resources went to the Beira Corridor, which could help earn foreign exchange for the national coffers—which were in Maputo, naturally.

What seemed to rankle Beirans most of all, though, was the

decision, taken in Maputo, that destroyed the city's prosperity—
the decision to impose sanctions against Rhodesia—and the
subsequent failure of the national government to help the city
recover. No explanation invoking other economic problems and
priorities could soothe Beira's anger over that.

How much of this resentment translated into support for Renamo? None, necessarily. At a major intersection in Beira, there
was a big sign celebrating ten years of independence and calling
for "the total liquidation of the *bandidos armados*." The sign had
been there for three years, and no one had defaced it. But it was
in Beira that I first heard someone say that the *bandidos*, if they
were serious about taking power, would lay down their arms and
start agitating against the government—start rumors, spark
campaigns, incite riots. Under the economic-recovery program,
each food subsidy removed and each devaluation of the currency
put a greater number of basic commodities out of the reach of the
ordinary worker, let alone the unemployed *afetado*. I actually
thought it was a miracle that there weren't food riots in every
town in Mozambique. But it was in Beira that I heard the stark
warning issued by the mother of a gung-ho Frelimo local secretary to her son: "Be careful, Frelimo is a chair of *caniço*." *Caniço*
means cane—the flimsy material with which most Mozambicans
were compelled to build their homes.

13

Frelimo was not a chair of *caniço*. On the contrary, it was one of the most stable, sophisticated political parties to hold power in postcolonial Africa. The kind of crushing military and economic pressure that had been applied to Mozambique since independence, first by Rhodesia and then by South Africa, would have brought down most governments anywhere. When Samora Machel was killed, a crisis of leadership seemed inevitable. But Joaquim Chissano, the foreign minister, was quietly elected by the Frelimo Central Committee to succeed Machel, and he took office without incident. A European diplomat who deals with many African governments told me that the Frelimo leadership's indifference to "the exhibitionism of power" was unique in his experience on the continent. The level of corruption in government was certainly, for Africa, spectacularly low. Joseph Hanlon, who was a student at the Massachusetts Institute of Technology and, from 1979 to 1984, a correspondent for the BBC and the *Guardian* in Mozambique, told me, "It's getting slightly worse now, but Mozambique is still less corrupt than Boston."

The widespread and sometimes extreme corruption in African governments is a product of, more than anything else, the shallow roots of the modern African state itself. European mapmakers drew the boundaries of African colonies with careful attention to the political balances of late-nineteenth-century Europe but very little attention indeed to the societies they were carving up into pieces or blithely cramming together. The

loyalties of most Africans remained firmly within their own, usually much smaller, communities: their tribes, clans, villages, and
families. At the end of the colonial era, when colonial boundaries
became national boundaries, these loyalties remained largely
unchanged. A job in one of the new state bureaucracies often
represented, above all, an opportunity to increase the wealth of
the clan, the family, the village, or the tribe. Thus, the most
pressing general task for many African governments has been to
create larger loyalties, to larger social and economic units, not
only in order to reduce corruption but in order to defuse what
has often been an explosive problem: internal ethnic conflict.
Few governments have been up to the task. The struggle to con-
solidate modern nation-states virtually overnight has already
spawned a long series of dictatorships, leader cults, and military
regimes plagued by corruption, incompetence, tribalism, and
chronic instability.

In Mozambique, where people speak a great number of languages and dialects and have long suffered from extreme underdevelopment, the sense of national identity was almost nonexis-
tent under Portuguese rule. Even the three outlawed nationalist
groups that came together in 1962 in Dar es Salaam to found
Frelimo each came from a different region of the country.[1]
Frelimo's leaders therefore concentrated from the outset on
reducing ethnic and regional differences among their membership, insisting, for instance, that the movement's guerrillas
learn one another's songs and dances. A white Mozambican who
was editing a magazine in the capital before independence told
me, "The nation is a dream of Frelimo's. It started with the
armed struggle, with the gathering of people from all over the
country." A favorite Frelimo rallying cry was "From the Rovuma
to the Maputo"—the Rovuma River forms Mozambique's northern border; the Maputo River is in the far south. Although Portuguese was the colonists' language, and many black Mozambicans—the country's population is 99 percent black—could
not speak it, it was adopted as the movement's lingua franca,
and later as Mozambique's official language, because it was seen
as a unifying force. (There was even a movement to make English the official language, since all of Mozambique's neighbors
are English-speaking, but the task of teaching the whole country
a new language was finally judged too daunting.) Unlike some

of its neighbors, Mozambique contained within its borders no very profound ethnic antagonisms;[2] and Frelimo, unlike other national-liberation movements in southern Africa, had no serious competitors. As Eduardo Mondlane, Frelimo's founding president, wrote, "Our problem was not one of bringing together major rival groups but of preventing factions from developing within."[3]

Factions did develop within Frelimo. Virtually from the beginning, disgruntled grouplets started hiving off. Extensive infiltration by the Portuguese secret police sowed confusion and mistrust, and many of the movement's early members disagreed with the decision to wage a *luta armada* (armed struggle) against colonialism. But the situation which compelled that decision was lucidly described by Mondlane:

> The character of the government in Portugal itself makes a peaceful solution inherently unlikely. Within Portugal the government has promoted neither sound economic growth nor social well-being, and has gained little international respect. The possession of colonies has helped to conceal these failures: the colonies contribute to the economy; they add to Portugal's consequence in the world, particularly the world of finance; they have provided a national myth of empire which helps discourage any grumbling by a fundamentally dissatisfied population. The government knows how ill it can afford to lose the colonies. For similar reasons it cannot afford to liberalize its control of them: the colonies contribute to the metropolitan economy only because labour is exploited and resources are not ploughed back into local development; the colonies ease the discontent of the Portuguese population only because immigration offers to the poor and uneducated a position of special privilege. Not least, since the fascist government has eliminated democracy within Portugal itself, it can scarcely allow a greater measure of freedom to the supposedly more backward people of its colonies.[4]

Guerrilla infiltration and underground mobilization began in northern Mozambique in 1963. Algeria provided military training, and in September 1964 the *luta armada* was launched.

The nearest thing to a serious rival that Frelimo faced was the Comitê Revolucionário de Moçambique (Coremo), an umbrella organization of Frelimo splinter groups that came together in Zambia in 1965. Coremo sent a small number of guerrillas into Tete, but never matured as a military force or a political movement. (Coremo, it may be recalled, was the group that sought to recruit Boaventura das Dividas in Nairobi.)

More serious threats to Frelimo were posed by a series of splits in the late 1960s. One of these was precipitated by Lazaro Nkavandame, a traditional Makonde leader from Cabo Delgado and the Frelimo secretary for the province. Nkavandame had been the president of a peasant cotton cooperative, founded in 1957, which became a focus for anticolonial activity on the Mueda Plateau. Driven into exile, he and his supporters founded the Mozambique African National Union, folded that organization into Frelimo, and, once the war had started, were crucial both to the recruitment of Makonde peasants and refugees for the guerrilla army and to the mobilization of peasant support for the guerrillas when they moved into Cabo Delgado. As Frelimo's "liberated zones" inside Mozambique grew, however, Nkavandame and his allies, who were known as "the chairmen," began to alienate that support. The chairmen owned shops and fields in the liberated zones, and they controlled the busy crossborder trade with Tanzania. They were accused of profiteering and speculation and of exploiting the workers on their farms. Threatened by the growing power of young guerrilla commanders with egalitarian ideas, the chairmen opposed Frelimo policies that sought to liberate young people and women from the "traditional" authority of older men like themselves.[5] Frelimo's creation of a women's detachment, in 1967, and its leadership's opposition to traditional practices such as polygamy, brideprice, and child marriage were especially disturbing to the chairmen. Unable to influence Frelimo's course, Nkavandame sought Tanzanian support for a Makonde separatist movement and, when that failed, returned to Cabo Delgado and tried to close the border to Frelimo's guerrillas. He was stripped of his responsibilities by the liberation movement in January 1969.

Another rebellion staged during the same period was led by Father Mateus Gwenjere, a Catholic priest from Beira and a teacher at the Frelimo school in Dar es Salaam. Gwenjere opposed Frelimo's policy requiring students to spend time in the liberated zones. He and his supporters contended that educated

Mozambicans were too rare and valuable to have their lives risked in the war zones, and that their time would be better spent pursuing their studies on scholarships abroad. Frelimo's leadership was concerned about the development of a nascent Mozambican elite with no commitment to the country's peasantry. This concern deepened as the Gwenjere faction began to make race an issue. Gwenjere tried to use the fact that a number of Frelimo's leaders were white, Asian, or *mestiço*—Mondlane's wife, Janet, a white American, was the director of the Frelimo school—to discredit the leadership with their Tanzanian hosts and with black-nationalist students. The leadership now saw its suspicions about Gwenjere's ambitions confirmed: he and his supporters hoped not to end racism and exploitation but simply to replace the white colonialists in the seats of power.

A dispute over the treatment of colonial soldiers taken prisoner seemed to highlight the differences between the black nationalists and what became known as "the revolutionary line." The black nationalists favored harsh treatment, even routine execution. The revolutionaries pointed out that most Portuguese soldiers were oppressed peasants themselves, and that an increasing number of soldiers in the colonial army were, in fact, black (so much for knowing your enemy by the color of his skin), and argued, successfully, for a policy of humane treatment.

Some of these differences in racial attitudes could be ascribed to the relatively cosmopolitan experience of much of the revolutionary leadership. Mondlane was an anthropologist with a doctorate from Northwestern University, at ease in the corridors of power; Marcelino dos Santos was an engineer, educated in Portugal and France; even Joaquim Chissano, the youngest member of the leadership, had been studying in Paris when Frelimo was formed. Such men could be expected to see the conflict in Mozambique in broad terms, and to recognize white allies when they saw them. But Frelimo leaders with far less education and cross-cultural experience, men such as Samora Machel and the Makonde guerrilla commanders Raimundo Pachinuapa and Alberto Chipande, were also firmly antiracist and antiregionalist—and fiercely opposed the sort of "false decolonization" they saw taking place in much of Africa, where the independence process had basically replaced the white elite with a black elite and left the impoverished masses as miserable as ever.

Frelimo was at this stage "two entities," in John Saul's formulation: "a conventional nationalist movement unable to secure an easy transition to power, and a revolutionary movement struggling to be born."[6] A number of forces were driving Frelimo in the direction of Marxism-Leninism, including the historical models for revolution offered by Cuba, Vietnam, the Soviet Union, and China; the military aid and training provided by the socialist countries (while the capitalist West was helping the Portuguese enemy through NATO); Mozambique's long and terrible experience with Portuguese-style capitalism, and the failure of capitalist theory to offer even a hope of rapid improvement in social and economic justice; the shortcomings, which were increasingly obvious, of the "African socialist" alternatives embraced by newly independent neighbors such as Tanzania and Zambia, where development plans based on romantic ideas of a classless precolonial Africa were rapidly coming to grief; and, finally, the internal conflicts with conservative factions such as the chairmen and the black nationalists. The experience of administering the liberated zones—and of resisting the chairmen's depredations—forced Frelimo's leaders to imagine more concretely the sort of country they were fighting to create. Being challenged by Gwenjere on the racial question compelled them to declare the primacy of a class analysis.

Although Nkavandame and his supporters were peasants from one of the least developed areas of Mozambique, and Gwenjere and his supporters were educated and nearly all came from urban backgrounds, their respective oppositions to the revolutionary line often took the same form. Both groups, for instance, opposed the idea of merged political and military leadership, preferring to see themselves as political leaders and to leave the extraordinary hardship, discipline, and danger of the *luta armada* to underlings. But the revolutionary leadership had decided that protracted mass struggle was the only strategy that could possibly defeat the Portuguese; that maximum identification with the peasantry and the war was indispensable both to the movement's success and to its political development (as Pachinuapa put it, "It was in the army that national unity was forged, that tribe, race and region were killed");[7] and that it could not afford a parasitic political class living far from the front lines. The conflicts with Nkavandame and Gwenjere both came to a head in 1968, with riots in Dar es Salaam that left Frelimo's offices sacked, one Central Committee member dead, and the Frelimo school closed. Barely a month after Nkavandame was expelled from the movement, Eduardo Mondlane was assassinated by a parcel bomb in Dar es Salaam. An investigation by Interpol and the Tanzanian police concluded that the bomb had been constructed in Lourenço Marques, probably by the Portuguese secret police, and delivered by Frelimo dissidents, possibly including Nkavandame. Nkavandame had defected to the Portuguese soon after Mondlane's murder.[8]

There was a succession struggle, ultimately won by the revolutionaries, represented by Samora Machel. The *luta armada* continued, with the liberated zones growing steadily. The Portuguese were a ferocious enemy. The secret police arrested, tortured, and murdered thousands of suspected Frelimo members and sympathizers. The colonial armed forces increased in the course of the war from 30,000 men to 75,000, and they came with fighter jets, bombers, helicopters, warships, napalm, chemical defoliants, and American counterinsurgency training. Frelimo, for its part, had only light weapons and land mines, but the guerrillas used them well, opening a western front in Tete and pushing south of the Zambezi to attack the Beira Corridor. In 1973, Frelimo forced the closing of Gorongosa National Park, then a world-famous big-game hunting ground that attracted 20,000 tourists a year. The morale of the Portuguese was abysmal. Although Frelimo had scrupulously avoided attacks on white settlers for most of the war, whites in Beira rioted in early 1974, accusing the army of failing to protect them. The military coup in Lisbon in April 1974 was clearly inspired in large part by the hopelessness of Portugal's colonial wars.

In Mozambique, ten years of fighting had produced a powerfully disciplined, unusually mature political movement with a leadership deeply committed to the idea of unity—to decision making by consensus.[9] The war had shaped Frelimo so decisively, in fact, that in 1989, a quarter of a century after the armed struggle was launched, nine of the ten members of the Frelimo Political Bureau were veterans of the *luta armada*.

There were Frelimo cadres who believed that the Portuguese collapse came too soon. The few Mozambicans with direct knowledge of Frelimo were nearly all in the northern part of the country, and many other contestants for power emerged in the chaotic months between the coup and independence. Gwenjere, Nkavandame, and other Frelimo deserters worked for rival parties. The new government in Lisbon wanted to hold elections, but Frelimo insisted on being recognized as the sole legitimate representative of the Mozambican people; when Portugal balked, Frelimo intensified the war against the demoralized colonial forces. Mozambicans were now flocking to join Frelimo, whose lack of political structures in most of the country was easily counterbalanced by the wild popularity that Machel and his comrades enjoyed as the liberators from Portuguese rule. Finally, in September 1974, Lisbon acceded to all of Frelimo's demands. No elections were held; instead, after a nine-month transition, power was simply handed over to Frelimo on June 25, 1975. At the Independence Day ceremony, Machel and the other Frelimo leaders wore their military uniforms.

The ecstatic expectations of most Mozambicans were matched by the enthusiasm of Frelimo. The exploitation of man by man would be abolished forthwith, and national unity forged. "We do not recognize tribes, regions, race, or religious belief," President Machel declared in his Independence Day speech. "We only recognize Mozambicans who are equally exploited and equally desirous of freedom and revolution." [10] Frelimo's nonracial rhetoric and racially mixed leadership failed to prevent the exodus of the Portuguese, who were more impressed, apparently, by Frelimo's Marxist rhetoric and by reports of antiwhite violence; but the prospects for a rapid transition from colonial capitalism to independent socialism must have seemed improved by the wholesale departure of the capitalist class. Abandoned plantations became state farms; abandoned industries were nationalized. Machel had announced that it was his ambition to make Mozambique "Africa's first Marxist state," [11] and in 1977 Frelimo formally rechristened itself a Marxist-Leninist "vanguard party." Twenty-year aid agreements with the Soviet Union and Cuba were signed—Machel often called the socialist countries "our natural allies." But Marxism, he insisted, had not come to Mozambique as an imported product. His own political education, Machel said, came "not from writing in a book. Nor from reading Marx and Engels. But from seeing my father forced to grow cotton and going with him to the market where he was to sell it at a low price—much lower than the Portuguese grower." [12]

The nationalization of medicine, law, education, rental property, and land ownership followed in rapid order, along with the dramatic expansion of the educational and rural health-care systems. The sharp decline of the economy caused by the flight of managers and skilled workers was slowed as thousands of Mozambicans began to receive the training and experience that they had been denied under the Portuguese. In November 1977, Michael Kaufman of the *New York Times* wrote, "The experience of Mozambique is only two years old and any instantaneous readings of revolutionary change are subject to revision. Still, there is evidence that the degree of mobilization and national purpose attained here is great and may be more durable than anything black Africa has known." [13] As the liberation war in Rhodesia ended, in 1980, and peace seemed a real possibility at last, Frelimo drew up an extraordinarily ambitious plan to modernize and socialize agriculture and industry, calling for the "radical transformation of our country." [14] By 1990, according to the plan, agricultural production would increase by 400 percent, with the gross national product rising by 17 percent each year. All peasants would live in communal villages and work on state farms or cooperatives. Mozambique would produce iron, steel, aluminum, trucks, tractors, and pharmaceuticals. There would be textile mills and huge modern factories throughout the country. The "victory over underdevelopment" would be won in a single decade.

Flying around Mozambique, an outsider finds it easy to empathize with the impulse of the new government to "jump over history." Most of the country presents itself as a gray sprawl of trackless bush. The sight of a road, a rectangular field—a building!—is, after an hour or two, a distinct pleasure, a tiny patch of order and hope. Yet Frelimo's approach to development, drawing on traditions both Stalinist and Portuguese, was centralized planning with a vengeance. Frelimo encouraged popular participation in politics (knowledge of Marxism was not a party membership requirement, and neither was literacy; the emphasis was on a candidate's standing in the local community), but there was no institutional brake on the leadership's passion for

monumental projects. As it happened, the huge foreign investment required for rapid industrialization never materialized.
The world recession of the early 1980s, Mozambique's perfectly
reasonable refusal to allow colonial-era levels of profits to foreign companies, and the failure of peace to arrive on schedule
(after South Africa assumed control of Renamo, and the war instead escalated) combined to defeat the ten-year plan even before it was announced.

In the projects that were launched, the lack of national infrastructure and trained personnel proved crippling. The state
farms were radically inefficient. Nationalization had been the
only feasible way to deal with abandoned large plantations, and
by 1980 state farms accounted for nearly all the country's tea,
sugar, and rice production; but in 1981 the Ministry of Agriculture admitted that not a single state farm was profitable.[15] The
government had imported thousands of tractors and three hundred modern combine harvesters from Eastern Europe, but the
new equipment was ill maintained and productivity remained
low. A socialist government could not superexploit workers the
way the colonial system had, a constraint which explained some
of the low productivity, but the state farm managers were also
less experienced than their capitalist predecessors. Continued
monocropping for export, moreover, required seasonal labor.
This prevented the establishment of a permanent rural work
force and the proletarianization of the countryside (only the proletariat, according to Marxist theory, can lead the transition to
socialism).[16]

Most Mozambicans live not in villages but on widely scattered homesteads. Under the Portuguese, people fanned out to
escape taxes and forced labor; traditional fallow-farming methods also require lots of land.[17] These living patterns make it impossible to deliver services—schools, clinics, clean water—to
rural areas, or to build mass organizations, or to foster almost
any kind of development. Frelimo's proposed solution was communal villages. Ten thousand villages were needed, it was estimated;[18] and by the early 1980s some 1,400 had been started.[19]
The access to health care and education was a great attraction
for peasants—especially women, who do the bulk of the family
farming in southern Africa and suffer the most from isolation
and illiteracy. But resources to support the new villages were

scarce, and the promises that persuaded people to move into them often remained unfulfilled. Worse, many peasants were forced into the villages, either by local officials eager to curry favor with Frelimo or by the military in areas where Renamo was active. And the fact that some communal villages were the same "strategic hamlets" that the Portuguese had used to try to keep the peasants away from Frelimo was lost on no one. The war was inadvertently speeding villagization, but villagization was inadvertently creating new social strata in the countryside, as families whose lands were close to the new villages profited and families whose lands were farther out suffered.[20] Eager to return to their ancestral lands, some of the residents of Frelimo's communal villages actually helped Renamo burn them down.

Communal villages were meant to be supported by cooperative farms. Cooperatives were the logical, though not the only, way to start modernizing peasant agriculture, but they required relatively complex organization and, if they were to make any technical advances over traditional farming, outside support. Again, the lack of training and resources undermined plans. Peasants still worked their own plots with more enthusiasm and to greater effect than they did the cooperative's fields.[21] "The peasants do not like communism"—this was a refrain I heard over and over in Mozambique.

But the starting point for what became known as "the peasant crisis" was the collapse of the rural trading network. The Portuguese *cantineiros* had abandoned the rural shops where peasants bought seeds, tools, cloth, oil, soap, salt, lanterns, and bicycles. Frelimo's efforts to keep the shops going failed. Peasants suddenly had nothing to buy with the money they earned from marketing their surplus, and the lack of seeds and tools made even subsistence farming increasingly difficult. The government policy favoring state farms did not allow for the hundreds of thousands of hoes that needed to be imported each year for family farmers. In the liberated zones of the north during the *luta armada*, Frelimo had been compelled to consider realistically the needs of the peasants it depended on for survival. But once it was in power, and relying on central planning, Frelimo seemed to begin to inhabit an imaginary country. The myth of the self-sufficient peasant, for instance, clearly informed the decision not to import enough hoes, and it left the government unprepared when the peasants suddenly stopped producing a surplus. Most Mozambican peasants were in fact heavily involved in the cash economy. The failure of the government to meet their needs led to a massive flight of peasants from the countryside to the cities, and to the disenchantment of millions who, in the words of one observer, "withdrew into a poverty-stricken form of self-subsistence, ever more vulnerable to the external shocks of climate, warfare and disease."[22]

Local Frelimo authorities were often out of touch with local people. In some areas, peasants joined the party and served as local secretaries, but the district administrators, who were the real authorities in the rural areas, were always outsiders. The deliberate pairing of northerners with southerners, of Makua-speakers with Ronga-speakers, which had been so successful during the liberation war, was carried over into state administration, and there it was a fiasco.[23] Overworked young officials were well versed in Marxism-Leninism, which they had learned at party schools in courses taught by foreigners, but they rarely had any more useful knowledge to share with their constituents. Some didn't even speak the local language. To many peasants, the difference between the party and the state was never made clear. With the new administrator living in the same house that the old colonial administrator had lived in, waited upon by the same servants, and trying to squeeze all too similar quotas of cotton and cashews out of the district, some peasants may even have wondered what the ultimate differences were between Frelimo and the Portuguese.[24]

The Portuguese, primarily through forced labor and forced cotton growing, had destroyed the self-sufficiency of peasant agriculture, but many aspects of rural African life—of "traditional culture"—survived colonialism in Mozambique. For a start, most Mozambicans retained their traditional religious beliefs. The mysteries of death, love, the land, and the weather; the rites of maturity, marriage, medicine, and burial; the structures of kinship, labor, inheritance, and authority—all these were still solidly embedded, for most Mozambicans, in a traditional society. When necessary, Frelimo worked with the traditional structures during the *luta armada*, forming alliances with popular *régulos*, *curandeiros*, and local headmen such as Lazaro Nkavandame; but the revolutionary movement was fundamentally opposed to this rival form of power.[25] After independence, Frelimo approached rural administration with what has since been called "the ideology of the tabula rasa."[26] Traditional society was "feudal." Religion was *obscurantismo*. Chiefs and *curandeiros* were shunted aside. The brave new day of scientific socialism had dawned. Reactionary practices that oppressed women—polygamy, bride-price, child marriage, initiation rites—were actively discouraged.

It was a novel approach to government in Africa. At a 1987 seminar on parliamentarianism in southern Africa, held in Botswana, delegates from a number of Mozambique's neighbors seemed astonished to hear the leader of the Mozambican delegation declare, "The traditional chiefs do not have any role to play in [Mozambique]. . . . We are not concerned with our traditional chiefs, but with the interests of the people." The seminar's moderator said, "In Botswana, we are afraid to interfere with our chiefs, because they would be very angry. What about your chiefs, were they not angry when you took away their traditional powers?" The Mozambicans were clearly not concerned about the feelings of chiefs.[27]

Botswanans did not, of course, have to fight a war to gain their independence. Zimbabweans did, though, and many of the Zimbabwean guerrillas who were based in Mozambique were also apparently nonplussed by Frelimo's attitude toward traditional authorities.[28] Some of the Zimbabwean commanders had received their military training in Warsaw Pact countries and no doubt shared some of the scientific socialist's doubts about shamanism and sorcery. But the Zimbabwean forces used spirit mediums and traditional chiefs extensively, and very successfully, in their conduct of the war;[29] and when independence came, celebration banners showed, above the image of the new prime minister, Robert Mugabe, the image of a female spirit medium, Ambuya Nehanda, who was hanged by the British in 1898 for her part in an early Shona anticolonial rebellion.[30] The Marxist government of Zimbabwe was also careful to give legal standing to a national association of traditional healers, and ten guaranteed seats in Parliament for traditional chiefs.[31] Neither of these syndicates had real power, but chiefs and soothsayers were groups that any prudent government would want to be able to keep an eye on, and would certainly not want to antagonize. The leaders of Zimbabwe were probably not surprised to hear that local chiefs and *curandeiros* were collaborating widely with Renamo inside Mozambique.

The same revolutionary purism that made corruption in high places all but unknown in Mozambique—while Zimbabwe's new leaders were fattening themselves (and their families, and their clans) at the public trough at a brisk pace indeed—seemed to blind Frelimo to what was happening in the countryside. The traditional structures that the new government tried to sweep away were not in fact feudal; they were not like the chieftancies in Afghanistan, which the Communists there unwisely took on: they were not broadly based, with the tenacious nexus of an organized religion. They could not deliver even basic commodities such as seeds and hoes.[32] But the *régulos,* the petty chiefs who had worked with the Portuguese, often remained, even after being deposed by Frelimo, the only people in their communities who had any experience in dealing with bureaucracy. They often still controlled access to cattle and land; they were still the "big men" in their neighborhoods. Just as important, many of them belonged to traditionally powerful clans—even, in some cases, to royal lineages—and were therefore the living links to the guiding spirits of the ancestors. As the war began to rage, and the general anxiety grew, many rural people naturally turned to the traditional authorities, and many of those authorities, just as naturally, were available to Renamo as allies.

The escalation of the war in 1981 caught Frelimo badly unprepared. Eventually, fifteen hundred *antiguos combatentes,* veteran commanders of the *luta armada,* were reactivated. They were ineffectual at best. After independence, many of them had been simply sent back to their villages, where they found their lives little changed. Being recalled to service gave them a chance to live in the larger world again, and many of the *antiguos combatentes* seemed less interested in fighting than in the perks that went with command. They were not above helping themselves to supplies, a weakness which exacerbated the army's logistical problems. It was no way to win a war, but the Frelimo leadership's reluctance to displace former comrades, its attachment to the idea that the nation's best values had been formed in the *luta armada,* delayed the needed housecleaning.[33] In the meantime, the peasantry was being exposed to an inept, unmotivated, poorly led, and poorly fed army. To many Mozambicans, "Frelimo" came to mean not the national-liberation movement, not the ruling party, not even the state—but a dangerous group of undisciplined soldiers. It was a disastrous political development. By 1988, the agitation of younger, better-educated officers for military reform (and for their own promotion) was finally bearing fruit, with the compulsory retirement of many *antiguos combatentes*, but immeasurable damage had been done.

Meanwhile, the country's economy had gone into an epic dive. A dire combination of war, drought, the peasant crisis, and the world recession of the early 1980s, which reduced prices for Mozambique's main exports, cut agricultural production severely. By 1986, the production of tea, a key export crop, had fallen to 5 percent of its 1981 level. Sugar exports were barely 30 percent of what they had been five years earlier, and exports of cashews, a major source of foreign exchange, had fallen by 80 percent.[34] With foreign-exchange earnings dropping, imports of consumer goods had to be sharply reduced. With nothing in the shops and markets, the metical was worthless, and the black market swelled monstrously. Food shortages in the cities became chronic, and in 1983 an estimated 100,000 people starved to death in the drought regions. Mozambique's foreign debt soared, while interest rates on the debt rose. Industrial production fell, for lack of equipment and spare parts—the shortage of foreign exchange striking again. Some of the economic collapse could be laid to Frelimo's policies, but the decisive factor was clearly the war. Similar collapses had occurred in other African countries, including some that had not experienced war or severe drought, and that were handed functioning, "turnkey" governments by their former colonial rulers. But the collapse in Mozambique was unusually thorough. By 1990, Mozambique was producing less than 10 percent of the food that its people needed,[35] and was widely considered the poorest country in the world.[36]

14

At a UNESCO seminar on the transition to socialism, held in Maputo, Carlos Cardoso, the director of Mozambique's state-owned news agency, was asked by a foreigner about *carapau*. The *carapau* is a small, bony, entirely awful-tasting fish that had become the only source of protein available to many Mozambicans. Cardoso's reply: "The *carapau* is a whale that has been through all the stages of socialist construction."

I had heard before I went to Mozambique that Cardoso was arrested for making this much-repeated crack. But when I met him and asked about it, he scoffed. He had made the remark; he had not been arrested. Such jokes had been part of Mozambican survival psychology for years. Everybody made them, including Frelimo militants.

For an outsider, the nuances of political fear can be among the hardest texts to read. Once I was driving in a provincial city. My passengers were an American relief worker and her Mozambican colleague. Approaching an intersection, I noticed people standing in the street and a soldier glaring at me, but I thought nothing of it until my American companion suddenly shrieked, "Stop the car!" I hit the brakes. "Get out!" she yelled. She leapt from the car and snapped to attention. It seemed that the Frelimo flag was being lowered outside the local party head-quarters on the other side of the intersection. "If you don't stop the car and get out," the American woman hissed, "the police will impound it and drive it around themselves while they 'get this cleared up.'" I noticed that our Mozambican companion was still inside the car. His colleague noticed it, too, and only under her furious glare did he slowly climb out and join us in the street, smiling to himself. Later, I asked him about the incident. He shrugged and said that, in the first couple of years after independence, there had been some public compunction around flag raising and flag lowering. But it had long since relaxed. "Nothing would happen to you if you kept driving," he said.

If the changing latitudes of political tolerance were unclear, it was at least certain that, in the early days of Mozambican independence, criticizing Frelimo was a very dangerous occupation. (For exiles not in the liberation movement, simply returning to the country could be, as Dividas knew, a life-endangering act.)[1] The rule of law—or, more specifically, democratic constraint on the arbitrary use of power—is a hard-won (and never complete, and never secure) condition in any society, achieved incrementally and rarely advanced directly by coup, revolution, or fiat. At independence, the rule of law in Mozambique was a stock that had been utterly debased by state-sponsored murder and mayhem. (For most Mozambicans, it had never existed in any case.) After the flight of the Portuguese settlers, there were three lawyers and not a single judge in the country. A makeshift system of revolutionary administration based on neighborhood "dynamizing groups" emerged to fill the authority vacuum. Alongside the heady experiment of self-government and the inevitable scramble for position in the new order, many political scores were being settled. Local administrators and local Frelimo committees had the power to sentence, without trial, any "opponents of decolonization" they happened upon to indefinite terms in rural "reeducation" camps.[2] Ordinary criminals, unemployed vagrants, Jehovah's Witnesses (their crime was their refusal on religious grounds to shout "Viva Frelimo!"), and "prostitutes" (some of whom were apparently just single women who, say, refused to sleep with a member of a neighborhood council) were among thousands consigned, along with suspected political opponents, to the reeducation camps.[3] Conditions in the camps were grim. Beatings and starvation were common, and an unknown number died.[4]

The worst abuses of due process ended, according to Amnesty International, after 1978, when the first laws establishing a new judiciary and legal system were adopted. At the local level, without the power to impose jail sentences, were customary courts known as Popular Tribunals. At higher levels, the judicial system, though still not fully staffed, was being professionalized. Nonpolitical trials were public and were generally reckoned fair. In political cases, however, indefinite detention without trial and trials in camera were still the rule. The state security service operated with no real accountability, and in 1979 a wartime high court called the Revolutionary Military Tribunal, composed entirely of military officers, was established. The death penalty was also introduced in 1979, and the Revolutionary Military Tribunal was empowered to impose death sentences for political crimes such as rebellion, sabotage, and agitation. Two days after the tribunal came into existence, it sentenced ten prisoners to death and all were executed by firing squad the same day. Over the next four years, sixty-two people were reported executed, all by firing squad.[5] In 1983, public flogging was introduced, and the number of crimes punishable by death was increased to include economic crimes. Although the reeducation camps were falling into disuse, it remained very dangerous to criticize Frelimo publicly.[6] And the standards of justice, not to mention health and hygiene, inside Mozambican jails remained, at least by Western norms, fearfully low. President Machel himself launched a "legality offensive" in 1981, inveighing against arbitrary arrests, torture, and other abuses and causing thousands of policemen, prison guards, and state security agents to be transferred, fired, or, in some cases, prosecuted. The courts continued Machel's offensive, and the local press even exposed instances of torture.

The legal and political picture was hopelessly distorted, of course, by the war. Summary executions were being carried out by the armed forces in the war zones, and there was a great deal of improvised imprisonment. A high-level delegation from Amnesty International visited Mozambique in October 1988, and announced that, as far as it could determine, there were no "prisoners of conscience" in the country's jails. There were, however, between 4,000 and 5,000 security-related prisoners—either captured Renamo fighters or alleged Renamo supporters.[7] An onerous (though haphazardly enforced) system of internal passports, which made it difficult for people to travel outside their home districts, was justified officially by the war.

Despite the war, the government produced a number of improvements in human-rights safeguards in the late 1980s. The Revolutionary Military Tribunal was abolished in March 1989, and prisoners accused of political offenses were again able to receive ordinary criminal trials. In September 1989, the right of habeas corpus was restored to political prisoners, and flogging was abolished.[8] A series of mass pardons released a large number of political prisoners, and in late 1990 the death penalty, which had not been used since 1986, was finally abolished. The heavy shadow of the reeducation camps was also said to have been removed from the land at last.[9]

But opposition to Frelimo remained a dicey proposition through the late 1980s. The equation of opposition with treason is standard fare, of course, in countries at war, but a more immediate problem with political opposition in Mozambique was that it was illegal. According to the constitution, Frelimo was the only legal political party. The press, moreover, was state-owned. The argument for one-party states in Africa usually rests on the notion that political parties have a tendency to become ethnic parties, which, in turn, have a tendency to destroy national unity. Frelimo had used this argument, along with both Leninist and Stalinist conceptions of the ruling party's role, to justify making Mozambique a one-party state. But Frelimo's idea of power really seemed to derive from, above all, the ideology of the tabula rasa, that ferocious dream of building a nation by denying, and thus eradicating, the differences among its people.

Janet Mondlane called it "Frelimotite." She pronounced the word playfully, but the undertone was serious. "You know, in Portuguese, the names of sicknesses often end in 'tite,' like *hepatite*. Well, Frelimotite is a local sickness. Many, *many* people here, including me, have been seriously affected by it. It's the inability to analyze, within a broader context, what goes on in Mozambique."

Mrs. Mondlane was a teenager from Downers Grove, Illinois, when she met Eduardo Mondlane, at a church camp in Wisconsin in 1951. After her husband's assassination, she continued to raise their three children in Tanzania, running a school and a hospital for Frelimo. After independence, she became Mozambique's director for international cooperation. She remarried in 1981 and left public service for a life of farming and writing west of Maputo. After the war forced her to abandon her farm, she accepted President Chissano's offer to head a newly formed Mozambican Red Cross. When I met her at her office in Maputo, I found a kindly-looking grandmother with long graying hair and a great easygoing laugh. She was wearing a brilliantly patterned African dress and worrying about software problems. Her native Midwestern English had acquired a few exotic trills and slurs. I asked her to tell me more about Frelimotite.

"It's as if you were put in a box in 1975 or 1977 and the box never opened," she said. "Some people just cannot get the original ideas of Frelimo out of their systems. They hang on to these extraordinarily unrealistic ideas, which have nothing to do with Mozambique. I mean, just look around. The rural areas have *suffered.* They never benefited from the big projects after independence, even though everything was supposedly being done for the benefit of the peasants. Now friends come to me and start talking about what's going to happen at the Fifth Party Congress, and I just say to them, 'You're still suffering from Frelimotite, aren't you?' It's absolute belief. For Mozambicans to catch it is understandable. They're not used to independence. They're used to dependence. But it's strange that I fell into it, too."

Mrs. Mondlane seemed to ponder this strangeness a moment, and then went on, "You see, it's different to get things accomplished here. Mozambicans are, in general, very laid-back. They are quiet and friendly, but they are also cautious, even fatalistic. They have such a long history of having their dreams not fulfilled. They feel they have to be laid-back just to avoid having their personalities destroyed by disappointment. So Frelimo always had to take the initiative, always be pushing and pushing. For some people in Frelimo, that became a way of life. But if you still hold on to the illusion that you can control everything, that Frelimo can control everything, then you are still quite sick. Because what *happens* is injustice, and the joy of living goes *out.*"

Mrs. Mondlane looked perturbed and sad. Along with its emergency service and health education, the Mozambican Red

Cross, I recalled, was working to improve conditions in the prisons. She sighed, then brightened. "The great thing is that it has taken the leadership only one decade to open up, to see that this business of being closed, of trying to control everything, just wouldn't work. Most places, it took decades."

In 1988, when I was in Mozambique, there was a great deal of excited comment in the embassies and foreign press about "Mozambican *glasnost*." José Luís Cabaço, then the deputy secretary for foreign relations on the Frelimo Central Committee and one of the party's leading theoreticians, said that that was a racist cliché. Mozambique, Cabaço told me, was far ahead of the Soviet Union in its creative reappraisal of the theory and practice of socialism, and Frelimo had always considered Yugoslavia and China more relevant models for its own development anyway.

The Frelimo leadership that I met was, in fact, remarkably self-critical. I asked Luís Bernardo Honwana, Mozambique's minister of culture, about Frelimo's attitude toward traditional society.

"We didn't realize how influential the traditional authorities were, even without formal power," Honwana said. "We are obviously going to have to harmonize traditional beliefs with our political project. Otherwise, we are going against things that the vast majority of our people believe—we will be like foreigners in our own country. I think we are gathering the courage to say so aloud. We will have to restore some of the traditional structures that at the beginning of our independence we simply smashed, thinking that we were doing a good and important thing."

Honwana, who was educated in Europe and comes from a prominent nationalist family—one brother was killed with Samora Machel; another was the chief of the air force—is the author of a celebrated collection of short stories, *We Killed Mangy Dog*, which explores, among other things, the collision of cultures in colonial Mozambique. "In most African families, even in the cities, some members have assumed Western habits and won't go to the *curandeiro* if they are ill, or confused, or need a change of luck," he told me. "Others will go. But when disaster strikes, even a Westernized family will always hold a council, and then they may decide to, for instance, placate their grandfather's spirit, which they may have neglected. Traditional beliefs are a point of reference for all those people caught in the middle of the road between Westernization and African society. In a state of flux like a war, the beliefs become even stronger. This war of ours has certainly underlined the shortcomings of our choice to ignore those beliefs. But we are hybrids, we so-called educated Africans, because we will react, sometimes violently, against the imposition of alien values, and yet we ourselves are often the agents of the imposition, all in the name of 'development.'"

Traditional society is conservative and not receptive to socialism, Honwana said. "But to most Mozambicans, independence is a socialist idea. That's partly the work of the Portuguese. When I was arrested by the colonial police for advocating independence"—Honwana spent time in prison, without being charged, in the 1960s—"they called me a Communist. But our starting point, you must remember, is always colonialism. On the one hand, fat gentlemen sitting on verandas and in the cafés in town. On the other hand, half-naked people performing forced labor. Everyone understands that this is unfair, that we must establish social justice for those who work. But socializing the means of production, changing the rules of the economic game— these are more elaborate ideas and are not widely understood. The nationalizations, the discouragement of the private sector— these were not popular policies, even at the time. Our assumption that we would build socialism through state-owned companies and cooperatives and so on was wrong, in any case."

Frelimo's lapse from the Marxist-Leninist faith took many years to complete. Signal events along the way included appeals to the West in the early 1980s for military assistance and emergency food aid, a decision to join the World Bank and the International Monetary Fund in 1984, and the imposition of the IMF-approved economic-recovery program in 1987. Private business was increasingly encouraged, private foreign investment desperately encouraged. Private schools were reintroduced, and some of the more unwieldy state farms were broken up and given away to private farmers and peasants.

But the wave of privatizations did not revitalize the economy, which remained stricken by the war and dominated by international aid. The aid industry became, moreover, a source of extensive corruption. Scandals and investigations repeatedly revealed theft and financial chicanery, not only in the government's aid-distribution agency but also in the armed forces and among Zimbabwean troops. Frelimo's reputation for clean government suffered, and recrimination flourished. At a December 1989 meeting of the People's Assembly—the Mozambican parliament—the general secretary of the semiofficial women's organization alleged that corruption went higher in the government than had yet been disclosed. "This reflects on all leaders and dirties the image of the entire government," she said. She mentioned the mass demonstrations that had been toppling governments in Eastern Europe, and said, "We will be confronted with the same sort of thing if we carry on like this. And all our necks will be on the block because of half a dozen crooks. I am prepared to lose my head for what I have committed, but not for what others have committed."[10]

Frelimo's dreams for Mozambique—universal, free, and equal health care; universal free education; public ownership; a fairer distribution of wealth—had failed. Health care was no longer free, had never been equal, and the system had been crippled by Renamo. The school system, too, had been crippled by Renamo, and the cost of textbooks, which students had to buy, had soared—while state spending on education had been cut so drastically, under the economic-recovery program, that by 1990 there were places in school for only 40 percent of children under sixteen.[11] The failure of Frelimo's dreams had sapped the party's strength throughout Mozambique. (Similar dreams had been dashed in many other countries, of course, including Portugal, where the socialist government that succeeded the dictatorship had been voted out in favor of a conservative regime, and an ambitious land-reform program had been all but abandoned.) Worse, the resistance to new economic and political initiatives was coming largely from the bureaucratic class that had developed inside the party and the government. This group naturally favored state projects over private enterprise, central planning over its alternatives. Frelimo's official commitment to "a revolutionary democratic dictatorship of workers and peasants" notwithstanding, many state and party decision makers clearly favored programs that benefited the cities, where they lived, over programs that benefited peasants. The higher ranks of the party and the civil service were still dominated by the families that were privileged before independence, and these people had largely seen to it that they themselves remained in Maputo, which was one of the few places in Mozambique where anything resembling a middle-class life could be had. The gulf between the comforts of the few and the absolute poverty of the rural and urban masses was as deep as ever.

Aware of the danger of becoming a party of state employees, Frelimo began trying to broaden its base. Between 1983 and 1989, membership nearly doubled, to more than 200,000.[12] To keep the party from losing touch with the private sector, the rules restricting the amount of property a party member could own and, if he was in business, the number of people he could employ were relaxed. Restrictions on polygamy for party members were also relaxed. Religious believers were permitted to join. The party's emphasis was still on ideology; its relation to the state was supposed to be that of the formulator of policy, of the desired result, which the state then tried to achieve. But the party was still talking about the achievement of scientific socialism, while the government never seemed to mention the subject. With private businessmen and devout Christians as active party members, the contradictions within Frelimo seemed to grow each day. The party's role, ensured by the constitution, as "the leading force in society" was in reality no longer clear-cut. By 1988, there were cabinet ministers who were not party members.

The revolutionary slogans on the walls were fading all over Mozambique, and nobody called anybody *camarada* anymore. A government minister was now His Excellency the Minister. In fact, Portuguese-style formalism had begun to reassert itself under Samora Machel, whose affection for hierarchy, though intermittent, could be intense. In a major speech on health, delivered in 1979, Machel, a former nurse, thundered, "Populism and ultra-democracy have been installed in the hospitals . . . there are no pyramids, no hierarchies." Machel called for special privileges for high officials, asserting, "The people like to see their leaders well treated, because they know the power they represent is the power that corresponds to their aspirations. . . . Is it right for a director to be in the same ward as his subordi-

nate? Is it right for the wife of a minister to be in the same ward
as the wife of a cook?"[13]

Machel's flamboyance seemed to overawe most Mozambicans, and a cult of personality—the fate of too many African
governments—had shown signs of forming around him. Joaquim Chissano proved a far less flashy, less intimidating leader.
He became known for letting people speak their minds at public
meetings. Machel was also known for encouraging people to
speak up publicly. If they had complaints about local officials,
for instance, he wanted to hear them. He would see to the cor-
rection of abuses that came to his attention, and woe betide any
officials who tried to punish citizens for speaking up. But if Machel, who was sometimes called "Mozambique's only authorized dissident," did not like what he heard, he cut people off.[14]
And there were many subjects with which he had no patience—
most notably, popular unhappiness with the overrepresentation
of whites, Asians, *mestiços*, and southerners in the top levels of
government. To Machel, this restiveness was just racism (or
tribalism, or regionalism) rearing its gruesome head.

Under Chissano, the subject of race was no longer taboo. At
public meetings, peasants and workers complained that only
blacks were required to do military service, and the president
tried to explain why this was so. (It was, in fact, a decision made
after independence, based on the suspect loyalty of many non-
blacks, apprehension about how well an integrated army would
function, and the fact that whites, Asians, and *mestiços* still
comprised the majority of educated Mozambicans—all perfectly practical considerations that starkly reversed Frelimo's
commitment to race-blind policies during the *luta armada*.) The
"Africanization" of the Frelimo leadership, in response to popular pressure, was speeded. There was dismay in some quarters
that race had become an issue in a party that had fought to remain nonracial, but in a country that was 99 percent black, it
was perhaps not unreasonable to expect that the political leadership should be largely black. The question was less one of race,
really, than one of culture. Ordinary Mozambicans wanted leaders who had some understanding of their culture—who at least
understood their languages. When President Chissano, who
speaks three Western languages and several African languages,

traveled in the provinces, he spoke not in Portuguese but, if he happened to know it, in the local language. "Our idea of unity has been forced to change," Luís Bernardo Honwana told me. "We've seen that we cannot build unity at the expense of identity, that unity does not mean uniformity."

The sudden collapse of the Communist regimes of Eastern Europe, and the deepening crisis in the Soviet Union, accelerated events in Mozambique. Warsaw Pact aid, which had been dwindling, vanished. (The Warsaw Pact itself soon vanished.) The Soviet Union withdrew its contingent of military advisers—who were estimated, as late as mid-1989, to number between 750 and 1,500[15]—and ended its vital supply of cheap oil to Mozambique. Newly unified Germany announced that it would continue most of the bilateral aid programs of the defunct German Democratic Republic in Mozambique, but the 16,000 Mozambicans working in East German factories and mines (their labor helping to pay their government's bill for East German arms) began to come under severe pressure to return home. Racist attacks by young German neo-Nazis on Africans and Asians sped the departure of thousands. Among Mozambique's longtime socialist allies, only Cuba, China, and North Korea remained significant. Cuba continued to supply an undisclosed amount of military aid, and thousands of Mozambicans continued to study in Cuba.

But it was difficult to imagine what the graduates of orthodox Marxist institutions in Cuba would make of Frelimo's Mozambique upon their return. The Fifth Party Congress, held in Maputo in July 1989, produced a platform that dropped all reference to Marxism-Leninism and class struggle. No longer would the state be "a revolutionary democratic dictatorship of workers and peasants." In May 1989, the students at Eduardo Mondlane University in Maputo boycotted their classes (it was the first time anything of the kind had occurred in independent Mozambique), protesting corruption and the poor quality of their food and accommodation. Then, in January 1990, a wave of strikes swept the country, beginning at *Tempo* magazine and the steel-rolling mill in Maputo in late December, and soon spreading to railways, hospitals, schools, buses, factories, and mines in other parts of Mozambique. Workers were demanding huge wage increases to offset rises in the cost of living. The government's response was, on the whole, restrained, although the director of the Maputo daily paper did find himself dismissed for providing "anti-Marxist" coverage of the events in Eastern Europe, and for "sensational" coverage of the strikes in Mozambique.[16]

Finally, a draft of a new constitution, drawn up by the Frelimo leadership and introduced in January 1990, was circulated for public review. The nationwide discussion lasted several months. The central questions were land ownership and the legalization of political parties. On July 31, President Chissano announced the Frelimo Political Bureau's support for the adoption of a multiparty political system. Two weeks later, the Frelimo Central Committee concurred. (The Central Committee came out against private land ownership, however, and the article that would have legalized it was dropped from the draft constitution.) In early November, the People's Assembly approved the new constitution, and it went into effect on November 30. Frelimo's legal monopoly on power was ended.

The new constitution was a resoundingly liberal document. Its 206 articles guaranteed universal suffrage in direct elections by secret ballot, the separation of state powers, freedom of the press, freedom of movement, and the right to strike. It abolished the death penalty, endorsed the market economy, and even changed the country's name—no longer would Mozambique be "The *People's* Republic of." (The People's Assembly would also get a new name: the Assembly of the Republic.) On December 22, a new law governing political parties was passed, and three new parties immediately sprang into existence: the Partido Liberal e Democrático de Moçambique, which described itself as antisocialist (but mostly sounded anti-Asian and antiwhite; it seemed to be dominated by black-nationalist *antiguos combatentes*); the Movimento Nacional Moçambicano, whose leaders had yet to move back from Portugal, where they had been living in exile; and Unamo, the former antigovernment guerrilla group and Renamo ally. Presidential elections were scheduled—optimistically, considering the war—for mid-1991.

Renamo was invited to lay down its arms, form a legal party, and contest the elections. A multiparty system had been, after all, one of the rebels' main demands. But Renamo, in a communiqué issued in Lisbon in early November, scorned the new constitution, calling it "null and void."[17] And the next day, only hours after the People's Assembly had approved the new constitution, and President Chissano had urged Renamo to stop the slaughter and compete in elections, the *matsangas* responded by attacking a communal village in southern Gaza province, where they killed twenty-five people and wounded twenty-eight others.[18]

15

Its response to the new constitution notwithstanding, Renamo was quite happy to take credit for the dramatic political and economic liberalizations in Mozambique. As Luís Serapião, then Renamo's representative in the United States, told me when I visited him in Washington, D.C., "The population is now enjoying the benefits of the existence of Renamo." Serapião cited the growth of private trucking companies as one of those benefits. It was an astonishing claim, considering that the main cost of running a trucking business in Mozambique was the excellent chance of losing trucks, cargos, and drivers to Renamo attacks. But then Serapião is an astonishing man.

Amilcar Cabral, the nationalist leader from Guinea-Bissau, once said that a revolution is like a train journey. At every stop, some people get on, other people get off. Luís Serapião got off the Mozambican revolution in 1968. He was a graduate student in the United States at the time. Frelimo was suffering its upheavals in Tanzania. The insistence of the revolutionary leadership that all students at Frelimo schools and on Frelimo scholarships should spend a certain amount of time inside Mozambique, either fighting or working in the liberated zones, was expanded to include all Mozambican students doing postgraduate work overseas. Serapião, who had been active in a pro-Frelimo student group in the United States, helped draft a statement denouncing the movement's leadership and attacking Eduardo Mondlane personally. The statement, titled "Mozambique: The Revolution

Betrayed," was sent to Mozambicans around the world. Its signers all became instant personae non gratae in the liberation movement and, after independence, in Mozambique.

Twenty years after his break with Frelimo, Luís Serapião, now a professor of African history at Howard University, was still fuming about the "Algerian gang," as he called the Frelimo leadership,[1] and still calling whites, Asians, and *mestiços* "non-Mozambicans." Serapião is a short, heavy-set, ebullient man. On the morning that I met him, he was wearing a brown sweater and a brown necktie over a yellow shirt. He was striding excitedly around his small office, which he shared with another teacher. "You see, the international trend is in my direction," he said. "People like you didn't come to see me before." Serapião said that he had been trying to lure Valeriano Ferrão, Mozambique's ambassador to the United States, into a public debate, as yet without success. His plan, he said, if the debate ever occurred, was to get onstage and then pretend not to recognize Ferrão, who is an ethnic Asian. "Then, suddenly, I would say, '*Oh!* I thought you were from *Pakistan!* Or *Bangladesh!*' That would do it! He would be destroyed!"

Serapião's notion that the Frelimo leadership, because it was composed mainly of whites, Asians, *mestiços*, ex-*assimilados*, and southerners from a few prominent clans, was therefore out of touch with large areas of Mozambican life had a certain validity. (Serapião, whose father was Ndau-speaking, is an ex-*assimilado* from Beira.) His argument would have had more power, though, if his own involvement in postindependence Mozambican politics had not begun in 1986 with his recruitment into Renamo by a white American named Thomas Schaaf. Schaaf was looking for a black person to speak for Renamo in the United States. Before Serapião's appointment, all of Renamo's external spokesmen had been white Portuguese.

The disarray of Renamo's external wing in Europe had left Serapião as the group's main international spokesman, a limelight he clearly relished. But Serapião had not been in Mozambique since 1965, and his ambivalence about his position was also easy to see. Perhaps his greatest regret was that he had turned against Eduardo Mondlane, in what he now called "a student overstatement." Renamo claimed to revere Mondlane, saying that Samora Machel and his Communist comrades had hijacked Mondlane's movement, which was moderate and nationalist. There were even Frelimo deserters in Renamo who spoke of the war as "the second phase" of the liberation struggle—Soviet colonialism, they said, had merely replaced Portuguese colonialism. As Western governments (including the United States) and Mozambique's neighbors began giving increasing support to the Frelimo government, they, too, made Renamo's list of the foreigners who had to be ejected from Mozambique. The few intrepid multinational corporations investing in the country were the latest additions to the list. Serapião and the other survivors of old schisms who had found their way to Renamo were sometimes dismissed by Mozambicans as "revolutionary debris." When I asked a young Anglican minister in Maputo what he thought of the "second phase" idea, he said, "Yes. This is the second phase of the liberation struggle. This is the past trying to rise up from the dead and reverse our independence, to take away our freedom."

Serapião's motives were perhaps less grandiose than that. At independence, he told me, "We were not contacted to go back." His disappointment on that score seemed to lead directly to the perverse pride with which he then said, "Of all the Mozambicans who stayed in the U.S., I am the one who hurt them the most." And then: "I was told by somebody high up in the U.S. government that Frelimo regrets not making me part of the team. So I am very highly respected within the Frelimo power structure. I am considered a nationalist. It's only the Algerian gang, they don't like me."

Serapião's difficulties with perceived "teams," "gangs," and other coteries seemed to be pervasive. In his scholastic career, he told me, he had had great trouble with "the academic network." "If you're not a member of the club, your work becomes untouchable," he said. Serapião's problems with his colleagues seemed to rise, at least in part, from political differences. In our conversation, he called a prominent American expert on Mozambique "an academic prostitute" because of his close relations with the Frelimo leadership. Serapião's work for Renamo had also caused him trouble at his own university, he said. The anti-apartheid movement was strong at Howard, where most of the students are black, and Renamo's association with Pretoria had caused students to look at him askance. But the pressure on him had disappeared, Serapião claimed, after President Chissano met with P. W. Botha, then the South African president. Still, the fact that he had tenure was indispensable, Serapião said. "Otherwise, I couldn't do what I'm doing." And his difficulties in getting his work published had apparently not been overwhelming. Before I left his office, he loaded me up with reprints of his articles and papers, chuckling with pleasure. Temporarily foiled by the combination lock on his briefcase while looking for a copy of a letter he had written to the *Wall Street Journal*, Serapião broke into a frenzied giggle, rebuking himself, "Luís! Luís!"

That was in late 1988. In January 1991, I phoned Serapião to see what he thought of the new constitution. Renamo was no longer calling the West to arms against Soviet colonialism, but Serapião (who had been demoted, after a falling-out with Thomas Schaaf, to director for further education, whatever that might entail; the new chief Renamo representative in the United States was a businessman named Julius Seffu) was still ebullient about the tide of history flowing his—and Renamo's—way. Since we had talked in his office, he said, Renamo had held its First Congress, at the Gorongosa headquarters, and he himself had attended, entering Mozambique secretly from Malawi, traveling by motorbike. He couldn't tell me much about what the Congress had done—there had been no official report produced, no program, nothing—but he was more excited than ever about his claim that Renamo now controlled all of rural Mozambique except the Beira and Limpopo Corridors, which were still being held by Zimbabwean troops. I asked about Renamo's objections to participating in multiparty elections being planned for later in the year. Serapião said that all the new political parties now appearing in Mozambique were frauds; they were really just creations of Frelimo. If that were true, I wondered, wouldn't Frelimo's strength at the polls be diluted? No, Serapião said. Frelimo was too clever to let that happen. But they were clearly all in it together.

Part Three

Malawi

16

Renamo claimed to receive clandestine support from half a dozen governments in Europe and Africa. "The United States is losing out to Europe," Luís Serapião told me. "Others are striking their deals." He mentioned the visit of Afonso Dhlakama to West Germany in September 1988. Serapião denied that South Africa was among the governments that supported Renamo, but he would not tell me what passport Dhlakama traveled on, because that would expose one of the countries that did help out. The subject of Renamo passports recalled a meeting of southern African leaders in September 1986, to which Samora Machel brought copies of new passports issued to Renamo leaders. The passports had been issued by Malawi.[1]

Malawi was a prime example of what Frelimo used to call "the neocolonial solution" in modern Africa. Formerly the British colony of Nyasaland, it had been ruled since its independence in 1964 by Dr. Hastings Kamuzu Banda, a populist dictator who spent forty-one years overseas—including thirteen years in the United States and fifteen years in London, where he was a successful family physician—before returning to his homeland in 1958, leading the campaign for independence, and becoming "Life President."[2] Banda sought to assure the British plantation owners in Malawi that their supply of cheap, docile labor would not slacken, and he did in fact set prices for peasant produce so low that both the plantations and malnutrition boomed. Banda and his allies also developed their own business interests. Malawi is a small, very poor country, but Banda and his friends became incalculably rich.[3] In the political arena, Banda strengthened the system of traditional chiefs, founded mass organizations for women and youth, and used these deeply conservative groups to identify and destroy any young politicians who came along with modern democratic ideas. In regional affairs (Malawi is bordered by Zambia, Tanzania, and Mozambique), Banda judged that the white-supremacist regimes of southern Africa were there to stay, and he threw in his country's lot with them.

And so Malawi became, in 1967, the first African country to establish diplomatic relations with South Africa—and, as of 1991, was still the only one to have done so. In 1971, Dr. Banda became the only African leader ever to make a full state visit to South Africa. Pretoria financed the construction of Lilongwe, Malawi's instant capital city, and supported the Banda government with loans. Malawi's police and armed forces were trained by South Africa (and by Israel and Taiwan), and South African tourists crowded the resorts along Lake Malawi, Malawi's main natural resource. With the Portuguese rulers of Mozambique, Banda's relationship was, if anything, even closer. In 1971, he became—just to keep his record perfect—the only African leader ever to make an official visit to the colony of Mozambique.

Malawi's "honorary consul" in Mozambique, named in 1964, was the Beira businessman Jorge Jardim. Jardim was the godson of the Portuguese dictator António Salazar; the owner of Beira's daily newspaper, *Notícias da Beira;* and a powerful figure within the colonial secret police. After the founding of Frelimo, Jardim persuaded Banda that, if he helped the Portuguese, he could stand to gain the entire northern half of Mozambique, a territory that surrounds and dwarfs Malawi; the colonists had never developed and so had little use for this territory, and Banda had long coveted it. The Portuguese gave Banda an old map of the region, purporting to show the size and importance of the ancient Maravi empire.[4] Banda later showed the map to Julius Nyerere, the Tanzanian leader, trying to convince him that much of Mozambique belonged historically to Malawi. (Nyerere ignored him.)[5] When some of the Frelimo dissidents who had founded Coremo in Lusaka broke from that group and started a small anti-Frelimo separatist movement, supported by

Jardim, Banda gave shelter to the dissidents.⁶ Their movement
was called the União Nacional Africana da Rombézia. Rombézia
was the name to be given to the new territory, stretching from
the Rovuma River on the Tanzanian border to the Zambezi
River in central Mozambique, that Banda hoped would become
part of a Greater Malawi.

The fact that the only economical routes for Malawi's exports
are two railway lines that run across Mozambique—one to
Beira, the other to the northern port of Nacala—also figured in
Banda's thinking. When he went to Lisbon in 1962, the magazine *Jeune Afrique* reported that he went "to trade the nationalists for the railway."⁷ Malawi collaborated openly with the
Portuguese security forces. The Young Pioneers, Banda's para-
military youth group, using radios supplied by the Portuguese,
patrolled the borders to stop Frelimo guerrillas from entering
Mozambique through Malawi. Those they caught were handed
over to the Portuguese. Malawi assisted the colonial army
with transshipments of fuel. Malawian gunboats, their crews
trained—and even, in some cases, commanded—by the Portuguese, patrolled Lake Malawi, which forms part of the border
with Mozambique, seeking to halt Frelimo infiltration. (Toward
the end of the war, Banda, seeing the direction in which things
were headed, finally allowed Frelimo to use Malawian territory
on a limited basis.)

After the coup in Lisbon, Jorge Jardim, who was suddenly a
wanted man, took refuge in the Malawian Embassy. He later escaped to Malawi itself. As independence came to Mozambique,
many ex-members of the colonial secret police fled to Malawi.
Some of them, along with some Frelimo deserters, were incorpo-
rated into the Malawian army, police force, and civil service.
Meanwhile, the União Nacional Africana da Rombézia, renamed
Africa Livre (also the name, perhaps not so strangely, of a radio
station that the Rhodesians had set up for the then-fledgling Renamo), was launching occasional armed attacks into Mozambique. Africa Livre remained a minor force, and was finally
folded into Renamo in 1981, after Renamo's then-new sponsors,
the South Africans, decided to open a northern front inside
Mozambique and to use their longtime client Malawi as a stag-
ing ground.

Renamo's attacks on the roads and railways in Mozambique

put Malawi in a bind. Sixty percent of Malawi's external trade passed through Mozambique. After Renamo cut the line to Beira in 1982, South Africa gave Malawi fifty heavy trucks.[8] The trucks were not enough to cover the shortfall, though, and when the line to Nacala was cut in 1984, Malawi was forced to export its entire 1985 tea and tobacco crops by air, at staggering cost. By then, the majority of Malawi's external trade, like that of its landlocked neighbors, was passing through South Africa.

Malawi's bind got worse after South Africa and Mozambique concluded the Nkomati Accord in March 1984. Calling upon its conveniently located ally again, South Africa transferred Renamo's main external bases to Malawi. The anti-Frelimo elements in Malawi's civil service and South African–trained security forces were apparently happy to be of assistance. Malawian buses and trains were seconded to carry Renamo fighters. Renamo began recruiting among Mozambicans living in Malawi. A heavy traffic of planes and helicopters into Mozambique was reported, and injured Renamo fighters were treated in Malawian hospitals. Renamo's startling military success in central Mozambique in 1985 and 1986, which included the capture of a number of district capitals, could never have been achieved without Malawi's help.

Samora Machel's display of Renamo leaders' passports, issued by Malawi, at his meeting with President Banda in September 1986—the leaders of Zimbabwe and Zambia were also present—was part of a concerted effort to force Malawi to end its support for Renamo. Machel threatened to close Mozambique's border with Malawi and even to place missiles along it. Although most of Malawi's external trade was passing through South African ports, it still had to transit the territories of its neighbors. Banda, while denying that he had ever supported Renamo, clearly took heed of his fellow leaders' feelings, and obliged them by expelling as many as 12,000 Renamo fighters in late September.[9] For Mozambique, the expulsion backfired instantly. Renamo launched its most successful offensive yet, driving toward the coast and Quelimane, with plans to cut the country in two and declare the northern half an independent republic: Rombezia, at last.

The Mozambican armed forces, supported by Zimbabweans,

managed to stop Renamo short of Quelimane, and in 1987 launched their counteroffensive. By mid-1988, government forces had retaken towns all the way to the Malawian border. The fighting had devastated central Mozambique, however, and driven hundreds of thousands of Mozambicans into Malawi. Suddenly, Malawi had one of the highest ratios of refugees to population in the world. The situation began to attract a great deal of international attention. Aid and relief groups poured into Malawi, along with foreign journalists. Malawi was not used to hosting journalists—Life President Banda was known not to care for them—and had long denied them visas.[10] But the spotlight was now too bright for that, and Malawi had been loudly claiming, after all, that it had nothing to hide. Renamo had been expelled.

When I arrived in Malawi, the government's Department of Information furnished me, unbidden, with an escort. As his superior explained to me, "Otherwise, someone might think you are one of the South African agents whom we are always being accused of harboring." My escort's name was Mr. Andsen. He and I arranged to meet in the bar at my hotel in the southern city of Blantyre. When I got to the bar, I approached the first likely-looking man I saw, and asked if he was Andsen. He smiled ferociously and said, "I think I am." Andsen wore a tight, three-piece, tan-colored suit. He looked about forty. He was powerfully built, with small eyes, deep-brown skin, a freshly shaven, bullet-shaped head, and a fixed expression that seemed simultaneously angry and eager to please. He had taken many journalists to the refugee camps, he assured me. We would leave before dawn the next morning.

I asked if I would need a coat and tie for the trip—the camps were in the southern lowlands, where it promised to be hot.

Andsen said I would. "Our Life President is a staunch supporter of ties," he said.

At least, I thought, he didn't say, "The Life President, Ngwazi Dr. Kamuzu Hastings Banda." I had heard that one could be arrested for referring to Malawi's leader by less than his full title.

(And my confidence in Andsen's knowledge of local law enforcement seemed justified when, a couple of days later, I was searching for him and asked a hotel clerk if she had seen him. "Do you mean that policeman who goes about with you?" she asked.)

Southern Malawi is the space between the prongs of Y-shaped Mozambique. (I've also heard it said that Malawi is like a dagger in the breast of Mozambique.) We were going first to the Nsanje district, which is at the extreme southern tip of Malawi, surrounded on three sides by Mozambique. We headed out early, as promised, dropping off Blantyre's high, wooded plateau through a long series of switchbacks into the valley of the Shire River. Having just come from Mozambique, I was impressed by all the bright advertisements for pain relievers, liver salts, shoe polish, and antimalaria medicines painted on the walls of houses and shops. Compared to Mozambique, which had never had an African small-business class, rural Malawi was a world of high-powered commerce.

The Shire River, which in that area forms the border between Malawi and Mozambique, was on our left. There were settlements on the near bank, but no signs of habitation on the far bank. I noticed three people in a canoe paddling toward Mozambique. "Those are Malawians," Andsen assured me. "They see that there is good land over there not being used, so they have planted some crops. They are gambling that the bandits will not come back." Andsen said that he himself had grown up in this area, and that when he was a boy he used to swim across the river to hunt kudu with a bow and arrow in Mozambique. The border had always been porous here, he said. People spoke the same language on both sides, and intermarried. Renamo, I knew, had until recently controlled all the land on the Mozambican side of the river. A report in the *Washington Post* only a month before had said that Renamo supplies still entered Mozambique by canoe across the Shire. Malawi was said to be trying to tighten up the border, but it looked wide-open to me. Clearly, the river was a busy place. Rice paddies and cane and vegetable fields flourished beside it, and I saw boys carrying strings of big, glistening, black fish.

Nsanje district had more Mozambican refugees—220,000 at the time I visited—than it had Malawian residents. Before we went to the camps, Andsen and I stopped to see the local district commissioner. As we drove into the Nsanje administrative center, I caught sight of a large, Victorian-style house set back in a grove of trees and surrounded by a high, chain-link fence. In a world of squalid, low-roofed shops and mud huts, the house, which looked to be in perfect repair, was a dwelling from another planet. I pointed at the house, and Andsen said, "Yes, that is for our Life President when he visits this area."

We found the district commissioner, a brawny, intense, hospitable man named Geoff Mwanja, in his office. He said that there had been two huge influxes of Mozambicans into Nsanje in the previous eight months. The first contained a large number of teachers and medical workers: "Such people are known to be Renamo targets." The most recent wave had been caused by Frelimo's aerial bombing. Pamphlets had been dropped in the days before the bombing, urging people to evacuate. I had read Renamo claims that its fighters helped civilians evacuate the areas bombed by Frelimo. I asked Mwanja about that. He gave a short, derisive laugh. He had never heard of Renamo's helping anyone do anything, he said. "The problem of Mozambique is not a group of gunmen taking over an area," he said. "It is the type of people who take over. Can they do anything besides operate a gun and destroy?" Mwanja sighed. "The problem of Mozambique is its whole history."

Mwanja had been in Nsanje two years. Just two weeks after he got there, he said, 30,000 Mozambicans had poured across the border in one day. "It was a really shocking experience, to see people who had had homes suddenly living under trees like antelopes. These people are coming from situations where they almost cease to be human. They are almost ready to grow hair all over their bodies!" Mwanja studied me sadly. "We cannot close our eyes to what we see," he said. "Because you have clothes, you must not think you are all right. That naked man? He is *you*. We are all involved. Man himself did this."

Mwanja's tone was pained, philosophical, not accusatory, but I squirmed under his gaze nonetheless. Somebody brought in a letter. Mwanja looked at it, smiled, and said to the man who had brought it, "Pompílio." To me he explained, "This is from a Mozambican man, Pompílio de Cipriano Gadimala, a driver from Quelimane who was kidnapped by Renamo. He escaped at night, and he showed up here wearing leaves and a long beard. He is very tall, and at first we thought he was a madman. He stayed with us for nearly a year and then went by bus to Tete. Now I see here that he has made it back to Quelimane. But I cannot read the letter, because it is in Portuguese." I took the letter from Mwanja. It was a polite, carefully written note thanking the commissioner for all his help while the writer was in Malawi.

We drove out to a camp called Mankhokwe. It was a vast settlement, a dusty sea of thatched roofs, reed walls, and people. There were more than 50,000 Mozambicans at Mankhokwe, and when we arrived, most of them seemed to be gathered around six small mountains of burlap sacks. The sacks contained beans, sugar, groundnuts, and maize flour, most of it donated by the United States Agency for International Development. Food distribution, a biweekly event, was in progress. The sound of the crowd was like a big river splashing through a deep canyon: continuous waves of deep and lively noise. Young Malawian officials were sweating over clipboards and checking registration cards as laborers doled out rations. Although most of the refugees looked underfed, I had seen people in far worse condition in Mozambique, where many of the camps for *deslocados* were accessible only by air. At Mankhokwe, there were flatbed trucks rolling in from Blantyre loaded with poles for building huts. Accessibility is everything in refugee relief. Lack of clean water was a major problem in the camps in Mozambique; the Malawian camps had wells, dug by the United Nations High Commission for Refugees. The clinics at Malawian camps had electricity. Some even had telephones. None of this was true when the first waves of refugees came, in 1986. At that time, I was told, the camps in Malawi were desperate scenes of starvation and disease.

The officials at Mankhokwe said that they were receiving, on average, about one hundred new refugees each day, and that another camp nearby was receiving about the same. Leafing through their registry, I noticed large fluctuations: four hundred arrivals one day, none the next. "If the roads were too dangerous the previous night, no one will come that day," an official explained. "If there is a big battle somewhere, or a big village is taken, then, perhaps a few days later, we get a big group."

At the clinic in Mankhokwe, we found a nurse from the French group Médecins Sans Frontières. She was twenty-nine, from Lille. She said that there had been a cholera outbreak at Mankhokwe, with many deaths, at the time she arrived, three or four months earlier, and before that a measles outbreak, which killed many children. At the moment, however, there were no major medical problems. "The *problèmes chroniques*—malaria, diarrhea, malnutrition, parasites—are present, of course, but *contrôlés.*" The Mozambican health workers at the clinic were very good, she added, and the refugees seemed receptive to education about health and hygiene. There were posters on the clinic's walls explaining, in English and Portuguese and in pictures, the proper way to rehydrate infants with diarrhea. As I studied the posters, I noticed, higher on the whitewashed mud wall, a sleek, blood-red gecko. In the moment that I watched the gecko, a bird attacked it. There was a short, terrified screech, the gecko was plucked from the wall, and the bird disappeared out the clinic's window.

Fernão da Costa Xavier was one of the Mozambican nurses at Mankhokwe. A quiet, substantial man in his sixties, Xavier had been working at a hospital in Mutarara, in the province of Tete, when Renamo overran the area in 1986. The rebels' arrival had not been unexpected—Xavier's wife and children had already fled to Maputo. The rebels destroyed the hospital at Mutarara, but did not, as it was feared they might, kill the patients who could not flee. In fact, Xavier said dryly, the *bandidos* fed the patients with some of his own slaughtered goats and cattle—it seems they were occupying a farm he owned. Xavier had fled at night, by car, with one of the workers from his farm driving a truck, carrying a mill engine but leaving behind the tractor, which was too slow. They had crossed into Malawi on September 27, 1986. In the two years he had been at Mankhokwe, Xavier said, he had seen hundreds of people he knew in Mutarara. They were still arriving to this day. His two married daughters had flown up from Maputo, but they had failed to persuade him to return with them. He was very busy here, Xavier said, and he did not want to return to Mozambique until the war was *over.*

Xavier was the only Mozambican refugee I ever met, or heard about, who had left the country by car. Most left on foot, with nothing but the clothes on their backs. Some lacked even those. A ragged group of newly arrived refugees huddled under a tree near some yellow reception tents at Mankhokwe. One man lay on his back on the ground, groaning with dizziness from the first salt he had eaten in months. I sat under the tree and talked with Manuel Zeca, who said he had arrived the day before, on foot. Zeca was a small, muscular, poised man of twenty-five, from an area of Tete called Nyangoma. He had been an assistant surveyor on a state cotton farm, he said, until Renamo destroyed the farm in 1982. He and his family had survived by subsistence farming until 1987, when Renamo kidnapped him and his wife. They managed to leave their child with her grandmother before they were marched to Sofala, where they became Renamo porters. The *bandidos* they lived with were well armed, Zeca said, but apolitical and unpopular. They raped local women, spreading venereal disease, and took food from the peasants. Zeca and his wife returned eventually to their *machamba* in Nyangoma, but the *bandidos* kept taking the food they grew. They had heard there was food in Malawi from others who had been here. So Zeca had come to see for himself. His wife could not come because she was pregnant. His plan was to build a house here and then go back for his family.

Six hundred thousand Mozambicans were not, of course, welcome to stay indefinitely in Malawi.[11] The pressure they exerted on local resources was severe. The trucks hauling hut poles to Nsanje had to do so because there were no suitably sized trees left in the area. Malawi's population had doubled in the previous twenty years—to eight million—and the country already suffered from an acute land shortage. The refugees, many of whom did not live in the camps but blended into the population, took yet more farmland out of production. Prices in the village markets were being driven up by increased demand. There had been no violent expressions of local resentment yet; but, according to a United Nations field worker I spoke to, it was only a matter of time. "When we dig a well in the camps, we must make sure to dig another in the nearby village," the field worker said. "We tell the Malawians they can use the clinics in the camps, too, and they do. But the Malawians suffer from hunger. The government forbids any studies, but it is known that Malawi has some of the highest rates for malnutrition and infant mortality in the world.[12] January and February are the worst time of year for the peasants in this area. They are always hungry then, and we don't know how they will react to seeing the Mozambicans still receiving free food every two weeks. And the Malawian refugee officials are so *idealistic*. We actually have to restrain them. Those in charge of education will request a desk for every school pupil. Then we have to remind them that there is not one desk for each Malawian child in school. There aren't even enough schools for all the Malawian children. The Mozambican children are taught in Portuguese, using the Mozambican curriculum, so that they can be ready to go home when the situation changes. No, there is never a shortage of teachers—teachers are always running here from Renamo."

As we drove on south, Andsen suddenly announced, "I would rather be a slave than a refugee." Earlier in the day, Andsen had asked me to stop at a number of shops and produce stands so that he could buy meat and vegetables that were not, he said, available in Blantyre. But there seemed to be nothing in Nsanje that interested him to buy.

Andsen's conversation was full of non sequiturs. After ten minutes of silence, he would suddenly blurt, "What does it mean, 'you manicured coward'?" This phrase came from a film that Andsen owned on videocassette, which he said was called *There Is Something Wrong in the Paradise*. Andsen loved this film to distraction. He tried many times to tell me the story—it had to do with racial politics on an allegorical island—but he always got tangled up in the details, and laughed so hard at his favorite parts that he never finished.

Andsen was also full of questions about American politics. He was interested in how Americans chose their leaders, and amazed at the disrespect that American leaders had to put up with. When I told him about a bicycle messenger who was turned away from the Justice Department offices in Washington because he was wearing a T-shirt that said, "Ed Meese Is a Pig," and explained that Edwin Meese was the head of that part of the government at the time, Andsen was astonished. He was even more astonished when I said that Meese himself later turned up at a picnic wearing the same shirt. Andsen shook his head and said, "Here, to be a leader, you must be a serious man." I considered asking him about all the serious men who must be looking hard at President Banda's palace now that Banda was over ninety—people had been predicting for years a post-Banda bloodbath—but I decided against it. I wondered if Andsen's own success in the Malawian system owed anything to his ability to wear a tight, three-piece suit in sweltering heat and choking dust. Or to the instinctive caution that made him answer the question "Are you thirsty?" with "I think I am."

Andsen's caution also showed in his opinion of my driving: *too fast*. We spent most of that day on straight, empty roads, and I didn't always see the point of crawling along. Andsen took to praising the discretion of the man from the *Wall Street Journal*, *who buckled his seat belt to drive across a parking lot*.

As we arrived at the southern border, the road ended. A row of Indian shops that had once catered to the border trade had been abandoned and ransacked. The railroad line, which had run alongside the road all the way from Blantyre, also ended abruptly at the border. The railroad here had once handled twelve trains a day between Blantyre and Beira, but it had been out of service inside Mozambique since October 1983. The destruction of Mozambique's railroads was somehow particularly horrible. It is such a poor country, it has so little to start with, and railroads, which are easily the most economical form of heavy transportation, have become prohibitively expensive to build. In the first three years of South African sponsorship, Renamo destroyed 93 locomotives and 250 railroad cars, and killed 150 railroad workers.[13] Even the great bridge over the Zambezi River had been destroyed. Now one train a day ran from Blantyre to Nsanje.

A young border guard, who said his name was Witness, told us that large numbers of people crossed out of Mozambique there, usually around dawn. He directed them toward the camps. There was a Frelimo post five kilometers south, he said, but everywhere on that side was a free-fire zone. He often heard gunfire, and a big battle had occurred the day before, with what sounded like aerial bombing, although he saw no planes.

As we were talking, I noticed a woman standing out in the brush on the Mozambican side of the border. Witness said, "That is Jacquina. She is Mozambican. She is mad."

The woman, who was wearing rags and a head scarf, watched us intently. She could have been thirty, or forty, or fifty. She had a basket in her hands. It sounded as if she was singing.

"She is always busy," Witness said. He gestured to some burned patches of land behind her.

I asked if it wasn't dangerous to be over there.

"Yes," said Witness. "No one else will go there. But Jacquina will spend all day there tending her fires, just as if she is going to farm."

Jacquina approached us. Her face was small and weather-beaten, her eyes small and green and sad. Her basket, I saw, was full of wild apples. She offered them to us without speaking. When no one reached for one, she handed the basket to Witness's young son. Then she started walking back into Mozambique, talking to herself.

Witness took an apple. "We call these *masau*," he said. "The people here like them very much. But they only grow in Mozambique. So only Jacquina gathers them."

We stood watching Jacquina make her way toward a set of fire-cleared patches of bottomland off to the southeast.

Contacting Renamo in Malawi was more difficult when I visited than it had been in previous years. With Andsen and I wasn't sure who else watching me, it was all but impossible. I had telephone numbers for some of the Portuguese businessmen who had moved from Mozambique to Blantyre or Lilongwe and were said to be Renamo supporters. None of them seemed thrilled to hear from me. They all wanted to know how I got their numbers. One said he would try to arrange a meeting with certain unnamed people, but it would take awhile. I didn't have awhile. There were in Malawi "sympathetic missionaries," who had on occasion arranged contacts between journalists and Renamo, but they were in the border areas, and they were also lying low. The Malawian government was making a show of support for Mozambique. Frelimo ministers were constantly visiting, and the Mozambican government's amnesty offer to Renamo fighters had been translated into English and published in all the Malawian papers. Frelimo, having come to value the information that the Malawians now shared with Mozambique, was even said to encourage Malawi's ongoing contacts with Renamo.

Without meaning to underline the new fraternal relationship

between their two countries, I arranged to bring an official from the Mozambican consulate in Blantyre along with Andsen and me on a trip to the eastern border. I wanted to try to cross into Mozambique to visit Milange, a district capital that had been recently retaken by Frelimo, and I figured a Mozambican official might be able to help out at the border.

The official's name was António Tauzene. He was younger, slighter, and more easygoing than Andsen. We drove through glorious fields of tea and coffee on the high plateau east of Blantyre. Eucalyptus and pine trees lined the narrow, paved road. I asked Andsen if the workers, whom we could see toiling with their white harvest sacks between the long rows of tea plants, were unionized. "No," he said. "We don't need that kind of thing." Tauzene snorted in the back seat, but said nothing. His government's attitude toward trade unions was actually not a great deal more benign than Malawi's. Workers in Mozambique were urged to exercise power through "production councils" that involved them in management, not through collective bargaining. Strikes were illegal.[14] But the great, white-owned tea plantations in Malawi were a true colonial holdover. In fact, wages were so low that many of the workers on them were illegal immigrants—that is, they were Mozambicans.

We drove around the south side of Mulanje Mountain, a 10,000-foot, waterfall-striped massif that looked blue, almost violet, in the morning mist. Rivers with lush banks poured off its lower slopes; boys splashed and hooted in the pools under the bridges. Hordes of white South Africans came to climb Mount Mulanje during the Christmas holidays, I had heard. I wondered where they stayed. The area was far more developed than Nsanje, with well-stocked shops, electricity in the more modern houses, even some small roadside restaurants, but no hotels. As we passed through a market town, Andsen mentioned that a Frelimo MiG had wandered off course during the big offensive in June and bombed this town, five kilometers from the border, killing a Mozambican woman and her child. Tauzene confirmed the story. We stopped to see the Mulanje district commissioner, could not find him, and proceeded to the border. Refugee camps flanked the road for the last mile or two.

The Malawian border guards, who had a neat, proper office inside a well-tended yard and garden, seemed nonplussed to see us. They wanted to know if I owned the car (it was rented), if I had a vehicle export permit, if I had the slightest idea what had been happening across the border in Mozambique. Andsen kept out of it, but Tauzene and I waved our arms for twenty minutes, got our passports stamped, and drove on into Mozambique, leaving Andsen playing checkers with the guards.

A small river, the Muloza, formed the border. On the Mozambican side, the border post had been shot up and cleaned out, but two officials were on duty. Behind the post, a soldier with an automatic rifle slung over his shoulder was pumping water by hand. He stared at us fixedly through an empty doorway. Tauzene persuaded the guards to let us pass, and we drove up a potholed road. We passed gutted buildings and overgrown tea estates. The grass beside the road was dangerously high, Tauzene thought—it could conceal a battalion of bandits—but there were peasants on the road, carrying sacks of grain on their backs to Malawi for milling, and several small encampments of Frelimo soldiers. The soldiers were gathered like acolytes around the shrinelike, tarpaulin-covered forms of tanks and tracked armored cars, and they, too, stared at us fixedly as we passed.

After a couple of miles, we came to Milange. Renamo had first attacked Milange in force in early 1986, and had finally taken the town in September of that year. The rebels had occupied the town for twenty-one months, and had been driven out less than three months before I visited. As the capital of the richest district in the richest province of Mozambique, Milange had been a beautiful town. Before the war, it had been a favorite day trip for the British planters in Malawi, who used to drive over with their families on Sunday afternoons for dinner.

But Renamo had laid waste to Milange with the same insane thoroughness that it had applied to Morrumbala. Except for the church and the rectory, which were untouched, every single building in town had been destroyed: stripped, smashed, burned, defaced. There were a few listless-looking people around. Tauzene asked them directions, and we eventually found the local Frelimo Party secretary, a serious young man named White Livison. He agreed to show us around. At the primary school, where a tire rim still hung from a tree in the yard, every door, window, windowsill, and roof tile had been removed, along with every bit of plumbing and wiring. Birds nested in the rafters in the classrooms. Even the blackboards were smashed. "RENAMO" was smeared on a classroom wall. On a roofless house across the road, "RENAMO MOTO" was scrawled. "Moto," Tauzene said quietly, meant "fire" in Chichewa, the local language.

We drove up a hillside to the administrator's house, a building of palatial outline that, after Renamo, looked like a piece of postnuclear Hiroshima. Across the hillside was the district hospital. We walked through its shattered corridors, broken glass and tile crunching underfoot. In the laboratory, every piece of equipment that could not be removed had been turned into an abstract sculpture of twisted steel. I thought I recognized an X-ray machine. The same thing had happened in the operating theatre, and in the maternity ward, where brightly painted flowers and slogans still decorated the walls: "Our Hospital Should Also Dispense Correct Ideas About Health and Hygiene." Higher on the hillside, we followed a young soldier in a black beret through stands of burnt sugarcane to a public swimming pool. The pool was tiled in sky blue and terra cotta, with a small amphitheater of steps surrounding it and a magnificent view of the town, the valley, and Mulanje Mountain. Even the brick dressing rooms next to the pool had been blown up. Alongside the path, the soldier showed me a primitive quail trap, made from broken chunks of cement, that he had set in the brush. There was not enough food in Milange, he said.

While we rested, admiring the view, I asked White Livison about himself. He said he came from Milange. Too young to have fought in the *luta armada*, he had gone away to a Frelimo Party school in 1982 and returned in 1983. He had been here when Renamo overran the town. There were 1,500 to 2,000 *bandidos*, he estimated. They were well armed but dressed in rags. They did not come from Malawi, but from their big base in Morrumbala, to the south. The few soldiers stationed in Milange had run away. Livison had been captured and beaten and forced to carry loot to the Renamo camps. He saw other people beaten, but no one killed. Then someone told him that the *bandidos* knew he was a party secretary and had marked him for execution. When the *bandidos* called a public meeting, and invited all the Malawian traders from across the border, Livison joined the crowd.

The *bandidos* wanted to trade the doors, windows, roofing sheets, maize, machinery, plumbing, wiring, and other wealth of Milange for soap, sugar, salt, and flashlight batteries. They wanted to set fair terms of trade. Agreements were concluded, and when the Malawians headed home, Livison, posing as one of them, went along. He stayed in Malawi for twenty-one months. At first, he said, the cross-border trade was brisk. Renamo set up huts on the banks of the Muloza, within sight of the Malawian border post, to expedite business. Renamo even sent recruiters into the refugee camps in Mulanje. And the Malawian officials, Livison said bitterly, never tried to stop any of it.

I had by now seen a number of towns, not only in Zambézia but farther south, across the Zambezi in Sofala, that had been sacked and stripped. All their removable wealth had also ended up in Malawi. By now, a fairly high percentage of the doors, windows, and so on in southern Malawi had to have come from Mozambique, courtesy of Renamo. I wondered how that affected local attitudes toward the war—I had heard that Renamo was popular in southern Malawi—and how the Malawian authorities regarded the trade. It seemed unlikely that they let it go untaxed.

I asked Livison how many people had returned from Malawi since Frelimo had reoccupied Milange.

Not many, he said. There was more food in Malawi. Milange was very fertile—there were fruit-laden papaya trees everywhere, and *machambas* were being started—but people were still eating only one meal a day. The international relief groups couldn't reach Milange, because the airstrip had not yet been repaired. In fact, only one military convoy had reached Milange since the liberation in June. It had come from Quelimane, and left a few military vehicles and one dump truck. The relief groups could come via Malawi, as we had, but that would be complicated, despite the current good relations between the two countries.

We returned to town and found the district administrator. His name was Captain Raimundo Rufino Kantumbyanga. He was a small, tidy man, ageless, polite, with a military bearing and ritual scars on his cheeks. Captain Kantumbyanga was a Makonde, from the Mueda Plateau, where the *luta armada* began and was largely fought. Captain Kantumbyanga had been fighting for his country, for Frelimo's idea of "Mozambique," for a long time. In fact, he had been in command in Milange when Renamo took the town. After retreating to Malawi, Kantumbyanga had been arrested. He spent two days in jail in Malawi, then was deported to Tete. Now he was back. We talked in his headquarters, a three-story building in the center of town. There was no furniture—not even a chair—so we stood. The smell of smoke was overpowering. Renamo slogans scrawled on the wall were half covered by sooty Frelimo posters and pictures of President Chissano. I could see, across the street, families cooking on the upper floors of a five-story building with giant holes in the outside walls. Down the street, a large, fancy building—it had once been the club for the tea planters' association—looked as if a bowling alley had fallen on it. The building was a casualty, Captain Kantumbyanga explained, of the aerial bombing that preceded Frelimo's liberation of Milange. The reconstruction of Milange, he said, would take many years.

Captain Kantumbyanga could not tell me how many people had been killed in the fighting around Milange, or how many were living with Renamo in the nearby hills. He said that there were still attacks in the area, but nothing serious, and that he had recently walked twenty-five kilometers to visit a newly liberated village and had encountered no problems. I got the feeling that Captain Kantumbyanga wondered how I had reached Milange and hoped I would not stay long. But he was an immensely calm man. He was also someone who clearly understood the war at a level that no outsider ever would. This wasn't the sort of understanding that would ever surface in an interview, though. Tauzene and I thanked him for his time.

A squadron of Frelimo soldiers was at the border post. Most of them were wearing red berets, which meant they were Soviet-trained commandos, who were said to be the best units in the army. They looked unusually tough and lively. Several had full beards à la Samora Machel. One had his hair in long braids. They were interested in us, and started teasing Tauzene, whose retorts made them laugh. I caught the word *mzungu*—white man—in the repartee, and afterward asked Tauzene about it. He was embarrassed. Finally, he explained, "Those fellows wanted to talk with me about Malawi, but one of them said, 'No, your white man is hungry, you must go.' It's because they see how white people are always eating, having tea, then eating some more, so they have the idea that white people cannot bear hunger like we can."

Quite right, of course. We picked up Andsen at the Malawi border post and went straight to one of the roadside restaurants in Mulanje, where I ate half a chicken, washing it down with grape soda. Andsen showed no curiosity about what we had seen in Mozambique. After lunch, we headed north, circling around the west side of Mulanje Mountain, which had turned gray-brown in the afternoon haze. Our destination was a refugee camp at a place called Phalombe.

It was a long drive on an unpaved road—what Andsen called "a dirty road." The countryside got dry and scrubby, with the only visual relief that magnificent nerd: the baobab tree in winter. We passed a mission, and I wondered if the padres were Renamo sympathizers. As we neared Phalombe, we passed a big, extremely neat *caniço* village. "Jehovah's Witnesses," Tauzene said. The village was obviously new and looked unusually well built. The huts were large, with separate cooking huts, separate shower huts with L-shaped entrances, granaries, gardens full of greens, wells with fences around them and stairways down into them, latrines that were clearly well reinforced. "They are very industrious," Tauzene said.

They are more than that. A veteran correspondent living in Zimbabwe once told me that the only thing that united nearly all African governments was their hatred and persecution of Jehovah's Witnesses. Frelimo had expelled thousands from the cities. Many of those Mozambican Witnesses had ended up fleeing from Renamo into Malawi, where the persecution was actually worse. A large number of Malawian Witnesses had been reportedly killed in 1967 for refusing to pledge allegiance to the Banda government, and more than one thousand fled into Mozambique.[15] The Witnesses living near Phalombe, I had heard, were Malawians who had fled to Mozambique and had recently come back—on the assumption that they would be safe from persecution if they lived near the big refugee camps that were getting all the international attention. If they actually had returned only recently to Malawi, they would have had to cross the border north of Milange—a truly mad act, since there were persistent reports that Frelimo had mined the area to discourage Renamo infiltration or refugee crossings or both.

Phalombe was a gigantic camp on a dusty, featureless plain. There was a soccer game in progress when we arrived, with dozens of players mixing it up in the long-shadowed late afternoon, and hundreds of onlookers. I remembered that the young Malawian officials at Mankhokwe camp had said, between recitations of figures for new arrivals, that their camp's soccer team was already the best in the district, regularly beating the local squads. "It's because the Portuguese were in Mozambique," one boy said ruefully. "The Brazilians, who are the best players in the world, were also from the Portuguese." In Maputo, while I was there, the Frelimo Political Bureau, including President Chissano, had played a local professional team in a challenge match. The professional team won, but it was generally agreed that the country's leaders had retained the precision passing skills developed in the *luta armada*. I wondered if Andsen would consider the leaders of Mozambique serious men.

Most of the people at Phalombe were from Milange. In the shade of a new hut, I sat and talked with three teachers who had lived with Renamo. Arlindo Gonçalves Zacárias, a soft-voiced man of thirty, said that his worst experience with Renamo had occurred before the rebels overran Milange. He had been walking with a friend in the countryside when they were accosted. The *bandidos* took his bicycle, his watch, and all of his clothes, leaving him in what he called his "bikini," and, because his friend was wearing a military tunic, which wasn't even his own, they killed him. Some months after Renamo took Milange, the teachers had been ordered to resume their classes, without books or classrooms, just by convening groups of children under trees. The district education director, a complicated, intelligent man who the teachers all agreed smoked too much marijuana, started working for Renamo, and he organized their schedules. The director ended up going insane, they said, and killing himself. The pressures of the situation were very great.

For Vasco Rafael Matrassina, a rather wizened man of thirty-six, the pressures had not ended. His wife and five children were still in Mozambique, he said. His father-in-law was one of the Milange *régulos* who had worked with Renamo. He had fled with the *bandidos* when Frelimo came, and he had taken his daughter and his grandchildren with him. But he had been foolish. Four other *régulos* had stayed, and they had not been punished. They were now working with Frelimo, trying to lure the people who were living in the hills with Renamo back to Milange. Matrassina only hoped that his wife would listen to them and not to her father. All the teachers agreed that it was too soon to go home, that they would wait here to see what happened.[16] Some of the people who had been here for two years were now marrying Malawians—they spoke the same language and had the same customs, after all—but they themselves would go back to Mozambique eventually, they were certain.

Andsen pointed out that it was getting late. We set off. As we left Phalombe, Andsen suddenly broke into song. Tauzene joined him. It was a rousing, rhythm-heavy tune, and the two men had the African voices to carry it. They sang a few verses, then broke off with hoots of pleasure. I asked Andsen for a translation. "It's a song in Shona," he said. "I learned it while I was living in Zimbabwe with my uncle. It is about a boy who joins the guerrillas. After he receives training, he comes back to his village and he chases away those people who he believes are collaborating with the Smith regime. He also kills some of them. Then he runs away before he can be apprehended. Then, after the independence comes, he returns again to his village, and the people are afraid of him. So he tells them, 'No. I am not a murderer. I only killed people so that you might be free. I killed so that you might eat. Please do not be afraid of me. I did it for you.' It is a very good song!"

Tauzene agreed heartily, and they belted out another chorus. It was a strange moment in African unity.

Late that evening, we straggled back to Blantyre, all parched and punch-drunk with exhaustion. Tauzene invited us into his house, where he served us drinks and we played with his children. Then his entente with Andsen broke down. It happened over an article about a Renamo defector in a Mozambican magazine that I was leafing through. For the first time all day, the mild and jolly Tauzene showed some political feelings as he turned to Andsen and said, "What about this business? I am not asking you as a diplomat, but man to man." He was referring to the deaths in Malawi, a few months before, of two Renamo lead-

ers.[17] The defector in the magazine article claimed that they had
been murdered by the Malawian authorities, on the orders of
South Africa, because they were part of a movement to wean Renamo from Pretoria. Malawi claimed that they had died in a car
accident, but the evidence for that was unpersuasive. Malawi
ended up changing its official story several times, and still refused to release the bodies to the families. The incident, which
had been picked up by the international press, showed clearly
that Renamo still operated in Malawi, and it suggested that
Malawi still worked for South Africa in the destabilization of
Mozambique. Andsen, suddenly glum, said he knew nothing
about it. Given the state's total control of the Malawian press,
that was actually possible.

Malawi's western border, about a hundred miles north of Blantyre, is marked not by a river but by an unfenced highway. On
one side of the road is Mozambique, where great sweeps of
grassy plateau, striated with rocky crags, stretch away to a distant horizon. Except for the mangoes and bananas growing in
the draws, the countryside, known as the Angonia Plateau, re-
sembles the Scottish highlands. In late 1988, when I saw it, the
Angonia Plateau, which had been heavily populated before the
war—its fertility rivals that of Milange—was completely empty.
Old Portuguese shops lined the road, roofless and burned, and
beyond them nothing, just empty land. Meanwhile, across the
road, only a swivel of the head away, the scene could have been
Indonesia. Round, thatch-roofed mud huts blanketed the hills in
close formation for as far as I could see. There were 300,000
Mozambican refugees living in this part of Malawi, yet these
were not formal camps. The Mozambicans had simply moved
over the border. The land on the Malawian side could not support the crush; and so, a United Nations field worker had told
me, people kept small fields on the Mozambican side, which
they risked life and limb to tend intermittently.

  The situation along the western border was intolerable, and
the Malawian government had recently proposed a solution.
The Malawians would undertake to seal off a small section of
Mozambique adjoining the border; secure it, perhaps with the
help of an international peacekeeping force; and fill it with re-
patriated Mozambicans. The area would be administered by

Malawi. The proposal seemed to be another outbreak of Greater Malawi fever. The United Nations agency to which it was made ignored it.

Malawi may be a geostrategic dagger in the heart of Mozambique. Its leader may have been eager to profit from the sufferings of his giant neighbor, even to violate the fundamental agreement among African states that national boundaries, for all their flaws (they are, in a sense, the most profound scar left by European imperialism on the continent), must now be immutable. But the peasants in the border regions undoubtedly saw things differently. They themselves were the blood that spilled from the socialist disaster into the neocolonial autocracy. The more fortunate found themselves looked after by men like Geoff Mwanja, in Nsanje. But what the peasants made of their plight, how they came to understand their country, with its arbitrary boundaries and endlessly murderous war, would finally count for more than the politics of their leaders. In the golden sea of huts there on the hilly western border, around the fires in the evenings, Chichewa-speaking people, Malawian and Mozambican, were telling each other stories. H. K. Banda's place in history was being decided there, along with Frelimo's and Renamo's. My own account would be published, and yet it would never have the power—or the ultimate impact on events—that those unrecorded Chichewa narratives would.

Andsen and I were headed for the international airport at Lilongwe. I was going back, for the moment, to Mozambique. Andsen seemed to have exhausted, finally, his store of hilarity from *There Is Something Wrong in the Paradise*. He yawned. I asked if he was sleepy. He said, "I think I am." There were women walking on the roadside wearing bright *capulanas* and matching head scarfs decorated with Life President Banda's lugubrious visage, taken from a black-and-white photograph, surrounded by garlands of flowers and corn. I had heard—another of the innumerable rumors that circulate among visitors to a dictatorship—that it was a crime to arrange one's *capulana* so that one sat on Banda's image. Andsen said it wasn't so.

Little boys kept thrusting sticks at the car as we drove past. The sticks had little dark objects skewered on them—cooked mice, Andsen said, a local delicacy. He wasn't hungry. Neither was I. He nodded off. As he dozed, I did battle with speeding church vans whose drivers seemed to think they carried a divine mandate around with them. The vans were full of well-dressed Methodists, Catholics, Lutherans, Baptists, and members of the Assembly of God. Christianity had penetrated Malawi far more successfully than it had Mozambique. When Andsen, who was a teetotaling Presbyterian, awoke, I asked him if any traditional religions were still practiced in Malawi. He said no, and went back to sleep.

Five minutes later, I saw three shaggy figures stalking along the road, two of them at least nine feet tall. They were dressed in long strips of torn cloth and burlap, with huge headdresses, and great ruffs of feathers around their shoulders. They looked as if they had wandered out of some Rastafarian Carnaval. They were carrying stiff, painted cow's tails, which they snapped in the air. One wore a bright-orange mask. Actually, they made Rastafarians look like British bankers. I slammed on the brakes. Andsen woke up, saw the giants, and laughed, very loudly and very nervously. "Nyaus," he said.

The Nyaus stopped when I stopped, and then started coming toward the car.

"Give them some money," Andsen said. "Give them something."

As they reached the car, the two tall Nyaus became nothing but, from our perspective, shaggy legs. The shorter one was cutting the air with his whisk. I couldn't see any of their faces, and they did not reply to my greeting. They took the change that I handed them without a word, and stalked away. Andsen said, "Go, go." The shorter Nyau turned and yowled like a cheetah as I began to drive away. One of the tall ones, in a breathtaking athletic display, *ran down the highway embankment*, swaggering casually on his stilts.

Somewhat shakily, I asked Andsen for an explanation.

"They are going to a funeral," he said quietly. "Or some celebration, where they will dance. They go to a cemetery to dress like that. You can never see them like that near their homes. If you come to them in the cemetery, where they have their initiations and private ceremonies, and you don't know their rituals, they may seize you and hold you there for as long as they like. In the olden days, they might simply kill you. They can still be a nuisance today. They sometimes attack people. When they put on those clothes, they are no longer human. They become like beasts.[18] You saw the short one snarl. And if a Nyau falls off his stilts, the others may just attack him. They are very proud of their ability. In Chichewa, they are also called *akapoli*, which means 'big dancers.' They are quite savage, really. This is the cemetery they are coming from."

Andsen pointed to a grove of trees a few hundred yards off the road. We were on a major highway, less than fifty miles from the city of Lilongwe. The main traffic was still in church vans.

Part Four

Maputo

17

Mozambicans have a gift for understatement. When they speak of the war that has destroyed their country, they speak of the *situação*. During the time I spent in Mozambique, talking mostly with victims of the fighting and the famines it has caused, by far the most emotional voices I heard were in Maputo. There, great bellows of rage and grief often woke me in the mornings. The sufferers were always the same South African and Portuguese businessmen, playing tennis on the courts below my hotel-room window.

Maputo did not feel like a wartime city. Its million-plus residents went about their business unhindered by military checkpoints—the indignities of which are a daily travail in many African cities, even in countries at peace. Hard news about the war was very scarce. *Notícias*, the daily paper, published brief accounts of how many bandits the army said it had killed lately, how many people it had liberated, what weapons it had recovered—that was usually it. Physically, Maputo had deteriorated since independence. Most buildings needed paint; many high rises—there were about a hundred of them—carried a patina of soot and scorch marks caused by cooking fires on the landings. Most shops and restaurants had the dim, bare look and unwashed smell of long disuse, and many had been abandoned. The streets were in disrepair—parts of Avenida Karl Marx, a main thoroughfare, practically required an all-terrain vehicle. A once-famous bullring on the airport road, now in use as a market, had grown profoundly grimy, like an old coal works. When it came to postindependence decline, however, Maputo was not in Beira's league, or even close. Much of the Lisbon-style neon still worked. The power was rarely off. The restaurants that were open had food; the shops that were open had goods to sell. Indeed, it was only on the first of several visits to Maputo that I noticed the city's disrepair at all. Compared with the rest of Mozambique, Maputo was Paris. It is, in fact, a handsome city, built on a bluff overlooking the ocean and Maputo Bay, its wide avenues lined with flowering shade trees— frangipani, jacaranda, acacia, flame.

A few years before, the war had crept close. At night, tracer bullets lit up the headland across the bay, and when the wind blew east, gunfire was heard downtown. Antipersonnel mines exploded on the beach, the highways and railways leading from the city were constantly being attacked, and the power was frequently off.[1] Food in those years was scarce—not entirely because of the war—and the shops were, from all reports, empty. But South Africa apparently declined to supply Renamo with the heavy artillery and air defenses that it would have needed to take and hold Maputo. The main theater of the war shifted back to the center of the country in 1986, and the worst shortages in Maputo ended with the beginning of the economic-recovery program. There were still attacks on every road and railway line connecting the city to the rest of the world, though, and they made life in Maputo feel islandlike, privileged, and somewhat unreal.

It may have felt like none of those things, of course, to the hundreds of thousands of people who had fled there from the countryside, or to the relatives they tended to stay with. Because of the influx, the high-rise apartment buildings in Maputo were extraordinarily crowded, with many three-room apartments sleeping twenty or more. At night, these buildings became a modern Pandemonium. Very few of the elevators worked, and the long-term, nationwide shortage of light bulbs ensured that most of the stairways were unlit. Because water pressure was often a problem, especially on the upper floors, water was carried in buckets up the stairs. During a climb of ten or fifteen floors, water spills. So the stairways were wet as well as pitch-black, and were jammed with jostling people, children playing, and rats. Dividas lived in a typical high rise. One night, his wife slipped on the stairs in their building. She was carrying their infant son in a *capulana* on her back. Mother and child both went to the hospital. The baby was in a coma for five days. When the ordeal was finally over—the baby recovered—I asked Dividas if they were considering moving. He said they wouldn't dream of it. Of the choices available, a Maputo high rise was, despite its drawbacks—the stairs, the stench, the crowds—by far the safest and most pleasant place for them to live.

Most people in Maputo lived not in the cement city but in the cane city, the archipelago of shantytowns that surrounds the capital. While the cement city commands a view of the sea and the harbor, most of the shantytowns are built on low ground, subject to seasonal floods. They are immense scenes of poverty and squalor, yet in the morning commuters emerged from them in the thousands, many in starched, pressed office clothes, hurrying down sand roads and dirt paths, through the thick wood smoke and low, cool sunshine, heading for the modern city. I went home for lunch one day with two residents of a shantytown called Maxaquene. Their names were Clara and José. They both worked as servants in a Danish guest house.

We went to José's house first. It was a tiny place, perhaps seven feet by twelve, built of reeds, with a low tin roof. José, who was in his early twenties, lived there with his wife and their two children. His father lived across a small, neat, tree-shaded compound, in an even smaller place. There was also a cooking hut and a flock of red-faced ducks in a pen. Inside, José's house was dim—it had no windows—but it was as tidy as a sailboat's cabin, with kerosene lamps all stored in a row, a formal tea set arranged on a shelf, José's bicycle tied to the ceiling, and a bicycle-racing trophy in the place of honor on the bureau. The contrast with the ramshackle, rough-trade exterior of Maxaquene was stunning. José entertained us with stories about his adventures on a recent trip back to his village in Xai-Xai, on the Gaza coast. It sounded as if he had spent the entire time dodging the draft. At one point, when soldiers stopped a truck he was traveling in, he had lain on the floor, covered himself with a *capulana*, and pretended to be too sick to speak. All in all, he was glad to be back in Maputo, where it was easier to get lost in the crowds. His job was a drag. He was underpaid and overworked.

Still, he was lucky to have it—unemployment in Maxaquene was high. And his wife had work, too. They wanted to build a bigger, cement-block house.

For lunch, we went to Clara's. She *had* a bigger, cement-block house, and it had electricity. Maxaquene was actually one of the better-developed shantytowns in Maputo. The Portuguese took no interest in the cane cities, except to try to charge their residents rent and, in the latter days of the *luta armada*, to sniff around for "terrorists" they thought might be hiding in the slums. After independence, rents were abolished, and Frelimo looked for ways to mobilize and develop the shantytowns. Maxaquene, which had a population of about 50,000, became the site of a pilot project that eventually brought—largely through the efforts of residents—streetlights, street names, public water taps, public telephones, a paved road for a bus route, and a small child-care center. In 1988, there still weren't many cement-block houses, or houses with electricity—and none with running water—but the clipped hedges and well-kept trails marked a still-"dynamized" *bairro*. Clara, who was twenty-six and had three children, was married to a policeman named Mateus. They, too, kept ducks in their yard, and had a tiny vegetable garden.

Their house, Mateus had made into a cheerful shrine to himself. On the turquoise wall of the main room—there was also a bedroom—his name was painted in large letters in red. Photographs of Mateus in military uniform were everywhere, and a pair of shoes—shiny black Oxfords, policeman's shoes—were hung on the wall, with shiny orange highway reflectors stuck inside them. When I asked Clara why her name was not painted on the wall, she said, "Machismo." She was a sharp-featured, wry young woman. With five years of primary school, she was underemployed as a servant and she knew it. Mateus, for his part, wanted to leave the police force, she said. The police were unpopular—people said that you were safer with the criminals than you were with the cops—but, for reasons too complicated to explain, he couldn't leave. While Clara prepared lunch, I leafed through Mateus's record collection. There was a lot of African jazz and pop, some Diana Ross, "Hot Soul Singles," reggae, an album of African National Congress songs, and, right next to it, an aging South African "Springbok Top 40."

Lunch was a casserole of potatoes and vegetables—a special meal, I assumed, for the foreign visitor. The free distribution of an array of rationed foods in Maputo had been cut back to just small amounts of rice, corn, sugar, and vegetable oil, and food subsidies had been eliminated under the economic-recovery program, thus driving prices out of reach for even the working poor. It was the usual harsh paradox of austerity measures in the Third World: that the shops and markets filled with goods at the same time that most people could no longer afford to buy anything. I had brought beer and soft drinks, but I wished I had brought more when I saw Clara's three children, her sister, Adelina, who was visiting from Xai-Xai, and Adelina's two children. The kids were excited to have Clara home for lunch. Middle-class Mozambicans, following Portuguese custom, normally go home from work at midday, and workers who can manage it do the same, but the bus to Maxaquene had, like most public transport in Maputo, stopped running, so Clara could only get home and back to work in the allowed two hours if she had a lift. I noticed that she and Adelina, who was smaller, rounder, darker, younger, and much shyer than Clara, spoke Portuguese together. They said, when I asked, that their mother tongue was actually Shangaan but that they spoke Portuguese around the children, who needed to learn it for school. Mateus spoke Makua, a northern language, and had learned some Swahili on a police-training course in Tanzania, so their house, Clara said, was normally a little Tower of Babel.

I asked Adelina what had brought her to town, and I was immediately sorry I had. She gave a pained look and glanced away. Clara said, "Adelina's husband was a mineworker in South Africa. Three months ago, while he was going home to Xai-Xai on his annual leave, the convoy he was traveling in was attacked by *bandidos armados*, and he was killed." Awhile later, I tried to break the silence that had fallen over the meal by asking Adelina if she planned to stay in Maputo. No, she said. She was already planning to return to Xai-Xai. It was nearly time to plant her *machamba*. Weren't the *bandidos* a problem in Xai-Xai? Yes, she said quietly, but the attacks that she had heard about were not yet near her *machamba*. They were still ten kilometers away.

Seeing the war in Maputo was often just a matter of asking someone a question. On another occasion, I ruined another lunch. I was staying in a United Nations official's luxurious apartment high above Avenida Eduardo Mondlane. That day, I was dining alone. As the cook—a heavyset, middle-aged career servant named Bernardo—was ladling out soup, I asked him in passing how things were in central Gaza, the area he came from. Bernardo set down the soup bowl, wiped his hands on his apron, stared at me unnervingly, and said things were terrible. It had become so dangerous that he had decided to bring his wife and four children to Maputo. But his wife refused to leave her mother, who refused to leave her land. He had decided to bring the children anyway, and to sell one of his four goats—the male—to finance the move. Just then, his goats were stolen from their herder by thieves posing as police. Bernardo paid the local militia 20,000 meticais (nearly forty dollars, at the official rate) to conduct a house-to-house search. They found three of his four goats, but not the male, and arrested the woman who had them. Bernardo decided not to press charges, because the woman was breast feeding and was also pregnant, and she promised to pay him, in installments, the 20,000 meticais. But now she was back in jail, having stolen from someone else, who didn't care that she was pregnant, and he, Bernardo, had no way to bring his children to safety in the city. Did I have any idea how dangerous it was in the countryside now? The *bandidos* could burst into your house at any time. And they would just start killing people, for no reason. Bernardo imitated a zombie hacking with a machete, supplying the sound effects himself—"Za! Za! Za!"—and getting visibly upset. That was what they did! They never said a thing! They just chopped people up! The robotic silence of the bandits was clearly the most horrifying part of it all to Bernardo. He kept imitating the chopping, his eyes bulging: "Za! Za! Za!"

Maputo's Central Hospital was just a block away from that apartment, and one-legged people, the victims of land mines, were always crutching along Avenida Eduardo Mondlane. One afternoon, I went into the hospital with an interpreter from the Ministry of Information, who had got us permission to speak to patients. There, the war was in one's face. Casilda Maquele, a sixty-three-year-old peasant, had been wounded by a bullet in an attack only six days before. It was the second time the bandits had attacked her village. Many people had been killed in this attack, she said, including her father-in-law. Her village, which was across Maputo Bay, was within sight of the city. Flávio Maria, a twenty-three-year-old mechanic in the army, had been wounded in an attack near the Swaziland border only five days before. One bullet had passed right through him—he showed us the open holes, front and back. Another bullet had already been removed, from his shoulder. This was the first day since he had been shot that he was able to move. Maria said he and his company had been defending a warehouse full of food. The battle had lasted seventeen hours. The bandits had finally succeeded in taking the warehouse. They had stolen the food and destroyed a lot of equipment. Maria expected to be moved soon to a military hospital and, when he was healed, sent back to the front. Where was the front? Almost anywhere outside Maputo.

Simião Natavele, a thirty-five-year-old ambulance driver, said he had been in the hospital four months. He had been riding in the cab of a truck in Cabo Delgado when it was ambushed from both sides of the road. The driver was unhurt and managed to speed away. When they got to a village, they found that six of the eight people riding in the back of the truck had been killed. Natavele was badly wounded, with three bullets in his upper legs and stomach. He had been transferred to Maputo for a series of operations. He still could not urinate. His wife and six children were back in Cabo Delgado. But his parents were here in Maputo, and they saw to it that he was fed. As soon as he was well, he would return to Cabo Delgado. Yes, Natavele said, he would continue to work as an ambulance driver. This was the third time he had been ambushed, but the first time he had been hurt. The bandits could not frighten him! Natavele seemed to be getting angry—not so much at the bandits as at us. He demanded to know why we were asking him these questions. He warned us, now clearly angry, that we had better not try to use his story for "propaganda." I didn't understand what he meant, and my interpreter couldn't enlighten me, but someone whom I asked about it afterward had a plausible explanation. Natavele probably did not want publicity as a defiant ambulance driver who could not be intimidated by Renamo, because that was a good way to get his name on a Renamo hit list.

The hospital was a hellish place, with a stench that forced me

to hurry outside periodically for fresh air. Patients were screaming with unsedated pain; sheets were stained red, brown, and
yellow; the wards were dirty and ill lit; legless men lay on the
floor in the corridors. And yet it was the best hospital in the
country, my guide assured me. "The last alternative before you
go to your grave," he said, with a gentle laugh.

18

Most of the foreign civilians living in Mozambique lived in Maputo. That amounted to a substantial number. "In the development racket, Mozambique is the trendiest place on earth," an American official in Maputo told me. "*India* has 150 people here, for Christ's sake." Shaking his head, the official called to his houseboy for more piping-hot cashews and cold beer. We were sitting in his living room, which was large, modern, and immaculate; the previous week's issue of *New York* magazine lay on the coffee table. Maputo's wealthiest neighborhoods—such as Somerschield, a leafy district from which even the Portuguese were once excluded by their British creditor-overlords—seemed to be populated almost entirely by foreigners. The government went out of its way to make them comfortable, reserving for them much of the city's best housing, even ceding tracts of well-drained land for the construction of whole new neighborhoods—arrondissements so blindingly clean they might have dropped out of the sky from Sweden. Because leaving Maputo other than by air was dangerous—a number of embassies, in fact, forbade their nationals to do so—many expatriates ended up living in a closely circumscribed world, bounded by house, office, hard-currency supermarket, the few restaurants that were up to foreign standards, and the company of their fellow expatriates. There were shopping sprees to Swaziland and South Africa to break up the routine, but the farthest that many foreigners ventured into local society was to join one of the old Portuguese yacht clubs that still moldered on the Maputo waterfront.

Few of the officials in the international organizations working in Mozambique were newcomers to the aid business. I was constantly running into foreigners whose résumés contained the same disaster zones: Southeast Asia, Uganda, Somalia, Ethiopia, Sudan. The American "aid professionals" would ask me how long I had been "in country," as if we were in Vietnam. Some of them seemed actively resistant to knowing any more about Mozambique than they needed to do their jobs. Others were more interested in the place, and yet the swimming pools of Somerschield often felt like a scene in Ross Coggins's satiric poem "The Development Set":

> The Development Set is bright and noble,
> Our thoughts are deep and our vision global;
> Although we move with the better classes,
> Our thoughts are always with the masses.[1]

One drollery making the rounds while I was in Maputo renamed our battered host the Donors' Republic of Mozambique.

The international organizations were doing vital work, of course, but their record in Mozambique was not unblemished. The dumping of rotten food and expired medicines that had led to major scandals elsewhere in the Third World was also happening here. Fifteen thousand tons of maize loaded at Le Havre, for example, had been found, on arrival in Mozambique, to be "totally unfit for human consumption," according to a 1987 study by the European Economic Community.[2] More troubling even than dumping was the damage being done by some aid to the already anemic local economy. Emergency food, which could take as long as nine months to arrive, was often earmarked by donors for areas that were oversupplied by the time the food came, while areas truly in need were left unsupplied. In places where farmers managed to harvest a crop, badly targeted aid could bankrupt local food producers.[3] And yet only a fraction of emergency food was actually being distributed free. Most was being sold, usually at prices set by the donors on the basis of local market value. After the economic-recovery program removed subsidies on basic foods in 1987, these prices could be prohibitive. A frequent result was that, as Joseph Hanlon noted, "the urban poor pay inflated prices for donated food."[4]

The competition among aid organizations could also get fierce. Some of their differences were honest ones, turning on questions of how to encourage economic development, or of how to minimize the debilitating dependence that so often accompanies aid, especially in places where people have been uprooted.[5] Other differences were pure bureaucratic turf war. One organization, using its financial clout, would pressure the government to certify it as the sole provider of prosthetic limbs in Mozambique, so that it could corner the lucrative fund-raising market. The losers in this sort of power play (the only real losers were the amputees, but they had no political clout) would then plot revenge. While I was in Maputo, accusations were flying that one organization was using photographs of another organization's project to raise funds in Europe, misrepresenting the project as its own. All this infighting gave rise to some fairly good name-calling. Rivals of the British organization Save the Children, which was very active and very effective, called it Shave the Children. Critics of World Vision, a Christian relief organization based in California, called it Blurred Vision.

Because the international organizations needed the Mozambican government as much as it needed them, relations between the two could be delicate. When I arrived in Quelimane, the director of the provincial emergency commission had just returned from three months of study in London. His trip had been paid for by an American organization that had recently begun operations in his bailiwick, a piece of magnanimity with which the other relief organizations working in Zambézia were decidedly not delighted.

There were also foreigners, known as *cooperantes*, who had moved to Mozambique after independence for political reasons. Most were socialists from Britain, Western Europe, Canada, the United States, or South Africa, and most worked for the government. Some had been associated with Frelimo since the *luta armada*, and many had dedicated the best years of their lives to building socialism in Mozambique. There were those who continued to hold out hope for the revolutionary project. One *coop-*

erante, reflecting on the war with Renamo, wanly (and incorrectly) pointed out to me that armed resistance to Bolshevism, some of it with Western support, did not end in the Soviet Union until 1926. But Frelimo's ideological swerve in the 1980s left a lot of *cooperantes* in the political ditch. Some left the country; some who had stayed seemed to me embittered but not sure how to express their displeasure—few, if any, were Mozambican citizens. *Cooperantes* tended to resent the new generation of expatriates—the technocrats who came to Mozambique with lucrative contracts, health insurance, regular home leave, and no visible ideals.

Many *cooperantes* saw the Western aid effort as a grand political demarche. They liked to point out that, in 1983, when parts of Mozambique were facing a famine, Samora Machel had had to go to Europe and make a number of "pro-Western" statements before the emergency aid he had been requesting for nearly a year was granted. (By then, it was too late for an estimated 100,000 people, who starved to death.)[6] The United States, it was often said, had become extremely popular with both the people and the government of Mozambique simply by dumping thousands of tons of surplus grain there. An American economist at Eduardo Mondlane University in Maputo told me that she held the United States, as a historic ally of South Africa's, partly responsible for Pretoria's war against Mozambique. South African destabilization dovetailed neatly, after all, with Western designs, since it "softened up" Mozambique for a repenetration by international capital. Many Frelimo militants shared this analysis, and many had certainly not forgotten American support for Portugal, through NATO, during the *luta armada.* But the leadership refrained from biting the Western hand that fed the people. "We are not destabilized for our socialist option, but for our independence," José Luís Cabaço, who had long been a leading Marxist voice in the party, told me. When I said to the American economist that hers was apparently a minority view, she sighed and said, "Mozambicans are too polite. It influences their vision, which is getting cloudy."

Among the *cooperantes* I met, some, it was clear, simply loved living in Mozambique, and even bore the privations of living on a government salary—depending on food rations, and so on— with a certain pride. Polly Gaster, an Englishwoman who taught at the Frelimo school in Dar es Salaam and now worked in the Ministry of Information, laughed easily when she told me that her apartment building was about to fall off a cliff. It was a ten-story, octagonal building, one of the dozens of its type hurriedly thrown up during the construction boom of the 1960s, and it was perched on the bluff above Maputo harbor. When the elevator worked, it banged hideously against the walls of its shaft, suggesting that something structural had changed. "Portuguese architecture," Polly said contemptuously. Her apartment, which was on the sixth floor, had been chosen by a technically minded neighbor as the site for hanging a plumb line. He had taped a piece of graph paper beneath the plumb and told Polly that if it moved more than a few millimeters, she needed to alert the neighbors—the building was ready to go. Unfortunately, the string for the line had turned out to be too stretchy, and the plumb now lay on its side on the graph paper—and the technical neighbor had gone off to Canada for a course. "Nao problema" is the all-purpose Mozambican phrase in a pinch, and that was what Polly said when she showed me the plumb. "I hope," she added. Then she showed me an old manual typewriter on a desk overlooking the harbor. Eduardo Mondlane had written part of his classic book, *The Struggle for Mozambique*, on that typewriter, Polly said. She looked at the machine for a minute. She tapped a key. "Mondlane had a heavy touch," she said.

While the government might, as an employer, still command the loyalty of *cooperantes*, it had an increasingly difficult time hanging on to educated Mozambicans, especially those who spoke English. Salaries in the private sector were far higher, and fields such as export-import offered great opportunities as state controls were relaxed. The employers of choice in Maputo, however, were the international organizations and the embassies. The director of Radio Mozambique's English-language service told me that the pressure on his staff of nine young Mozambicans, all of them trained by the BBC in London, was so great that he had no choice but to schedule their shifts "so as not to interrupt their moonlighting," Otherwise, some of them would undoubtedly have left state radio for jobs in the aid industry at three times their government salaries.[7] The popularity in Maputo of the United States was, in fact, only partly attributable to the amounts of aid it sent—the United States was, in the late 1980s, the largest single foreign donor to Mozambique. There was also the Americans' role, in various forms, as a major local employer.

It wasn't always so. In 1975, when Mozambique raised its flag for the first time as an independent nation, the United States was pointedly not invited to the ceremonies. (Neither were its NATO allies France and West Germany.)[8] Diplomatic relations between the two countries were only established six months later, and direct economic assistance to Mozambique was soon ended by the Carter administration as a protest against Frelimo's human-rights abuses.[9] These cool relations froze almost solid after a South African commando attack on a Maputo suburb in January 1981 killed fourteen people. Accusing the CIA of providing intelligence to the South Africans, Mozambique expelled six American Embassy personnel and accused nine others who had already left of having been CIA agents. The incoming Reagan administration retaliated by refusing to name a new American ambassador.

The thaw began in late 1982. East-bloc aid and military training were not keeping pace with the deepening military and economic crises in Mozambique, and the Soviets had rejected Mozambique's application to become the first African member of the Council of Mutual Economic Assistance. The Reagan administration's policy of "constructive engagement" with Pretoria, while being reviled in most of Africa as an unholy friendship with apartheid, began to be regarded in Maputo as a possible opportunity. Perhaps the Americans could get their good friends the South Africans to ease up on their ruinous campaign against Mozambique. The Nkomati Accord, brokered by the United States, formalized this desperate hope; even after the discovery of Pretoria's ongoing support for Renamo had turned "Nkomati" into diplomatic shorthand for South African treachery, American policymakers continued to cling to the Accord as the lone bright spot in U.S. policy toward southern Africa in the mid-1980s. The Machel government was also being helpful, the Americans felt, in the then-stalled negotiations over Namibian independence, mediating between them and the Angolan government. Frelimo, for its part, was banking so heavily on the good will it was accumulating in Washington that it actually declared its support for

Ronald Reagan's reelection. And Mozambique was rewarded for its tractability with increasing amounts of aid. In 1985, Samora Machel traveled to Washington to meet Reagan. The two men got on famously, from all accounts. In its 1985–86 foreign-aid budget, the administration even included a small amount of "nonlethal" military aid for Mozambique.

Alerted, at least in part, by this unusual request for military aid to Marxists, American conservatives got interested in Mozambique. A full-page advertisement in the *Washington Times* urged President Reagan not to meet with Machel. Even as the two leaders chatted, Republican legislators (Senator Malcolm Wallop of Wyoming, Representative Dan Burton of Indiana) were introducing a bill to provide five million dollars in military aid to Renamo. As the *Washington Post* commented, "It may have been the first time Congress was ever asked to arm both sides in a civil war." [10] Both proposals for military aid were defeated, but right-wingers were now aroused, and the administration's routine request for economic assistance to Mozambique was nearly rejected as well.

Policy toward Mozambique *was* an anomaly, a glaring exception to the "Reagan Doctrine," under which the United States gave aid to insurgents in Nicaragua, Afghanistan, Cambodia, and, most pertinently, Angola. Right-wing critics labeled Mozambique a "Soviet client state" and ridiculed the idea that such a government could ever be "weaned away" from Moscow. The State Department contended that Frelimo's "turn to the West" was genuine and that Renamo was not, in any case, a legitimate alternative. After the Clark Amendment, which had prohibited American involvement in the Angolan war since 1975 (but had apparently been circumvented by deals with third countries—notably Saudi Arabia—to channel assistance to the Unita rebels),[11] was repealed by Congress in 1985, clearing the way for large-scale aid to Unita, the State Department's Africa Bureau was obliged not only to drop its opposition to Unita aid but also to clarify, repeatedly, the differences between Unita and Renamo. Yes, both had received extensive backing from South Africa, but Unita had a strong ethnic and regional base and provided at least some services to the people living in its territory. Unita, it was argued, would cut its ties with Pretoria if it could; Renamo had no comparable independent streak. The

State Department's arguments met heavy resistance. Renamo had powerful supporters in the CIA and in the administration—including William Casey, the CIA director, and Patrick Buchanan, the White House communications director, who actually had his photograph taken in a meeting with Artur Janeiro da Fonseca, the Renamo secretary for foreign relations.[12] Yet the State Department somehow managed to keep President Reagan persuaded that Mozambique was a special case.

In 1986 and 1987, conservative senators—led by Jesse Helms, Republican of North Carolina—held up the confirmation of Melissa Wells, a career foreign-service officer nominated as ambassador to Mozambique, for eleven months in an effort to shift U.S. policy in Renamo's direction. Referring to the State Department's contacts with South Africa's then-outlawed African National Congress, Helms told the assistant secretary of state for African affairs, "[A]ll the State Department has to do is say, 'We are going to do the same thing with Renamo that we do with the ANC.'"[13] In another bizarre attempt to link the struggle in South Africa with regional policy, the Senate voted to deny aid to any SADCC country that did not explicitly renounce a gruesome method of execution known as "necklacing" (a gasoline-soaked tire placed around a victim's neck and set afire), which was then being used in South African townships to punish suspected police informers.[14] The bloc opposing Mrs. Wells's confirmation eventually grew to include such mainstream figures as Robert Dole, Republican of Kansas, who was at that stage campaigning for the 1988 presidential nomination—and using a strategy that apparently included a Mozambique position designed to appeal to the extreme right. But Mrs. Wells maintained, throughout a process that included 246 detailed written questions from Helms, that Renamo was not a nationalist movement and was not worthy of American support. And the bloc opposing her confirmation finally disintegrated after the July 1987 massacre of 424 civilians in Homoine was reported.

But a frightful laundry list of right-wing American sects and organizations had become interested in Mozambique by then. From the Family Protection Scoreboard in Costa Mesa, California, to the End-Time Handmaidens of Jasper, Arkansas, every far-right fringe group and would-be mercenary in America seemed to want to send Bibles or worse to the Renamo "freedom fighters." The Reagan State Department became the unlikely target of ceaseless attack from the extreme right;[15] and a ramshackle system of "privatized intervention" sprang up, shuttling supplies and light weapons into Mozambique, usually via Malawi.[16] The trial of Ian Grey, the young Australian missionary convicted in Maputo in 1987 of spying for Renamo, offered chilling glimpses of the fanaticism of the Christian fundamentalists—most of them Americans—who supported the rebels.[17] The congressional Iran-Contra investigations did not reveal whether William Casey's network of clandestine supply operations to Third World insurgencies extended to Mozambique—though Lieutenant-Colonel Oliver North's testimony did contain a tantalizing reference to his group's failure to achieve "unity" among the "resistance" in Mozambique.[18] In the face of this strange, multifaceted onslaught of zealots from America, nearly all the Mozambicans whom I asked about it seemed remarkably calm. José Luís Cabaço just said that, yes, there were "sectors" of the United States actively destabilizing his country, but they were not the important sectors, and they certainly did not represent any aspect of American policy.

Ambassador Wells, I gathered, was hugely popular. The Mozambican press had followed her nomination controversy closely, so she was already widely known, and admired, by the time she arrived. And her performance in situ had only increased her local standing. She spoke Portuguese and was experienced in Africa, knowledgeable about Mozambique, and endlessly energetic, traveling the length of the country to see things for herself and adopting local projects. From the news reports, it seemed there was hardly an orphan in Mozambique who was not at risk for the American ambassador's kindness. The first time I met her, she was enthusing about an African dance Mass she had seen, and advising me on the pitfalls, which she had learned firsthand, of attending an amnesty ceremony for ex-Renamo fighters. She was a tall, handsome woman, with the easy manner and the steady gaze of a very good poker player. She was a serious reporter, known for personally investigating important stories, asking hard questions, and making detailed notes. And she was taken seriously by the Mozambican government. Virtually the first thing President Chissano did after meeting with South African president P. W. Botha in September

1988, in a historic attempt to revive the Nkomati Accord, was call in Mrs. Wells for a briefing.

The American Embassy as a whole was on surprisingly good terms—suspiciously good terms, Jesse Helms might think—with the Frelimo government. Indeed, the American diplomats seemed ready to try almost anything to wean Mozambique away from communism. I overheard the deputy chief of the United States mission instructing that a card be printed up, in Portuguese, to accompany three bottles of Scotch that he had lost in a tennis wager to the Frelimo minister of finance. It seemed that they had a regular doubles game on Sunday mornings. The card would express a wish that the minister and his partner would be as gracious in defeat as they had been in victory, and it would be signed with Frelimo's revolutionary slogan, "A Luta Continua"—The Struggle Continues.

19

—

The long beach running north from Maputo used to be a favorite weekend campsite for white South Africans. They parked their campers and pitched their tents in among the shaggy pines behind the beach, and the Mozambicans called them "banana Boers," because all they ever bought from hawkers was bananas. Everything else they needed—except, perhaps, black women and prawns—they brought with them. For prawns, they went to the Costa do Sol, a cavernous old restaurant at the north end of the beach, which, in 1988, was still open, still run by the same Greek couple that had run it since the 1940s, still had child beggars haunting the parking lot, and still served great piles of fresh prawns to a clientele that was largely white and foreign. The Costa do Sol was actually the northern limit of the area within which many expatriates in Maputo were permitted to wander—the Scandinavians were not even allowed to go there after 7 p.m. The land mines that exploded on the beach in 1986 were in among the pines where the South Africans used to camp. There were also, in colonial days, primarily for the amusement of the South Africans, a stock-car track behind the beach and a miniature golf course. Both were now closed and overgrown, although the golf course survived as Mini-Golf, another of the handful of Maputo restaurants that expatriates frequented. The most striking remnant of the area's tourist heyday was a huge building, at least twenty-five stories high, near the old racetrack. The building was going to be a hotel, but it was unfinished at independence, and the Portuguese builders, before abandoning it, had poured cement down the pipes and down the elevator shaft. And so the building had stood, empty and rusting in the sea breeze, a rather heavily symbolic skeleton, since 1975.

The Portuguese settlers committed a great deal of sabotage and vandalism before they left Mozambique. They killed cattle, wrecked machinery, drove tractors into the sea, destroyed records and repair manuals, and, above all, spirited wealth out of the country. An estimated 150 million British pounds was illegally exported immediately before and after independence.[1] The owners of Boror, one of the world's largest coconut-farming companies, simply "loaded the entire 1975 copra crop, worth 2 million pounds, on to four ships and sailed away, never to return."[2] Like Renamo's destruction of infrastructure, the damage caused by this pillage was magnified by the underdevelopment from which Mozambique already suffered. In the case of the Portuguese, of course, it was only the last blow in a battering that had lasted nearly 500 years.

And yet some Portuguese stayed on in Mozambique after independence—by 1988, the number was perhaps 20,000. The level of racial tension in the country was, from all indications—including my own experience—remarkably low. Mozambicans who traveled to South Africa were shocked at the racial attitudes they encountered there. A young Mozambican who had been living in Soweto for two years, and who had just returned to Maputo, told me he had been horrified by some of his friends and neighbors. "Those people just *hate* whites," he said. "It is as if they have no moral education. The Boers have just treated them like animals." In Zimbabwe also, where many more whites stayed after independence, the air was still thick, comparatively speaking, with racial resentments. Even high Zimbabwean government officials engaged in public race-baiting—an unimaginable practice in ferociously antiracist Frelimo.

Most of the whites in Mozambique were in Maputo. Among the Portuguese who stayed, a small minority were actively pro-Frelimo. A few had been members of clandestine Frelimo cells during the *luta armada*. The existence of white leftists in Mozambique was sometimes attributed to family traditions retained from the days when Lisbon deported political opponents to the colonies, but in fact some Frelimo officials had seen their entire families leave without them. A high proportion of young whites, enthusiastic about either the popular revolution happening around them or the prospect of having the family house to themselves, or both, stayed. But when food shortages in the cities became so serious that even whites—who had no access, after all, to a family *machamba*—began going hungry, more left.

Paulo Oliveira, who was born in Portugal and raised in Mozambique, was one of the young whites who started having problems in the years after independence. But Oliveira's problem, as he recalls it, was not hunger. It was politics. He was studying engineering at Eduardo Mondlane University, and he didn't see why he was required to take courses in Marxism-Leninism. After he quit college and left Mozambique in 1979, Oliveira became a journalist in Lisbon. In 1981, he joined Renamo. He later moved to South Africa to run Radio Free Africa, the Renamo radio station. Upon the signing of the Nkomati Accord in 1984, the station was closed, and Oliveira returned to Lisbon, where he edited the Renamo magazine—it was called *A luta continua*. He became Renamo's spokesman in Europe and, in 1986, Renamo's diplomatic representative and delegate to Western Europe. But differences with other Renamo leaders, and with the group's South African sponsors, led, in late 1987, to Oliveira's resignation. Several of his former associates were murdered over the next few months. With his own life clearly in danger, Oliveira defected to Frelimo in March 1988 and flew to Mozambique.

When I went to see him, in August, he was staying at the Rovuma, a big, modern, well-maintained hotel in downtown Maputo, owned by the Frelimo Party. I had obtained his address from the Ministry of Information, but Oliveira had apparently heard nothing about an interview. He was wary when I knocked on his door, but eventually he let me in.

He was a big, pale, ponderous, fair-haired man, with a sad face, shaky hands, and smoke-yellowed fingers. His quarters were clean but bleak. He spoke very slowly, in English, and he slowly warmed to his subject. Oliveira had a reporter's interest in dates, numbers, details, and the spelling of names. Although the press conferences at which he had appeared after his defection had been effective as Frelimo events, they had not engaged all his journalistic faculties. With me, Oliveira could get *into* his subject. After an hour or two, he ordered beers from room service, and when I said I had to leave, he seemed disappointed. I said I would return the next day; and when I did, there were half a dozen quart bottles of beer already cooling on the air conditioner.

Oliveira mainly talked about the conflict within the Renamo leadership between what he called the "Washington-Paris axis" and the "Pretoria-Bonn axis." He and others in the Washington-Paris group had been trying to develop a credible political structure for Renamo, he said, with ties to the West, particularly to the United States. The South Africans, not wanting to lose control of Renamo, had been opposing this effort by various means, including murder. Oliveira described some of the killings in chilling detail. He had been with Orlando Cristina, the first Renamo secretary-general, when he died, in South Africa, shortly after being shot, and he could name both the gunman and his accomplices. He even had photographs of the wreckage of the car in which Mateus Lopes and João da Silva Ataíde—both leading members of the Washington-Paris group—died in Malawi.

Oliveira was wonderfully thorough in his descriptions of his life while running the radio station in South Africa, recalling the names, ranks, and quirks of the South African officers who handled Renamo; the standing orders to destroy with phosphorous grenades everything in a Renamo camp near the Mozambique border if the camp were attacked, either by Frelimo or by South Africa's own African National Congress, because such an attack would bring journalists flocking; the strict segregation of the Mozambicans from the Angolan and Zimbabwean dissidents also being trained in South Africa; the clashes between Renamo and Pretoria over the release of Soviet hostages taken in Mozambique; the many times that he and his comrades, in an act of solidarity with the fighters, stayed up late waiting for supply planes that had gone to Mozambique to return; and the music, Mozambican national languages, and English that he, Oliveira, had introduced to Renamo radio programming.

After returning to Lisbon, Oliveira continued to work with the South African military. Brigadier Charles Van Niekerk, Pretoria's chief liaison to Renamo—he was also an adviser to the Portuguese colonial army during the war against Frelimo[3]— told Oliveira in Lisbon in 1987 that he wanted to renew Renamo radio broadcasts inside Mozambique, and he had two South African technicians install a fax machine and a cipher machine for Oliveira to use while communicating with South Africa. But Oliveira had become thoroughly disillusioned with Pretoria by that stage. He had, after all, been told years before by a South African colonel that Pretoria had no intention of letting Renamo take power in Mozambique, and he had seen no reason to doubt the colonel's assessment since. It was Oliveira's affiliation with the Washington-Paris group that ultimately forced him to leave the movement, and then, after several death threats, to take refuge in Mozambique.

He had not spent an easy five months since defecting. Two small teams of black Mozambicans, apparently working for South Africa, had tried to assassinate him. The Maputo police had captured one of the teams in a stolen car after they ran over and killed a couple on a motorcycle. Submachine guns and Oliveira's photograph had been found in the car, and the team, which had apparently already killed an African National Congress member since coming over the border from Swaziland, revealed under interrogation the existence of the second team. Oliveira, for his own protection, had been stashed away in the northern province of Nampula for two months. Now he was back in Maputo, and he was lonely and bored. He wanted to get out of the Rovuma; he wanted to go to work. He had been unable to get his personal belongings back from the Ministry of Security. The minister himself said he could have them—the goods included books, papers, and videos that were essential for a book that Oliveira wanted to write—but the actual keepers of the material would not release them. He could not get a driver's license. He was not receiving his mail. He had registered for classes at the university—which no longer, he was glad to see, even had a faculty of Marxism-Leninism—but the Ministry of Security had screwed up the transport and security arrangements. He missed his girlfriend and had just told the minister of security that he would return to Portugal, despite the dangers, if some of his demands were not met soon. He would accept a scholarship to resume his engineering studies in Brazil, England, or the United States, but not in the East bloc.

Oliveira was reading, I noticed, a Portuguese translation of Jim Morrison's poetry—a sign, I thought, of true desperation. I was astounded by the lack of security around him. No one had questioned me when I arrived at the Rovuma. No guards were posted on the landing. Oliveira was obviously being left alone. He had even gone out recently with some old friends, he said, who still belonged to the Maputo Air Club—Oliveira had been a recreational parachutist in palmier days. Pretoria aside, were there not many, many people in Maputo who had all the reason in the world to want to attack Oliveira, the former front man for the group that had murdered perhaps a hundred thousand Mozambicans? Could he really be safe going out in public?

I was reminded of a scene that a *cooperante* in Quelimane once described. Half a dozen *amnistiados*, Renamo fighters who had taken advantage of the government's amnesty offer, were sitting on a bench outside a government office, waiting to receive clothes or food or blankets. A crowd of fifty or sixty had gathered around them. In Quelimane, it was a safe bet that half of that crowd had either been driven from their homes by Renamo or had had family members displaced, injured, kidnapped, or killed. So the emotions running through the people there were presumably very powerful. But they did nothing, they said nothing. They simply watched the ex-rebels, silently. The *cooperante*, who had been working in Quelimane for years, was at a loss to explain it. Did the crowd's restraint represent an extraordinary political maturity, or was it just extreme passivity?

Mozambicans did sometimes act in mobs. In Maputo I heard about incidents in which some poor sod was denounced as a *bandido armado* in public and was attacked on the spot—even killed—by an enraged crowd. After Samora Machel's death, a mob had attacked the Malawian Embassy and the South African trade mission. In an extraordinary incident in Beira—it surely could have happened nowhere else in Mozambique—a protest by handicapped war victims, in December 1990, turned violent after the protesters looted a government warehouse, then marched on a police station, where they stole weapons, beat up a policeman, and hijacked a truck. The police counterattack, which killed one man, was condemned even by the official news agency.[4]

And yet Paulo Oliveira was safe. After I left him at his hotel, I made my way to the office of the national airlines. I wanted to buy a ticket to Quelimane. The airline office was scruffy and crowded and reeked of unwashed bodies and some low-grade species of despair. Behind the counter, half a dozen grim, over-worked clerks dithered among piles of paper and food, occasionally consulting crumpled little cardboard calendars and disintegrating fare books and talking on battered, ancient phones with uninsulated wires sprouting from the receivers. Strange scraps of English military shorthand—"Whiskey November Bravo"—flitted through their muttered Afro-Portuguese. Mostly, though, the clerks just sipped coffee and chatted to each other and ignored the desperate pack that surged and clamored on the public side of the counter. I was getting jostled and was struggling to keep my patience. Nobody else seemed to be in any danger of losing theirs, of course. That, I thought, was because they were Mozambicans. What had Janet Mondlane said? People here *had* to be laid-back to avoid having their personalities destroyed by disappointment. I could see that my hope of buying an air ticket that day was going to be disappointed—if only because the office was scheduled to close in two hours, which was less time than it would take to get a clerk's attention, never mind buy a ticket.

I weighed going out to the airport. There was a ticket counter of sorts out there, and the airports in Mozambique were famous for their efficiency. People said that was because Armando Guebuza was minister of transport and communications. Guebuza, it was said, scared everybody who worked for him so badly that they all performed superhuman feats to avoid his wrath. *He* was famous, in his way, for *not* being patient. (He sounded like an African Dona Amélia—someone who regarded the whole country as his Hotel Chuabo.) In fact, Guebuza's nickname, "Vinte-Quatro/Vinte" (24/20), derived from his days as minister of the interior in the period after independence, when every white resident whom he suspected of counterrevolutionary activity heard the same order: "Vinte-Quatro/Vinte." They had twenty-four hours to leave Mozambique, and they could take no more than twenty kilograms of possessions with them. Twelve years later, black Mozambicans still chuckled admiringly when they explained how Guebuza got his nickname. It was Guebuza who had told Dividas when he returned to Mozambique that the government would be watching him (and Guebuza who had directed the disastrous Operation Production)—and yet even Dividas had described him with affectionate respect. Indeed, he himself subscribed to the Guebuza explanation for the relative efficiency of the country's airports. Unfortunately, I had no way of knowing whether the ticket counter at the airport would be open—and no way, for that matter, of getting to the airport.

That evening, at my hotel, I met an American doctor who had just arrived in Mozambique the day before. She was reeling from her first glimpse of the country. It seemed that her delegation had been visiting the emergency room at the Central Hospital when the victims of a Renamo massacre in a district just north of Maputo began arriving. "The doctors and nurses were simply amazing," she said. "I mean, if dozens of badly injured and dying people suddenly started showing up in an American emergency room, it would be a very big deal. But nobody batted an eye. They just kept working, dealing with whatever came in, and they were doing an incredibly good job."

The coolness of those doctors and nurses, the silence of the crowd in Quelimane watching the *amnistiados*, the patience of the people in the airline office, Paulo Oliveira's personal safety—these were all signs, it seemed to me, not of any special maturity or extreme passivity but of the almost inconceivable adversity that most Mozambicans had endured.

20

All of southern Mozambique lives in the shadow of the neighboring giant, South Africa. When Lourenço Marques was built, in the late nineteenth century, it was to serve the mines and industry of the Transvaal as a port. The Portuguese colonial government sold its main exploitable resource, cheap labor, to the South African mines, and the Portuguese settlers were endlessly dependent on South African goods and know-how. Even when the Portuguese built the Cahora Bassa dam, a huge hydroelectric project in northwestern Mozambique (it is the largest dam in Africa, the fifth largest in the world), its design ensured that the bulk of its electricity would go directly to South Africa, and that Maputo would still have to get its electricity from South Africa. After independence, Frelimo sought to reduce economic ties to South Africa, arranging, for example, to sell the oil from the Maputo refinery (which had been built to serve South Africa) to Brazil, to buy chlorine for the capital's water supply from Brazil, and, after Zimbabwean independence, to buy coal and grain from Zimbabwe.[1] But the economic integration of southern Mozambique with South Africa was very thorough—by 1977, South Africa had already replaced Portugal as Mozambique's largest supplier of imports, and was also the source of 80 percent of the country's hard-currency earnings[2]—and most of the few gains made in reducing dependence were reversed as Mozambique's economy was buried by the war. Mozambique supported international economic sanctions against South Africa but, like a number of other states in the region, was in no position to impose sanctions itself. Indeed, comprehensive international sanctions clearly needed to include provisions for increased aid to Mozambique and its neighbors.

In Maputo, the giant's shadow was deep indeed. Television was full of South African programming: Afrikaner schoolchildren chanting a martial tune between clips of sports bloopers (gymnasts missing their launch on the long horse) and dog tricks (a poodle on a jet ski, a Doberman catching Frisbees in the park). At the market, every second product—even the onions—came from South Africa. Although Pretoria had sharply cut the number of Mozambicans allowed to work in the Transvaal mines, men all over southern Mozambique still wore the gum boots and hard hats issued to miners. The deepest part of the South African shadow, though, was military. In 1974, the South African Army, acting on the orders of Defense Minister (later President) P. W. Botha, actually prepared an invasion to prevent Frelimo's accession to power, and an armored column reportedly reached the Mozambican border before it was disabled by troops sent by Prime Minister B. J. Vorster, who was pursuing a détente with black-ruled Africa at the time.[3] Maputo is only forty easily traversed miles from the South African border, so it is understandable that Frelimo military strategy after independence concentrated at first on preparation for an invasion. Although the real threat turned out to be another guerrilla war, South Africa had launched a number of raids into Maputo and its suburbs. In 1981, South African commandos simply drove across the border and destroyed three houses in a Maputo suburb, killing thirteen members of the African National Congress and a Portuguese bystander.[4] In 1983, a dozen South African jets strafed two Maputo suburbs with special fragmentation rockets, killing three factory workers, a child, a soldier, and one member of the ANC (he was washing a car) and injuring forty other Mozambicans, most of them women and children.[5] Later that year, commandos bombed the ANC office in Maputo.

Mozambique was virtually helpless against this sort of attack. South Africa's armed forces dwarfed those of all its neighbors combined. South Africa could mobilize half a million troops (the Mozambican Army had, as noted, fewer than thirty thousand men); it had ten times the number of combat aircraft

Mozambique did and twenty times the number of armored fighting vehicles.[6] It also had vastly superior firepower—including, according to many reports, nuclear weapons. Some of Frelimo's supporters, including Fidel Castro, were triumphalist in their view of the liberation struggle in South Africa, believing that military and economic pressure could cause the apartheid regime to fall relatively quickly.[7] But Frelimo's leadership was obliged to be realistic about the balance of forces both in the region and inside South Africa, and President Chissano clearly believed that he had to work out a modus vivendi with Pretoria. It was toward that end that he had been trying to revive the Nkomati Accord. Chissano also seemed to believe that the capitalist democracies, although they had historically been Pretoria's allies, might now be persuaded to help South Africa's neighbors survive the external shocks of apartheid's death agonies.

Inevitably, people in Maputo ended up doing a lot of South Africa watching. The politics and responsibilities of certain military figures in Pretoria—not only Brigadier Van Niekerk but also Major-General Van Tonder, Colonel Breytenbach, and Colonel Grobelaar—were as well known among the Mozambican intelligentsia as they were among observers in South Africa. The changing strength of a hard-line faction, say, on the politico-military State Security Council was charted closely in Maputo, because it would likely have consequences for the war in Mozambique. While I was in Maputo, a popular explanation for apparent contradictions in South African policy—for instance, Pretoria's eagerness to provide security for the Cahora Bassa transmission lines that Renamo sabotaged[8]—had South Africa taking a "corridor approach" to Mozambique; that is, continuing to sponsor widespread disruption and destruction while securing a few corridors, like Cahora Bassa and Maputo's harbor, for its own use.[9] The harbor, it was said, was being eyed in connection with sanctions-busting schemes that Pretoria was developing.

Pretoria's relations with Renamo were, naturally, the subject of abundant speculation. Every *deslocado* or *amnistiado* who could describe a South African supply drop, every mysterious parachute recovered from a lake, every helicopter overflight, or suspicious movement in the Comoros Islands (a tiny country, less than 200 miles off the northern coast of Mozambique, whose leader was close to South Africa but whose obscurity made it a highly deniable transshipment point for Renamo-bound supplies)[10] fed the Renamo-Pretoria rumor mill in Maputo.[11] South African motives were dissected with Thomist care. In July 1988, four American journalists flew in to central Mozambique to interview Afonso Dhlakama.[12] The journalists refused to reveal what country they had flown from, but it was clear that their trip served the purposes of both Renamo—the story that appeared in the *New York Times* actually ended up in the Renamo propaganda packet—and South Africa, which was always at pains to publicize Renamo's *other* sources of support (the role of the Comoros was first revealed by Pretoria). The American stories met Pretoria's objectives by stressing the fact that the reporters traveled on a plane that also carried laptop computers supplied to Renamo by an American businessman.[13] There were reports that the journalists believed their trip was arranged over the *objections* of the South African military, a quaint notion which led to speculation that Pretoria had played them a nice game of journalistic three-card monte. There were even reports that Afonso Dhlakama was actually living in the Transvaal at the time and was flown into Mozambique for special occasions, such as the interview with the Americans.[14]

The place in Maputo for foreigners to hear this kind of political scuttlebutt and soothsaying was the Hotel Polana. A grand colonial pile, the Polana was built on spacious grounds overlooking the sea just along the bluff from President Chissano's house. Since foreign delegations, officials, journalists, businessmen, and international-aid workers awaiting other housing all stayed at the Polana, the local elites were obliged to put in regular appearances there. The hotel ended up showcasing all the peculiar contrasts of late-revolutionary Mozambique. The doormen wore grandees' full-length braided uniforms, while the front desk sold a postcard captioned "Luta Armada." (The photograph on that card contained an unusually honest image of African bush war: just a line of peasants walking barefoot on a trail through dry grass and sun-baked dirt with heavy-looking bundles on their heads.) One evening, in the Polana's restaurant, I asked José Luís Cabaço about how the party planned to handle the confrontation with the power of the national bourgeoisie that the growth of the private sector would inevitably cause. Cabaço, a portly, genial, urbane man with a gray Vandyke, who was a construction executive in Lourenço Marques during the *luta armada* and used his position to photograph strategic sites for Frelimo under cover of commerce, stroked his beard, laughed, and said, "I am cleaning my gun." He was sitting with a beautiful young woman from the Italian Communist Party, who had come to make arrangements for a visit by her boss, Giovanni Berlinguer. Because Cabaço was educated (in sociology) in Italy, he handled the visits of dignitaries from Italy. His most recent guest had been Pope John Paul II. The Pope's visit was generally considered a big success, not least because His Holiness did not call for talks with Renamo, as the government had dreaded he might.

The main action at the Polana, though, was capitalist. Businessmen from all over the world hustled through the lobby, dealing out their business cards, and huddled with government officials over lawn tables beside the swimming pool. As Mozambique ostensibly opened its doors to private foreign investment, everybody and his corporate brother seemed to be scrambling for the Land Rover franchise, the office-computer franchise, the oil-exploration and mining concessions. Mozambique's natural wealth—which includes large coal reserves, iron ore, and some of the world's largest deposits of tantalite, not to mention vast tracts of arable land—has been virtually unexploited.

And yet all the wheeling and dealing I observed might have been an illusion. There was another wave of foreign-investment interest after the signing of the Nkomati Accord, but the investment itself never materialized. Even South African businessmen who had pressured their government to make peace so that they could get back into Mozambique lost interest when they saw the extent of the war's destruction. In fact, the only real money to arrive had been four million dollars for the construction of a new, heavily fortified South African trade mission, which was just down the street from the Polana. Many of the accents to be heard around the hotel were South African, some of them belonging to quite voluble characters, happy to explain how they were already using Maputo to get around certain Western trade sanctions.

The true composition of foreign investment so far was probably best reflected in rumors that Italy was preparing to resume construction of the great sabotaged hotel along the beach north of Maputo. It was being said that the Italians planned, when the building was completed, to fill it with the offices of international-aid organizations. Most foreign investment in projects outside Maputo simply had to await improvement in the *situação*.

One of the few companies that could consider doing much in the meantime was a British firm, Defence Systems Limited, and that was because it had its own security expertise. DSL, which provided security for New York's John F. Kennedy Airport and many American embassies, and was training the troops, both Malawian and Mozambican, assigned to guard the rehabilitation work on the railway between Malawi and the northern port of Nacala, was a much-desired partner in joint ventures. Its chief, David Maxwell, a former member of the elite British military unit the Special Air Service, was living with his wife in a superb ocean-view suite at the Polana.

One place where commercial opportunities were not restricted by the war was offshore. Samora Machel was said to have been unhappy with Soviet overharvesting of Mozambican prawns, and the Japanese now had the franchise. I met a young Greek businessman who was trying to wrest some of the prawn business away from the Japanese. He was a soft-looking fellow with light, frizzy hair, wearing a red Lacoste golf shirt. He was the scion of a ship-owning family, he said, and he had spent a month in Maputo negotiating to lease two coastal tramps to the government. He wasn't actually interested in the deal for the boats, he said, but wanted the industrial marine business license, which he would need to introduce a prawn boat. "My father always says, 'Where is the Japanese, there is the money.'" The reason he had been a month in Maputo—which he absolutely hated and compared to "prison," because he could find nothing to do there—was that the Japanese had gone to the government and blocked his business license application, so that in the end he had to settle for a semi-industrial license, which would not permit him to introduce a prawn boat.

"But Mozambique is a virgin country," he said. "And now is the time to get in. As soon as this war ends, there will be a lot of money to be made. In five years, you can make enough to live for the rest of your life." The great thing about Mozambicans, he said, was that "they are still so cheap. You can get them for nothing." The workers on the coastal tramps would be paid less than a hundred dollars a month, and the bribes that officials wanted were absolutely laughable. The minister with whom he had negotiated for the coastal tramps—which would be leased, with Greek captain, mate, and mechanic, for three thousand dollars a day—had asked, very meekly, for a personal commission of ten dollars a day. "They are *so stupid*," the Greek marveled. "They are like *this*." He knocked on the brass frame of a coffee table. It would all change soon enough, of course. Official extortion in Nigeria had become so onerous that his family had had to abandon a lucrative ship-fueling business there. As he spoke, the scion spotted a Japanese family across the lobby lining up for a group photograph. He studied them unhappily for a minute, then erupted, "Aren't they ugly!"

I asked if he was planning to make his own fortune in Mozambique. He said his wife would never agree to live there, and changed the subject, wanting to know if I could give him the name of a good bookie in New York. He already had a great bookie in Los Angeles. He could place bets with him from anywhere in the world, even Maputo. He had been ecstatic, by the way, to hear that Ben Johnson had been stripped of his Olympic gold medal, because he had had money on Carl Lewis. His personal favorite sprinter, though, was still Calvin Schmidt. He loved America, he really did. His family had spent every Christmas for the past twenty-five years in Caesars Palace, Las Vegas. It was a perfect venue—it was *built* for celebration. As for the family business, he said, "I am only interested—" He stopped himself. "Not 'I'—'my father'—I am nothing. I am only rubbish. Mozambique is only a rubbish little business for my family. That is why they send me."

I checked into the scion's story about bribing a minister to lease the coastal tramps, and concluded that it was just something he had fabricated to make himself feel better.

He was also wrong about there being nothing to do in Maputo. Even for those whose Portuguese was not equal to the rowdy, thriving amateur theater, there was plenty of entertainment. I heard good jazz, saw spectacular national dance, and discovered the work of some powerfully talented painters during a tour of the National Museum and, later, on visits to studios. In the museum's basement, there were rows of old Portuguese paintings of kings, queens, and archbishops stacked in their heavy, gold-flake frames—the curator said they had been taken down from the corridors of public buildings, and were of no interest now, but someday they might be, to someone—while the main rooms of the museum bristled and roared and sang with contemporary African painting and sculpture. The mood of the major postindependence works was pervadingly anguished and sad. "It has been a time of suffering," the curator said simply. There wasn't a scrap of Socialist Realism in sight, or even of political themes. Walking down the street near the museum later, I came across a group of Makonde sculptors under a tree in a scruffy backyard, and I stopped to talk.

The Makondes are known throughout Mozambique for their ferocity, independence, sculpture, and dance. The sculptors in the yard said that they had been living in the northern city of Nampula, having left their homeland on the Mueda Plateau because the war had made it too difficult to get their work to market. The National Museum had invited them to Maputo to produce some work for a forthcoming show in Paris, which the museum hoped would set to rest any question that Makonde sculptors produced only airport art. The sculptors had been dubious, but one of them had finally come to Maputo to check it out, had seen the yard with the tree, had pronounced the tree a good one, and had persuaded his mates to come ahead. They had been there several weeks now, working in the yard, living in the adjoining house—there were six or seven of them, all men. They ranged in age from their twenties to their fifties, but all had a similar quality of great self-possession. Several had filed teeth, and all had ritual scars on their cheeks. A couple of the sculptors were quietly working, but, since it was a Sunday, most of them were taking it easy, listening to the radio and getting ready to go to the big football match, Mozambique versus Egypt, at the stadium that afternoon. They seemed happy to show me the pieces they had made since coming to Maputo.

All were more or less pillar-shaped, carved from logs of ebony or sandalwood, and they stood from three to six feet high. Some were realistic, showing families or villages all connected in a totemic tangle in a style known as *ujamaa*. Others were more fantastic, full of animals and extraordinary changelings, and still others were almost abstract, with breasts and hooves and teeth emerging only occasionally from a rarefied skein of polished wood. All were of extremely high technical quality, and each told a story. The sculptors told me the stories of their pieces. One was about a widowed devil who, having lost her husband in the war, was now wandering with her madcap suckling. Another was about a village besieged by enemies angry about the amorous exploits of one of the villagers among their women; if you knew where to look, you could see the Lothario showing how it was done. Most of the sculptures were about the sorrows visited upon human beings by the four-eared, bug-eyed, snake-bodied devils that live in the mountains and frequent the roads on dark nights. Did such devils also live in Maputo? The sculptors laughed. Of course they did.

Part Five

Manhiça

21

Everyone knew that the highways out of Maputo were not safe to travel. Reports of Renamo ambushes had been almost daily fare for years. Of course, ambushes can happen only where there is traffic, and the fact was that the highways around Maputo were full of traffic. People had to get from town to country, and so they took their chances. Most of the traffic was in convoys with military escorts, but going by convoy was no guarantee against attack. Convoys were regularly ambushed. In October 1987, at least 278 people were killed in one attack on the national highway fifty miles north of Maputo.[1] In such circumstances one's conception of what is safe collapses into a basic equation: if we got through, it was a safe trip, whether the bus behind us was attacked or not.

In September 1988, I rode up the highway from Maputo to Manhiça, a rural district where Renamo was very active (the highway massacre the previous October had occurred in Manhiça), with Lina Magaia, an official in the Ministry of Agriculture. Lina drove the route every week, and she did not like to travel in convoys. "If something happens, you cannot get away," she said. "All the cars and trucks start to run into each other." So we set off unaccompanied in her van, a new, charcoal-gray, four-wheel-drive Mitsubishi Pajero, our only armament an automatic pistol on the seat between us. It was an overcast day. My plan was to spend a few days in Manhiça, where Lina worked as a sort of all-purpose rural-extension officer.

The soldiers at the checkpoints all knew Lina. They called her Mama Magaia and tried to bum cigarettes from her. Those we passed on the highway waved. At one checkpoint, she talked for several minutes with a commander. They spoke Shangaan, which left me out, but they were obviously discussing the road ahead. Lina gave the commander a pack of cigarettes. We saw a couple of convoys heading for the city but no traffic going our way. The land we were passing through was deserted. It looked like farmland reverting to scrub. We came to a large, spooky cleared stretch, in an area called Pateque. I had been told in Maputo by a local journalist that Pateque was one of the most dangerous stretches of road in the country—he said he would not travel it for anything—but Lina said his information was outdated. "This was the worst part of the road," she said. "So I went to President Samora—this was in 1985—and I asked if there wasn't something he could do to improve the security here. His solution was to bulldoze the forest away from the road, to improve the visibility. You see, now you have time to take some action *before* you are ambushed." It was true: there were no trees within several hundred yards of the road, and few places for attackers to hide. All the bulldozing had revealed a number of burned, bullet-riddled farmhouses. Lina pointed out a group of empty huts and said, "Those were used to house miners traveling between South Africa and their homes. Then the bandits used them as hiding places before their attacks."

Beyond Pateque, at a place called Maluana, the forest came back to the edge of the road. Lina said, "Now I cannot talk. I must pay attention." I began to notice burned, overturned vehicles along the shoulder of the road. Lina started driving at a very high speed—seventy-five miles an hour or more. We screamed around curves and didn't slow down even when we came to an army checkpoint. The soldiers hurried out of the way, seeming to understand. After several miles, we came to a group of inhabited houses, a place called Esperança, and Lina finally slowed down. She reached into my bag, pulled out a fifth of Scotch I had brought, and, with my permission, took two slugs from the bottle. She sighed. "Now we can relax," she said.

I felt fairly safe with Lina. She had been working in Manhiça since 1982 and knew the area well. In fact, she had been going there, she told me, since she was a child. Her mother was from

Manhiça, and Lina had used to visit her grandmother there. She had watched the war come to Manhiça, and in 1986 she had moved her four children back to Maputo. Now she usually saw them and her husband only on weekends. But she had not considered abandoning her work in Manhiça, she said.

Lina was, at forty-three, a formidable woman. She came from a prominent southern clan, the Mabjaia—the Portuguese had had trouble pronouncing the name; hence the modern form, Magaia. Her uncle was Mozambique's ambassador to Swaziland; her brother was the editor of *Tempo* magazine. Lina's father, a teacher, had become *assimilado* when she was eleven, thereby enabling her to go to a state school in Maputo. She had studied economics in Lisbon on a scholarship until the 1974 coup and then had left to join Frelimo in Tanzania. There she received nine months of military training and rose to the rank of sergeant. The war ended before she saw combat, and she left the army in 1977, but there was still, I thought, plenty of military dash to her manner. She handled a pistol as if she had been born with one in her hand. On the day we drove to Manhiça, she was dressed entirely in black—sweatpants, sweatshirt, boots, beret. She was big—tall, and a good 200 pounds—with a big, husky voice and an enormous laugh. She had a mobile, expressive face and a quick tongue—not, all in all, the deferential bearing found among most African women in southern Mozambique. Lina also had a quick pen. Her weekly column for *Notícias*, the Maputo daily paper, was popular for its attacks on incompetent officials.

We reached Manhiça in the afternoon and found a large convoy, perhaps a hundred vehicles, getting ready to leave for Maputo. The people in the cars and trucks all smiled when they saw us arriving safely from the south. Manhiça is a pretty town, spread out on a green plateau above the Incomati River. The cement town probably has 2,000 residents, the cane town many times that. The main commercial street, which is the national highway, is flanked by old-fashioned pillared sidewalks. Two small hotel restaurants compete for the carriage trade. We turned off the highway and followed a dirt road out through the cane town, where little children started rushing at the car, all shouting excitedly, "Lina Magaia! Lina Magaia!" Lina pointed to a row of burned houses. "The bandits attacked here two weeks ago today," she said. "They burned forty-seven houses, and they wrecked the office of our farm, Ribangue, which is just coming up here. But the attack was a victory for our militia. They killed four bandits and captured a bazooka and a Mauser."

We arrived at Ribangue, a dilapidated farm headquarters at the edge of the plateau (the fields were down in the flood-plain), and were met by Domingos Jasse, a solid-looking, mild-mannered man with a glass eye, whom Lina introduced as the head of defense for the farm. (She later told me that Jasse had lost his eye in the *luta armada*. He had been living in Malawi when the war started, had gone to Tanzania to join Frelimo, and had fought for ten years as a guerrilla in his home province of Niassa.) Jasse showed me the damage to the farm's office— burned files, a burned desk—and gave me a blow-by-blow account of the attack two weeks before. The farm's militia, consisting of eighty-seven people with only five automatic weapons, had received word that an attack was coming and had moved out into the fields. The *bandidos*, they knew, were after the food, seeds, tools, bicycles, and other goods stored in the farm's magazine. When they entered the office and started smashing it up, the militia ambushed them. Two militiamen were injured when a fleeing *bandido* threw a grenade, but otherwise it had been a rout. The *bandidos* had left one body behind, and it had been handed over to the man's family, who lived nearby, but the militia now knew they had killed three more, because a young woman whom the *bandidos* had kidnapped—they had kidnapped eleven people from the adjoining cane town during the raid—had returned and told them so. She also said that the *bandidos* had had a kidnapped peasant carry one of their wounded, and had killed the peasant when the wounded man died. The *bandidos* had beaten up the young woman, and they had given her a message for the people at Ribangue: they would be coming back for their bazooka and their Mauser and to place flowers on the grave of their fallen comrade. Jasse showed me the bazooka and the Mauser, now stored with the other valuables in the farm's magazine. The *bandidos* would have to fight very hard to get these back, he said quietly.

Lina said she only wished that the newspapers covered militia victories the way they covered highway massacres, and then she showed me around the farm. There were pigsties, a hen-house, a duck farm, a large shed full of rabbits, and 600 acres of corn, beans, cabbage, bananas, and other crops. The fields were divided into small family plots, which suggested a cooperative farm, but Lina denied that Ribangue was a cooperative. It was "a project," she said. Whatever it was, she was clearly in charge of it. She upbraided workers who had not fed the chickens, went over salary sheets, and scolded the salary clerk for not paying out raises that had been set. When I asked if she received a salary herself, she said she did, but added that she did not get paid if the farm did not make a profit. Though the fields at Ribangue seemed to be flourishing, Lina said they could be far more productive. The main problems were irrigation and drainage. They badly needed a backhoe to reopen drainage ditches that had been neglected since independence. Lina wondered if I would ask Melissa Wells to help her get a backhoe. We met a man in rags in a beanfield. He grinned when he saw Lina and handed us two ears of roasted corn, which we chewed as we went bumping around the muddy roads of Ribangue.

I was supposed to stay with Lina in Manhiça, but she already had three houseguests, North Korean technicians working on an irrigation project, and they panicked when they heard that an American was coming. They were afraid, Lina said, that if their embassy heard that they had stayed in the same house as an American—or were even seen speaking to one—they would be in big trouble. They could be sent back to Korea and could lose their jobs. I had passed the North Korean Embassy in Maputo a few times and had been impressed by the tone of a display in the front yard—it was all photographs of the recent visit of the Great Leader, Comrade Kim Il Sung, to Ulan Bator, Mongolia, with captions, in English, pointing out the "rapturous" crowds waving "fervently" while wishing long life with "infinite respect" to an old, dour-looking fellow in a gray suit. So I was sympathetic, and happy to stay in a house around the corner from Lina's. (But Manhiça is a small town, and on my third day there the inevitable happened: I ran into the Koreans on the street. Without thinking, I waved. They blanched and turned away, and we all just pretended that it hadn't happened.) It was a small, bare, three-bedroom cement house that, from the outside, might have been in a postwar working-class neighborhood in Fresno. The whole street had that look, in fact. Two young men who worked at Ribangue also stayed in the house.

I was thoroughly confused by everything I had heard about the war in Manhiça, so that evening Lina brought over a huge map of the Manhiça district and we spread it out on the floor. The map, which had been drawn in 1969, was outdated but terrifically detailed, showing every house and hut in the district. Renamo had first come to Manhiça in force in 1984, Lina said, crossing from South Africa into the sparsely inhabited western parts of the district. She showed me wild swamplands, far from any road, where the bandits had established their first big encampments, and the routes they had used to move into more populated areas, and where they had first started preying on the national highway. The map clearly showed why the stretch of highway at Pateque had become so dangerous: there were many miles of heavy forest cover on either side of it, with no roads and no villages. A second major group of bandits, Lina said, had come to Manhiça from the north, after a Frelimo offensive in Gaza in 1985. They had moved down the left bank of the Incomati, preying on the villages in the valley and in the sandy, forested hills between the river and the coast. (The name *Incomati* is the Portuguese version of Nkomati. The famous Accord was signed where the river, which rises in Swaziland and then flows northward into South Africa, crosses the border into Mozambique; ironically, the first Renamo force to enter Manhiça was probably sent out of South Africa in accordance with the then-new "nonaggression" pact.) The Incomati River describes a long, lazy loop inside Mozambique until, as it passes Manhiça town, it is flowing south. The coastal hills across the river from the town were a roadless maze, full of hideouts, and, Lina said, the empty beaches beyond them were ideal for resupply by sea.

I wondered why, if the bandits had come from far away, the family of the fighter killed at Ribangue was living in Manhiça. Lina said that the composition of the local Renamo bands had changed over the years. The commanders were still all Ndau-speakers, from the north, but now many of the troops were local men. In fact, Lina believed that there were no longer any large Renamo bases in Manhiça but instead just a number of small bands with excellent radio communications, which enabled them to mass for large attacks and then disperse. She showed me on the map where the bands tended to camp, where they went for water and food, where they attacked at different times of day, where army offensives had secured some areas, where villages had been burned, where others had been abandoned. And as Lina waxed military in her descriptions of the fighting over the years, the tactics and countertactics used in Manhiça, one thing became clear, even to nonmilitary me: Renamo could not be defeated. Even in Manhiça—though it is near the capital, has a railway and a highway running through it, and is, for Mozambique, relatively developed and heavily populated—there were vast, roadless areas where guerrillas could hide. It occurred to me that if the entire army were brought to the Manhiça district—which constituted less than 1 percent of Mozambique's area—its 30,000 soldiers might have a chance of actually securing the district, of making it safe for the people who lived there to grow their crops and live their lives without fear of attack. *Might.*

And Lina, to my surprise, agreed. But the army was not the answer, she said. There would never be enough soldiers to defend Manhiça. No, the answer was militias: local people, well trained and well armed. They were fighting to protect their own property, and so had a level of motivation that soldiers would always lack. What was more, they knew the area, and they often had advance word of Renamo attacks. Many people were disenchanted with the popular militia—the Territorial Defense Force, it was now being called. They said that militiamen were dangerous, drunken, undisciplined thieves. That attitude, which made Lina furious, had been most cruelly manifested, she said, at a meeting in Manhiça the previous Saturday. Local private farmers and shopkeepers had gathered and, at Lina's urging, had agreed to support the reorganized district militia, but at the insulting level of 1,000 meticais (less than two dollars) a month each. Lina was still spitting mad about the outcome of the meeting. "We *must* help ourselves," she said. "The army cannot help us. The security in this district could be much, much better. The bandits are not really so strong here." The Italians, who funded two of the four foreign-aid projects in Manhiça (there were also a West German project and the Korean irrigation work), kept and fed *their* own militias, defending *their* projects. They had considered leaving the district after a series of attacks, but they had been persuaded to try militia defense; and it, according to Lina, was working. The least that local property owners could do was match the faith of foreigners in local people! Militias, I gathered, had been the subject of some of Lina's columns in *Noticias*.

It was getting late. I had noticed, under the bed where I would be sleeping, an AK-47 Soviet assault rifle, and I asked Lina about it. She said, "That is for your self-defense, in case the militia fails." She checked to make sure that the rifle was loaded, showed me how to set it on automatic fire, and said good night.

Thinking about it afterward, I wondered why Lina had said, "in case the *militia* fails." The town was full of regular army. Earlier in the evening, in the commercial district, I had seen hundreds of people bedding down for the night on the canopied sidewalks. They were from the cane town, Lina said, and from nearby villages; they were afraid to sleep in their homes. Every few yards, a young soldier had sat, cradling an automatic rifle, guarding the sleepers. And open trucks full of soldiers were cruising the streets, the soldiers singing lustily. They were letting people know, Lina said, that they were being protected. They had already come past the house several times.

As I was getting ready for bed, I asked one of my housemates, a quiet young man named Alexander, why Lina had not mentioned the army when she left.

Alexander, who had studied animal husbandry in South Africa and, as a result, spoke English, looked at me strangely and said, "You have heard her. She believes that the militia, not the army, must protect us."

I asked Alexander if he had a gun.

"No," he said.

I asked him what he thought about my having one.

He shrugged. "The chap who usually sleeps in that room keeps that gun. I think it is not a good idea."

I poured Alexander a glass of Scotch and asked him why.

He said, "Because when the bandits come, they don't come just one or two. They come one or two hundred. You cannot fight them alone. And if they see you have a gun, they will consider you the enemy."

I found it hard to believe that Renamo ever came to that part of town, much less in a force of hundreds, and said so.

Alexander stared at me. "They come," he said.

I asked him when Renamo had last come into the center of Manhiça.

"The last time they killed many people here in the cement town was January 12," he said. "They broke into the shops on the national road and they killed eleven people. But the last attack we suffered here was three months ago—in June. They came into this road." Alexander gestured at the Fresno-like street outside the window. "I was alone here, and I was sleeping, and nobody came to warn me. When I woke up, I heard the bandits singing and firing their guns. I ran outside. There were hundreds of bandits marching in this road. They were beating drums, firing guns in the air, and shouting. It was very dark, so I just stood next to the house and said nothing, and they said nothing to me. They were singing, and they were shouting, 'Where are the men in this town? Where are the soldiers? We are the men in this town!' They went to the national road, and they looted the shops. They took clothes, and they just left their old clothes there in the road. They even took the curtains from the hotels. No one was killed in that attack. But that was when the last white people living here in Manhiça town left. They owned the hotels, and I think they didn't want to see the bandits next time wearing clothes made from their curtains."

I repeated the bandits' question. "Where *were* the soldiers?"

Alexander waved a hand toward the river. "The bandits came from three directions at once," he said. "Everybody ran in the fourth direction, including the soldiers. Why should they stay and fight? The bandits are so much stronger." Alexander regarded me seriously. "We have a very bad situation here," he said, finally.

We finished our drinks and said good night.

Later, lying in bed, I tried to recall if I had heard anything about militiamen standing guard nearby. Was there even any militia *to* fail? The month before, there had been a major militia failure a few miles south, at an agro-industrial complex called Maragra. Lina had been very upset about it. From 1982 to 1986, she had been the deputy director of Maragra, and she had created and trained the militia there herself. It had repulsed a number of Renamo attacks, and the reputation it gained had caused many people to move to Maragra. But then, in August, a late-night attack had caught the Maragra militia napping. Six hundred Renamo fighters had overrun the complex, killing twenty-one people and wounding many. The most horrifying aspect of the attack was that a number of teenage boys *from* Maragra had joined the bandits in looting the homes of their neighbors and had departed with Renamo. Lina had been lamenting the Maragra militia's fatal overconfidence, but the community's problems clearly went far deeper than that. The war in Manhiça contained a large amount of delinquency, apparently, and nonpolitical banditry, as well as organized military activity, possibly supported by South Africa. The threat hanging over Ribangue sounded like an Appalachian family feud or an inner-city gang fight—"We're comin' back for our Mauser, and we're gonna put flowers on our buddy's grave!"

I decided that, Alexander's wise words notwithstanding, I liked having a rifle within reach. Somehow, perhaps by reducing, if only symbolically, my sense of vulnerability, it made the possibility of sleep slightly greater. Still, I slept poorly. The problem was not so much that I was thinking about a Renamo attack as that my bed's mattress was thin and lumpy and had a horrible odor that seemed to get stronger every hour. Finally, after a long night, roosters began to crow, birds began to chirp. The dawn revealed a small, too blue room—blue walls, blue curtains—and slowly transformed the assault rifle from a dream-dark lifeline into a battered, prosaic old gun.

Manhiça was typical of nothing in Mozambique. Officially, it wasn't even part of "the emergency." None of Maputo province was. There was, therefore, no free distribution of food or clothes in Manhiça. In truth, while no one was starving in Manhiça, there were plenty of unofficial *afetados* and *deslocados*. There was also large-scale unemployment, caused by the cutbacks in migrant mine labor in South Africa. For generations, young men from Manhiça, and from all over southern Mozambique, had been forced to work in the mines for some years before they could start farming and raising a family; it was the only way to earn enough to buy cattle, land, and a house, and to pay bride-price. All the people driven by the war from the remote areas of the district into the towns had, in combination with the legions of the unemployed, created intense pressure on the land. Again, this kind of pressure was unusual in land-rich Mozambique. The highway, the railway, the abundant water, the soil's fertility, Maputo's proximity—all made Manhiça a special case. And the fact that it was in the far south, where the people spoke Ronga and Shangaan, and had been exposed to modern life and ideas, made it, politically, natural Frelimo territory—in contrast to many other parts of the country. And yet, paradoxically, as I traveled around Manhiça, I began to feel as if I were seeing all of Mozambique's problems, and all the patterns of the war, in perfect, murky microcosm.

The murk here, as everywhere, shrouded not only the war but local farming and living arrangements. Lina said that communal villages had been a failure and that the only one still functioning in Manhiça was a model project that received special government support; and yet we visited at least two other communal villages that seemed to be functioning. Both were building schools, and both had militias. I never did find out what sort of operation Ribangue was. Every time I asked someone working there who owned the farm, the answer was "Lina." Lina, however, denied owning it. What had probably happened was what had happened on many cooperative farms: the Ministry of Agriculture had ended up running the show, with little or no formal declaration. In any event, Ribangue was just one of many projects that engaged Lina's attention. Her job description was simple, she said: she was supposed to find out what Manhiça's farmers needed, and then go to the government to try to get those needs met. But her actual work seemed to involve everything from importing bicycles (the trading network in Manhiça, like that almost everywhere in rural Mozambique, had collapsed since independence, and Lina believed that she and the Ministry of Agriculture needed to take up some of the slack), through diagnosing crop diseases, to training militias.

There were many kinds of farmers in Manhiça: subsistence farmers, wealthier peasants, small and large private farmers, Portuguese, Chinese, African, and those on cooperatives and state farms. Lina's decisions about where to focus her assistance were critical, and highly political. Was she still working toward Frelimo's revolutionary goal, "the socialization of the countryside"? Lina seemed impatient with the question. The former economics student pointed out that Marx had never said that agriculture had to be collectivized, and, as for Lenin, "He had his own cultural-historical situation to deal with, and we have ours." Private farmers, she conceded, were a long-term problem, but Frelimo's medium-term goal was simply to reduce the social and economic gaps between farm workers and their employers. And the government's short-term goal was even simpler: to increase production.

This was Lina's obsession as well as the government's. She talked farm talk with every farmer we saw: the tomatoes killed by the frost; the rice that was getting too much water; the ominous yellowing of the onion tops. She constantly rued her own lack of technical expertise. She needed surveyors, a hydraulic engineer, and an agronomist. First, though, she needed vehicles for them. And, since they would probably have to be foreigners, she needed houses. There were no houses suitable for foreigners available in Manhiça, so new ones would have to be built. Lina also dearly wanted to establish a farm-equipment shop in Manhiça, selling seeds, pesticides, and pumps, perhaps offering pump and tractor maintenance and repair. She was very excited about the possibility of growing rice in the bottom of a lush valley she showed me, but she was in despair over a mealybug infestation that was destroying the district's cassava crop—she had no idea how to combat it. She would give *anything*, she said, to have an agronomist here in Manhiça.

Lina's politics did show sometimes. In a communal village called Malavele, we stopped to inspect a school under construction. It was a set of prefab buildings, financed by the Italians, being put up by a crew from Maputo. Later, in another communal village, called Muinguine, we looked at another school under construction. It was being built by the villagers themselves out of bricks made with a simple press from earth found next to the school. Not only would the bricks be more durable than the Styrofoam-core walls being used in Malavele, Lina said, "but imagine how those Styrofoam walls will burn when the bandits decide to destroy that school! This school the people of Muinguine will defend and maintain because they have financed and built it themselves. This is my favorite village in Manhiça!" Lina also loved the Association of Agriculturalists of Muinguine. They were a group of twenty small farmers—not peasants but teachers and shopkeepers and mechanics who had acquired parcels of good land, forty or fifty acres apiece, on the right bank of the Incomati when the white owners fled after independence—and they had pooled their resources and bought a new tractor from the government. When they weren't using the tractor, they rented it out to nonmembers for 4,000 meticais (about seven dollars) an hour. Lina and I spent several hours with some of the Muinguine farmers, bumping around their fields in Lina's van, with Lina asking questions and taking notes.

Afterward, she exulted about the success, the forward-looking self-sufficiency of the Muinguine farmers. Had I seen their tractor, how well it still ran? I had seen it, and the sight had recalled something José Luís Cabaço said: "Our first goal was to promote the self-capacity of the peasants. But our fascination with modern technology led us into a great contradiction. We made a big investment in mechanization, but we forgot culture. The people making the decisions are urban, technically oriented. They have always been around cars, so they know the sound of a motor that's not running right. But if you put a peasant who is thirty years old into a car, no matter how well he is trained, he won't hear the motor the same way an urban person hears it. The relation between man and machine is a cultural relation. The concept of maintenance is not learned in a training course. It takes a generation. So we introduced tractors, creating a dependency on the systems of support for the tractors—exactly what we did not want. And then maintenance was neglected, and we lost most of the tractors!" The loss had been greatest on state farms, where workers felt the least responsibility for the new machinery. There seemed, I thought, no danger that the Muinguine farmers would neglect *their* tractor.

Wandering the back roads of Manhiça with Lina was part celebrity tour. Everywhere we went, the children ran at the van shouting, "Lina Magaia! Lina Magaia!" Peasant women gazed at her adoringly as we sped past. Lina looked entirely unlike any of the other women I saw there. They wore *capulanas* and head scarves; she was now wearing blue jeans, pink elf boots, and a loose lavender knit blouse, the short sleeves of which kept blowing back over her shoulders. And yet she seemed beloved: the longer we drove, the more the back of the van filled with gifts of onions, bananas, lettuce, carrots, sugarcane. Many bundles were placed there by unseen hands while we were out tramping around in the fields.

Not everybody was ecstatic to see Lina. Several times, we came upon individuals with whom she was unhappy—"these so-called technicians they send me," she called them. They were all young men, and they all looked stricken on being found lounging behind a warehouse when they knew they were supposed to be out building a dam. After two or three of these scenes, Lina began to fume. Her biggest problem, she said, was the difficulty of delegating authority. Nobody wanted to make any decisions, so nothing got accomplished when she was not around. People had such terrible work habits! It was a hangover from colonialism. Because of slavery and forced labor, people had the habit of conserving their energy for their own *machambas*. That was why communalization had not worked. Frelimo had made a huge mistake at independence when it allowed people to start believing that life was going to be easier.

I had heard about the onset of "commandism" in relations between officials and peasants, and Lina clearly had a serious case of it going in Manhiça. Her interactions with people were hard for me to read, though. She seemed to chew out all comers without fear or favor. She was obviously a diva, self-involved and imperious. But most of her conversations were in Shangaan, so I understood nothing that was said, and several times, just when it seemed to me that she was riding roughshod over everyone, some worker would answer her more robustly than I expected, get a big laugh from everyone listening, including Lina, and then press his advantage, getting more aggressive and winning more laughs. Lina's moods were mercurial. While she was driving along in silence and I was watching her from the corner of my eye, I could see expressions of tenderness and ferocity and perplexity pass over her great fleshy features, alternating along with her thoughts.

"Do you see why I love Manhiça?" she said, sighing and waving a hand out the window. We spent most of our time in the floodplain on the right bank of the Incomati or up on the rich green bluff at its edge, but when she asked that question, we were crossing an exquisite open plain known as the Mozambique Valley. A eucalyptus windbreak ran alongside the road, which traversed brilliant fields of rice and sugarcane. "Only war could cause famine here," she said. "It's a naturally *rich* place. And it all makes me so sad. This farm here used to be João Ferreira's place. He was my favorite farmer. He worked so hard. He was going to be a Mozambican Inácio De Sousa." Inácio De Sousa, a white man, had been the biggest farmer in Manhiça.

"But João was killed last year, along with two friends, on the way home from a wedding." Lina pointed out a young *mestiço* man in a battered cowboy hat who was climbing out of a truck. "That is João's brother-in-law. He is trying to run the farm, but he is very, very young. All this unnecessary suffering!" Later, on the edge of Manhiça town, Lina pointed to an abandoned house set back in the woods. "This is where João and his friends were ambushed," she said. "The bandits hid in that house. After shooting them, they slit their throats, and took all their clothes, leaving them naked."

I asked Lina if she had ever been ambushed. She said she had not. Several times, she had come upon the scene of a fresh attack, though, and had ferried dead and wounded in her car. She had also been involved, she said, in the defense of Maragra during Renamo attacks. I asked if she had ever been threatened personally by Renamo. She had once heard that the local bandits were hunting "the lady who wears black and organizes the militias," she said. "That was when I always wore black. But they never found me." Another time, in Tete province, she had heard a captured *bandido* say, "This is a real war. It has even been written in a book." She assumed that he meant a collection of her stories about Renamo atrocities in Manhiça, which had originally appeared in *Tempo* and had then been published as a book called *Dumba Nengue*. "Dumba nengue" was a local expression. It meant, literally, "Trust your feet," and in Manhiça it referred to farming areas that had been abandoned but were sometimes visited by former residents, who came to gather fruit and nuts and were always ready to flee from Renamo. The stories were full of murder, torture, rape; of people burned, beheaded, thrown down wells. Ten thousand copies had been published in Mozambique and had quickly sold out. *Dumba Nengue* had also been translated into English and published in the United States. It was still the only local book about the war. But Lina didn't know whether the bandits in Manhiça knew that she was *that* Lina Magaia.

I got a sense of how Lina might have collected the stories for her book when we asked a farm worker in a field for directions. He had a tiny, hoarse voice, and he had trouble speaking. Lina asked him what had happened. He said that the *bandidos* had caught him near Palmeira and had slit his throat. He lifted his head so that we could see the scars. They went from ear to ear, and were at least an inch wide. It was hard to see how he had survived.

Later that day, while we were on the way to Palmeira—it's a small town on the national highway in the northern part of Manhiça—things briefly got tense. Lina spotted three men with rifles standing on a curve in the highway ahead of us. There were burned vehicles overturned along the side of the road. It was obviously an ambush spot. Lina stepped on the gas, we both slid low in our seats, and we went flying past the men, who did not move. "Those might be bandits," Lina said, as we slowed down to normal speed. "Sometimes they will come out and simply stand by the road, waiting for a truck carrying food, or a bus, or any vehicle they want to ambush. People think they're the militia. There is no way to know." We stopped at the next village to ask around. Eventually, we found an old man who said that the men *were* militia. They had been stationed out there because of all the attacks on the curve. Afterward, Lina grumbled, "But is anyone feeding those militia? Is anyone paying them? If they are not being paid, how will they get food? And what will they do when they get hungry?"

We were going to Palmeira to see José Inácio De Sousa, a son of Inácio De Sousa. Inácio, who died in 1976, had been such a respected farmer, Lina said, that Samora Machel himself had given the eulogy at his funeral, praising his honesty. Most of the white and Asian farmers in Manhiça had left after independence. Others, like a Chinese shopkeeper who owned a big banana farm we had seen near Muinguine, lived in Maputo. The Portuguese farmers in Manhiça had been prosperous, unlike the illiterate European peasants who settled in, say, the Limpopo Valley, to the north. The most prosperous among them, though, had been Inácio De Sousa. He had controlled the entire banana market in Maputo. And José Inácio—who was popularly known as Zeca—was still here, growing bananas and rice, raising cattle, and running a large mill and rice-cleaning plant in Palmeira, where he lived with his wife and child. We looked for Zeca in Palmeira and were told he was in the fields. We drove out to a large, beautifully laid-out, well-drained banana farm and found Zeca on an access road, driving a new white Japanese pickup truck with a black roll bar.

He joined us, and we took a tour of his farm. Zeca was a trim, unassuming man of thirty-three, wearing tinted glasses. He had a crooked, modest smile and a quiet voice. Lina and he talked trucks for a while—she needed to borrow some. Then I asked him about how the war had affected his operations. Zeca looked out across his fields. Finally, he said that the farm and the mill in Palmeira had both been attacked many times. The farm, for instance, had been attacked last year by a force of about 150 men. The farm had a good militia, with forty full-time fighters and fourteen part-time fighters, trained and equipped by the army, paid and fed by Zeca. In the early days, Zeca himself had taken the militia to search for *bandidos*. People in Manhiça, he said, tended to believe that the *bandidos* were "bulletproof," and he had wanted to show his men that the *bandidos* were mortal. Fortunately, he said, they never found any. But they began to hear about other militias that had killed *bandidos*. Zeca's militia took heart, and Zeca retired from active duty. In last year's big attack, the farm's militia had killed eleven *bandidos*, according to people who had escaped from their camps, and they had gravely wounded many more. Six tractors and two pumps had been burned, but no militiamen had been killed, and only a few were wounded. Most of the great success of the defense was attributable to the fact that the militia had heard about the attack in advance from escaped captives.

Palmeira had suffered even larger attacks, Zeca said. The most recent one, three months before, had involved three hundred *bandidos*. Zeca and his family had just gone to Maputo that afternoon. His wife and child were now staying in the city, waiting until things calmed down. One militiaman had been killed in the last attack on Palmeira, and many people in the nearby communal village had been killed or kidnapped. But the *bandidos* had been repelled before they reached the mill, which they no doubt wanted to loot and burn. Again, the militia had had advance warning. Zeca had since put up an electrified fence around Palmeira, and powerful lights, which shone all night out into the fields. He was thinking about doing the same thing on this farm. It was all very expensive, though.

I asked Zeca about his family. He said that he had two sisters who had moved to Portugal after independence, but that his mother and his brother still lived in Maputo. His brother was a pilot.

I asked Zeca about his relations with Frelimo. He said that he had lost a little land to a communal village and that his taxes had gone up. They were now 45 percent of profits. Otherwise, he said, he had had no problems with the government.

Lina erupted: "I love this man. He is doing so much for my country, and he loves this land."

I asked Zeca if he had ever been approached by Renamo.

He was silent for a minute. Then he said, "Twice." The first time had been in 1984. A well-dressed black man had come to him in Palmeira and asked for a lift to Maputo. He said that his car had broken down in Manhiça town. He had left it there, and, he said, he had come to see Zeca especially. He was cool, Zeca said, but he had nervous eyes. Then he changed his mind and said that he didn't want to go to Maputo after all, but wanted to stay the night. Zeca said he could. Then the man changed his mind again. He wanted to go to the coastal town of Bilene. Zeca put him on a bus to Bilene. Then Zeca thought about it, and sent the militia after the bus in a truck. They brought the man back, Zeca questioned him, and the man gave him a new story. Now he was coming from Sofala. He mentioned several Portuguese farmers and businessmen whom Zeca knew there. Zeca had heard enough. He took the man to Manhiça and handed him over to the police. Someone said the man had a room at one of the hotels in Manhiça, so the police went there. In the room, they found several South African and Swazi passports issued to various black men, some photographs of Samora Machel and other Frelimo officials, and a Renamo document transferring the man from Sofala to Manhiça for "research."

"That means that he was sent to approach white farmers, to see who might support them," Lina said.

The second approach to Zeca had been only five months before. A man had come to him asking for a job. He said he had been living in Matola, a suburb of Maputo. There was something fishy about the references he gave. Zeca had him searched, and, again, the searchers found a Renamo document, transferring him from Matola to Manhiça for "research."

It was all very strange, if only because the De Sousa farm had a big reputation with the *bandidos* in Manhiça as a government redoubt. Among Renamo's captives, anyone known to work for De Sousa was usually killed, because the De Sousa militia was considered a major enemy.

We were passing through a newly planted banana field. Lina stopped the van, and we all climbed out. Lina had been asking Zeca questions about his farming methods between my questions to him about the war. Now she wanted to know how he had dug the large, regular holes in this field, each with a young banana plant growing nicely inside it. Zeca reminded us that we had seen a machine up at the farm headquarters, attached to the back of a tractor. That was a special machine for digging such holes, he said. Somehow that was the last straw for Lina. As we climbed back into the van, she burst into tears. She sobbed and sobbed, while Zeca and I sat and squirmed. Through her tears Lina began to rage against, of all things, government bureaucrats. They sat in their offices in Maputo and issued idiotic orders that did nothing but screw up the people trying to work in the country. They called a meeting to enlist support for the new militias without proper preparation, on the wrong day, undermining the entire project. They set ridiculous production goals that did nothing but oppress the people trying to produce, and they arbitrarily reorganized successful projects, destroying them in the process. They sent her stupid, lazy, so-called technicians instead of a real agronomist who could teach her things like how to dig proper holes for young banana plants. Lina was sad, she was furious, and, for the first time in her life, she was *tired*.

Zeca and I tried to comfort her. She eventually stopped crying, wiped her face with the back of her hand, took three belts of Scotch, laughed lightly, and resumed driving, plainly in a much better mood.

The Cubans thought highly, everybody said, of the Territorial Defense Force. It had worked for them at the Bay of Pigs. Other military advisers in Mozambique were less enthusiastic. Cuba had a strong central government and few remote areas. In Mozambique, creating militias with loyalties that were primarily local—to the farmer or factory owner or administrator who fed and paid them—carried the risk of fostering warlordism.[2] It also seemed like a backward step in the overall effort of nation-building, the struggle to create larger, national loyalties. But, again, this had been Frelimo's deepest political problem since independence: how to reconcile local realpolitik with abstract modern ideals. And the military reality was that, in many places, the regular army was useless. In Manhiça, in March, Renamo had overrun an army training barracks in the southern part of the district virtually without resistance, capturing a large number of weapons.

The army could also be worse than useless. Lina and I went to see the one *cooperante* living in Manhiça, an Italian named Giovanni. We found him at his warehouse, very near the spot where João Ferreira and his friends had died. Giovanni was a dapper-looking fellow about forty years old. When Lina asked him how he was, he said, "Fine. Now." His smile was tight. I thought I saw his hands shaking. Lina asked him what he meant. Giovanni said that he had been driving in from Maputo on the national highway earlier that afternoon and had come upon an ambush. A group of soldiers was looting a truck between Maluana and Esperança. He stopped and made a U-turn. The soldiers spotted him and started shooting at him. He got away without being hit, and reached Manhiça by back roads.

Later, Lina said that Giovanni must have meant *bandidos*, but I had heard him say "*soldados*." Lina sighed hugely and said that it was a major problem: the soldiers were ill fed. She had often had to feed them herself. But the situation was improving.

It had been a long day. Lina was right when she guessed that I might want a bath. She was also right when she guessed why I hesitated when she suggested it. She came to check out the facilities where I was staying, and she emerged from the bathroom with her face a mask of fury and shame. She went looking for my housemates, and I heard her out in the kitchen shed berating someone fiercely. All I caught was the word *barbarity*. When she returned, she muttered that she would take me to her friend's house for a bath—the damn Koreans were already back at her place.

We went to an old house on the highway, in the center of town. I got a bath—in water heated over an open fire—and afterward sat talking with some of Lina's friends, including a shopkeeper, a young man who worked for a parastatal agricultural company called Diprom, and a part-Chinese farmer named Abraão, whom we had met earlier in his fields. Conversation centered on business and the war. Like Lina, the shopkeeper and Abraão had their families in Maputo and drove back on weekends. Abraão said that he had 150 acres and a tractor, and employed fifty-eight people, and also owned a fishing boat in Maputo. But Abraão was not a capitalist, Lina said, because he actually worked the land. In fact, he wasn't making any profits from farming and would do better to invest his money elsewhere. I asked Abraão if he was really such a good citizen that he made his investment decisions according to party directives about production, and he laughed. He wasn't a party member, he said. He just loved to work on the land. But Abraão was not against Frelimo, Lina said. She studied him. Abraão grinned. "He prefers to have an independent position," Lina said. (I later learned that Abraão had fought with the Portuguese during the *luta armada*, and that would have disqualified him from party membership even if he had wanted it.) Each time the conversation came around, as it seemed to do often, to the government's failings in agriculture and commerce, I noticed that the others turned to the man from Diprom, taxing him with their complaints, rather than Lina. Lina, meanwhile, was trying to persuade Abraão to open a shop for his workers—he said he would do so if he could get his work force up to two hundred and if he could be assured of security—while Abraão was trying to persuade me to try to interest individual American investors in becoming partners with small Mozambican farmers like him.

Later that evening, we ended up down the street at the Hotel Castro—no relation to Fidel, Abraão assured me, so Americans were welcome. It was a lively bar and restaurant, with drunks falling about, a jukebox, a number of trucks parked out front that had not made it into the last convoy of the day, and soldiers posted at the doors. We ate steaks and mealie pap—a cornmeal mash that is the southern African staple—and drank local beer. The Castro's proprietor, a sharp-eyed woman with big gold earrings, joined us and then entertained us by coolly ejecting some of her more boisterous customers. I inspected the new curtains—the Castro was one of the hotels relieved of their dry goods by Renamo in June—and met a large number of Lina's friends and associates. At one point, a song by a Brazilian pop singer named Roberto Carlos came on the jukebox, and Lina's face became a vision of bliss. She had owned this record when she was seventeen, she said. She used to have parties at her house and play this record, and she and her friends would dance. Roberto Carlos was singing a Portuguese version of Dion's "The

Wanderer," and Lina did a hilarious imitation of herself at seventeen seriously bopping. "You know, Bill, when I am not working, I really love to play," she said.

There were a number of soldiers in the bar, some of them drinking, some of them dancing in front of the jukebox. Few of them looked over eighteen. Abraão studied the crowd critically, then said, "There are only two good soldiers here tonight." He pointed out two older, serious-looking characters, both sober, alert, erect, and well dressed, standing at the edge of the room. One wore a greatcoat. Both wore pistols. I later noticed two young soldiers with pink flowers in their berets, and for no particular reason I pointed them out to Lina. Her smile disappeared. She called one of the soldiers over and spoke to him long and quietly. After he left, she called over one of the watchful officers and spoke to him. He left, and I asked Lina what was happening. She said that the young soldier had said that he and his friend had just completed a British training course in Zimbabwe, and that they had received the flowers in their berets as graduation gifts. That might be true, she said. Or the flowers might mean that the boys were spies for the bandits. The bandits might have told them to wear flowers so that they could be recognized and would not be killed accidentally in an attack.

I was shocked to hear what I had started, and a few minutes later I went outside for some fresh air. I had seen the soldiers with the flowers in their berets go out a minute before, but I did not find them on the hotel steps. The guards in front of the hotel were extraordinarily young—they looked like children—and they wore big, unnervingly cowled East German helmets. I asked one of them where the boys with the flowers had gone. He smiled, held up his hands, and hit the insides of his wrists together. It was the sign for "arrested."

Some hours later, I found myself back on my evil-smelling mattress, still horrified by what had happened. I had heard before about Renamo attacks in which certain soldiers suddenly turned their caps around backward, were not shot at, and, when the battle was over, left with the enemy. People said that Renamo had spies everywhere, even in the army. But the boys in the bar with the flowers in their berets seemed to me so clearly what they said they were. (I later asked a British defense attaché about the course in Zimbabwe. He said that the training officer was from the Fusiliers, who wear a hackle, a red-and-white plume, in their cap badge, and that the training officer did indeed award a hackle, or the best locally available equivalent, to his graduates.)

The incident had led me into a series of bar conversations about the army, some of them even more disturbing than the arrest of the young soldiers. I had asked one of my companions what he thought could induce a soldier to spy for Renamo, and he had said, "To many of these boys, there is no difference, the bandits or the army. They are taken in just the same. They are never let go, even though the army says they only have to serve two years. We hear that the bandits are starving, but we *know* the soldiers are starving. They do not get enough food."

I asked if he had ever heard of soldiers ambushing vehicles on the highway.

He sneered and said, "They do it. And they are the most dangerous, because they don't want to leave witnesses, so they try to kill everyone. The massacre at the Third of February—that was soldiers." The Third of February was the village near the spot where the big highway massacre had occurred the previous October. Rocked by this news, I asked two other solid Manhiça citizens, as discreetly as I could, who they thought had committed the massacre at the Third of February. Neither blamed the soldiers, but only one blamed Renamo. The other said, very sadly, "I don't know." (A number of diplomats had flown by helicopter to the scene of the massacre. When I got back to Maputo, I asked one of them what he thought. He said that the army had provided very poor protection to the convoy that was attacked, and that there was a chance—a *chance*—that soldiers had joined in the looting, which lasted for hours.)

The man who had accused local soldiers of committing the massacre was, at the same time, sympathetic to soldiers. He said, "Not only is the soldier hungry but his family, wherever they are, they are hungry, too. And he knows it. And his wife knows that if he is killed she will get nothing but a pension for six months. The soldier you see is the same man who was struggling to survive, to see his future, to understand his situation before he came to the army. He has not stopped thinking. And so he must ask himself, 'What am I fighting for? So that a few officers, high officials, and the bourgeoisie can eat meat, drive cars, and live in nice houses, while we eat beans, if we're lucky, and our families starve, must walk everywhere, and sleep on the bare earth?' Lina loves the soldiers. But have you seen her telling them that they are the victims of injustice? Have you seen her telling the peasants that? No, and you won't hear her telling them that. Because there is nothing that she can do about it, and they will only look at *her*."

Was this what Renamo was telling people in Manhiça?

The man sneered again. "Renamo? Who is Renamo?"

It was a good question. I had been struck by the disparity between the intrigues Zeca De Sousa had described—the shadowy characters carrying Renamo transfer papers and engaged in dubious "research"—and the world of the Manhiça *bandidos*, such as I had glimpsed it. Although most Renamo fighters were, like most Mozambicans, illiterate—even important commanders, according to Paulo Oliveira, were illiterate—there were levels of Renamo where written records were kept, as several captured caches of documents had shown. But there were other levels, probably including some of the Manhiça bands, where records were not kept, and Zeca's experiences suggested that the communication between, say, the Manhiça bands that battled the De Sousa militia and whoever sent the "researchers" to sound him out was poor at best. I had been surprised to see, near Maragra, an undestroyed bridge over the Incomati. It was in an area where Renamo had been active for years. When I pointed it out to Lina, she said that the bandits did not try to destroy infrastructure in Manhiça, but simply tried to kill and terrorize. It made me wonder just what their orders, if any, from outside Manhiça were.

Local conditions dictated who Renamo was locally. The mass unemployment caused by the cutbacks on the South African mines and the hopelessness that it bred in many young men were, I had heard, a major aid to Renamo recruitment in Manhiça. The belief that the *bandidos* were bulletproof was common throughout Mozambique; Renamo fighters, and especially Ndau-speakers, were believed to have powerful magic. And yet the main Renamo magician in Manhiça, who gave the fighters their power, was, according to Lina, a local woman named Nwamadjosi. She was the widow of a former *régulo*, and she was considered a great *curandeiro*. The "advance word" of attacks which Zeca's militia always got suggested that there was a steady traffic of local people between the Renamo camps and government territory. Nwamadjosi was an attraction, apparently, helping to swell Renamo's ranks; perhaps she was drawing more ordinary business as well. I somehow doubted, in any case, that her line of goods included extolling the virtues of democratic elections or, for that matter, of Afonso Dhlakama.

Trying to fall asleep, I began to see the war in Manhiça as a battle between two titanic women: Lina and Nwamadjosi. It was a silly idea—and it wasn't silly at all. Beyond the fact that they fought on opposite sides, with very different weapons, Nwamadjosi casting spells and invoking the spirits of the ancestors, Lina importing bicycles and writing books—beyond everything they might be made to represent in the wider world of ideas, politics, values—there was the fact that each of them was a locally powerful individual. Lina was not Frelimo's sole representative in Manhiça, or even, necessarily, its most important one, but she was clearly popular. She was in no danger of becoming a warlord in Manhiça—that wasn't why she favored militias—but in another place, at another time, it would not have been inconceivable. She and Nwamadjosi circled one another like lions in a dim clearing in my head as I drifted off.

In the morning, I discovered that, after our long evening in the Hotel Castro, Lina had gone home and written a letter to the minister of agriculture about the things the farmers needed in Manhiça; a letter to the local military commander about the problem of nonstandard uniforms, with particular reference to the beret-flower incident; and most of her weekly column for *Notícias*. I had seen her houseguests leave for work, so I ventured to her house for coffee and found her tapping on an old portable typewriter at her dining room table. The night before, she had groaned, held her great head in her hands, and said, "I smoke too much, I drink too much, I eat too much, I never sleep, I am *so tired*"—but that morning she looked infinitely fresher than I felt. Her beret seemed set, in fact, at an even more rakish angle than usual. She asked me to give her a few minutes to finish the column. It was addressed to a director at the Ministry of Health who had still not handed over an ambulance that the Mozambican Red Cross had given to Manhiça more than two years before. This was a fantastic modern ambulance, with blood and oxygen on board, and the director apparently believed that it was too good for a little one-horse district like Manhiça. But Manhiça was where the war was *happening*. This was where people were getting wounded, and a high-tech ambulance was needed to keep them alive. The director's behavior was a perfect example of office-bound Maputo thinking, and Lina was flaying him without mercy. She wanted that ambulance!

Lina's house was airy and bright, and crowded with potted plants. Pictures of her mother and her children covered a bureau top; one of the children, I knew, was a war orphan she had adopted. Although the bookshelves were nothing like the shelves in her house in Maputo, which groaned with the works of Faulkner, Camus, and dozens of Portuguese and Soviet authors, they were well stocked with technical books, mostly agricultural science. A mud-caked surveyor's tripod stood in a corner of the living room. The wonderful old map of Manhiça covered one wall. Mozambican pop music was playing on a radio, and in the kitchen Lina's cook was chopping vegetables. I glanced into Lina's bedroom and saw, propped next to her bed, an AK-47. Also, a pistol on the night table. And a very large knife.

The map of Manhiça, which I had consulted several times since coming to the district, had helped me form a picture of the area with sufficient detail in it that, while we wandered the fields and back roads, I rarely worried about the possibility of an ambush. There were places and times of day that were dangerous. Otherwise, the risk was remote. Once, we had come into a small compound on the bank of the Incomati, near Muinguine, and I had asked a woman living there—she was one of several wives of a wealthy peasant—whether she and her family were not afraid. They were in a spot where, from everything I had heard, the *bandidos* were certain to pass at night. She said that the *bandidos* did sometimes come at night, and for that reason they sometimes slept at Muinguine. (I had actually been hoping to see a hippopotamus in the river there. Lina had told me that tourists on their way to the beach at Macaneta, which was nearby, used to honk their car horns, which aroused the hippos' curiosity, to bring them out on the banks. The tourists were long gone, and salt water had penetrated far up the Incomati during the great drought of 1983–84, forcing the hippos, as Lina put it, "to hide themselves," but the water in the river was fresh again now, and the hippos might be back. I was embarrassed to ask Lina to honk her horn again, though—and it was getting late in the day to linger in that area.)

I studied the map on Lina's wall. We were planning to return to Maputo that afternoon, and Lina had said that she did not want to take the highway. Apparently, Giovanni's had not been the only report of an attack on the highway between Manhiça and Maputo over the past couple of days. Instead, Lina wanted to take a dirt road that ran along the bluff on the Incomati's right bank. It went through more heavily populated areas. It was dangerous at night, but in the daytime there was only one bad stretch, a few miles south of an army training barracks— not the barracks that had been overrun, Lina said, but another one. I found the barracks Lina meant, and the dangerous stretch of road, on the map. The back road did look less vulnerable than the highway, and the bad stretch looked short.

We spent most of the day running around Manhiça. Lina was planning to go overseas on a speaking tour, and she was worried about Ribangue. The stock operations were poorly managed, and the militia needed to be ready for the next attack. She and Domingos Jasse went over his preparations several times. We ran into the local military commander on a road in the cane town, and Lina and he had a talk about the need for standard uniforms for soldiers, thus obviating her letter. We went down into the fields at Ribangue, where Lina pondered the blighted cassava crop. "Sometimes I feel that it's me against the land," she muttered. "And I don't know which one will win."

Finally, rather alarmingly late in the day, we were ready to leave Manhiça. We set off on the dirt road, through the cheering columns of children: "Lina Magaia! Lina Magaia!" We passed through Maragra, Lina's old headquarters, where a vast old sugar refinery stood silent, closed for lack of spare parts, and the rows of worker housing, their residents nowhere in sight, looked like a town still in shock from the Renamo attack of the month before. Lina was driving very fast. Suddenly, in the woods south of Muinguine, she slammed on the brakes. As we slid to a stop, hundreds of young men surrounded the van. They were jogging in the road, running straight out of the low sun—that was why I had not seen them. They were recruits from the nearby training barracks. They were all bare-chested, and they all had their heads shaved, and they came at the windshield in waves, all with hypnotic marathoners' eyes, their skin shining in the dusty golden light. They were singing: a deep, swinging, African chant. The recruits swarmed past the van, and when they saw Lina, they tapped the van's roof, but they did not alter their chant. As the last of them passed, I saw that Lina's face was lit with a beatific smile. She put the van in gear, sighed, and said that she really regretted having left the army. "I think I have the military mentality," she said. She liked the order and discipline of military life, and she believed that military discipline had a role to play in the economic development of Mozambique.

The road turned to sand as we approached the stretch where an ambush had seemed possible. Lina showed me how to release the safety on the pistol and told me to hold it between my knees. I wondered about the wisdom of my blazing away at any attackers—maybe they wouldn't start shooting if they thought we were not armed—but I figured that Lina knew more than I did. The road dropped into a gully, the sand got deeper, and I felt a sense of menace that I had not felt before in Mozambique. Lina was battling the sand, which slowed us to walking speed. It was already dusk in the gully. The crest of the far slope was lined with abandoned houses. Although it probably took less than a minute, it seemed to take hours to climb the slope beneath the houses, the van screaming and lurching in the sand. I didn't need to be told that any attack would come from the houses. The worst moment occurred when we emerged from the gully into a scatter of abandoned, bullet-riddled buildings and had to round a slow, blind corner. Nothing happened, and we were soon speeding down a gravel road, each sending regards to our separate deities.

The Scotch was all gone, but we promised ourselves a stiff drink in Maputo. Lina tried to raise someone on her two-way radio. She was going to be late delivering her column, and she wanted to reassure her editor. I had heard that Lina had sometimes called Samora Machel himself on her car radio. She laughed when I mentioned it, shook her head, and said, mostly to herself, "Samora, Samora." She gave up on the radio. I asked if she ever called President Chissano on the radio. Lina said, "I never have. I have other ways to talk to him." She nodded at the typescript on the seat between us. It struck me that Lina had been producing engagé journalism—writing with consequences—ever since she was the only black child in her class at school and was jailed for three months, at the age of seventeen, for publishing an anticolonial poem. The gravel road curved and came up onto the highway. We were now out of Manhiça, and out of ambush territory. The soldiers at the checkpoints seemed surprised to see us. Lina handed out cigarettes, and we headed for the city.

While the buildings multiplied around us, Lina said, "So you have seen Manhiça. People here in the city will tell you Manhiça is too dangerous. They put their hands on their heads and say, 'Oh, all these tragical things!'" Lina did a good imitation of a Maputo worrywart. Then she said, "Yes, there are tragical things, but that is why we must fight. We must not abandon Manhiça." We skirted the crowded, smoky edge of the cane city, passed the American Embassy, the Hotel Polana, and the South African trade mission, and drove down into the center of the cement city. Outside the editorial offices of *Notícias,* Lina called to a man standing on the sidewalk. She handed him the typescript of her column and asked if he knew where the editor's office was. He said he did. That was all she needed to hear. Lina made a U-turn, and we went to find a drink, agreeing not to talk—at least, not that evening—about tragical things.

Part Six

Outside

22

The white rulers of South Africa for many years described themselves and their country as the object of a "total onslaught" by the forces of communism, led by the Soviet Union. Their response, fully formulated by the late 1970s, was a "total strategy" that included the militarization of South African society and the military, economic, and political destabilization of their neighbors. This "aggressive counter-offensive," as Magnus Malan, the South African military chief, called it,[1] was launched with particular ferocity against Angola and Mozambique, which Malan called "the Soviet Union's puppet states."[2] In the military arena, Pretoria had suffered a major defeat in Angola in 1975, when, despite its best efforts, the Movimento Popular de Libertação de Angola gained power. This setback led to a shift in South African military thinking, away from conventional warfare and toward the use of surrogates—Unita in Angola, Renamo in Mozambique—and an embrace of what was by then being called, in the United States and elsewhere, "low-intensity conflict." It was a high-intensity embrace. In 1987, Steven Metz of the U.S. Army Command and General Staff College described Pretoria's total strategy as "the most sophisticated development of low-intensity doctrine in the world today."[3]

The United States had itself been developing strategy for unconventional intervention in the Third World since shortly after World War II. In the Philippines, Iran, Southeast Asia, and Latin America, the techniques of destabilization, counterinsurgency, and proxy conflict—"total war at the grass-roots level," as the chief of the U.S. military advisers in El Salvador called it[4]—had been tested and refined.[5] Some of these efforts were mounted to support perceived allies, others to destroy perceived opponents, and still others simply to weaken and manipulate all parties and thus keep matters under American control. The Kurds fighting for independence in northern Iraq, for instance, were in the early 1970s the beneficiaries of American covert aid funneled through the Shah's Iran. Later, after the aid was abruptly cut off, they discovered that they had been simply used to play off Iran against Iraq, that they were, in fact, considered—in the words of a CIA memo that came to light—"a uniquely useful tool" in Henry Kissinger's vintage power politics.[6] The Americans had no interest in seeing the Kurds *win*—just as the South Africans had no interest in seeing Renamo win in Mozambique.

But it was American intervention in Latin America that seemed to inspire Pretoria the most. As a South African government radio broadcast put it in 1982, "There are growing parallels between the security role of the United States in South and Central America and that of South Africa in this part of the world. The correspondence arises from similar motives: the promotion of stability and the strengthening of democratic forces against communist subversion. . . . As the most advanced and powerful state in the region, South Africa has a special responsibility towards it. . . . A Monroe Doctrine is needed for southern Africa."[7]

For all the "parallels," however, between American support of the Contras in Nicaragua and South African support of Renamo and Unita, there were also important differences, most notably of accountability. The U.S. Congress, reflecting popular opinion, cut off aid to the Contras; and the Reagan administration's efforts to circumvent the ban led to a major political crisis. A main tenet of the theory of low-intensity conflict, as developed in the United States after the Vietnam War, was the need for secrecy, for "deniability." The object was to be able to fight wars *without* popular support and without public debate. Exposure, as in the Iran-Contra scandal, was always potentially disastrous. The Pretoria regime, while not immune to scandal and its repercussions, had far fewer democratic checks on its behavior.

What was more, the white minority to which it was ostensibly answerable gave no sign that it objected in any serious way to the campaigns against Angola and Mozambique.

The campaign against Mozambique must be considered, from Pretoria's standpoint, a huge success. The ANC was ousted. The Frelimo government was crippled. The economy was destroyed. The specter of a thriving black socialist state on its borders had been exorcised. The dreaded Soviets were no longer even in the picture. It seemed impossible that South Africa could have any reason to continue to support Renamo—except that Pretoria had played such a potent game of cat-and-mouse for so long, especially since the signing of the Nkomati Accord, that "the target nation," as the destabilization theorists called Mozambique, could never really be sure it was safe.

But the ground had also shifted under Pretoria. The "total onslaught," which had for so long been used to justify internal repression, external aggression, and claims on the strategic sympathies of the capitalist democracies who would not want to see South African minerals fall into Soviet hands, was no longer available as a sustaining myth. P. W. Botha, the dour doyen of destabilization, was replaced by the less bellicose F. W. de Klerk, and the slow dismantling of legal apartheid accelerated. In 1990, the ANC was legalized, Nelson Mandela was released from prison, and the ANC's armed struggle was suspended. Strategic confusion seemed to reign in Pretoria as the possibility of majority rule became increasingly real. Surely no one in power could be bothered with pursuing that old sideshow in Mozambique *now*.

And yet the war went on.

The end of the Cold War produced new ambiguities not only for Pretoria's security establishment. The superpower rivalry had helped pour arms into countries like Mozambique, Angola, Ethiopia, and Somalia, hastening their devastation, but it had also served to focus a certain amount of international attention on Africa, an attention which, when East-West tensions eased, soon drifted away.[8] A large share of Western relief and development aid was suddenly going to Eastern Europe. Throughout the Third World—which now seemed due for a name change—it was feared that a "unipolar world" would condemn poor countries to a greater indifference than ever on the part of the industrialized nations. In Mozambique, "donor fatigue" was being widely cited for a catastrophic shortfall in emergency aid in 1990.

The end of the Cold War also seemed to highlight the superficiality of Western concepts like communism and capitalism when transplanted to Africa. The "Marxism-Leninism" and "international proletarianism" of Frelimo were as rigorous as any ruling-party ideology on the continent and had clearly made sense as a framework for national liberation and development in the early days of the revolution, when a "new society" was being born and the chiliastic appeal of radical egalitarianism must have been irresistible. And yet, for all its local applications, Marxism was, *pace* Samora Machel, a European product; and when it no longer made sense, and some form of capitalism seemed to become the only economic and political model with a future, Frelimo switched tracks with breathtaking ease. The real issue, after all, was development, the proposed transformation of an impoverished sprawl of Africa into a modern nation.

Could it be done? *Was* the ultimate goal to become like Europe? Machel saw as clearly as anyone the importance of political and psychological liberation for Africans—he even called Frelimo's reeducation camps "Camps for Mental Decolonization"—but he was also attracted to the colonial-style discipline of the Hotel Chuabo in Quelimane. Colonialism in Mozambique and elsewhere created a local mission-educated elite. The difference between an elite and a revolutionary vanguard can be slight—just add radical ideology. Vanguardism has inherent weaknesses—it fosters passivity and authoritarianism—and the victories won by a vanguard in the name of the people rarely end up empowering the masses. But the social and economic distance between the elite, whether it calls itself revolutionary or an aristocracy, and the great mass of illiterate peasants remains the most striking political fact in a place like Mozambique. Thus, there was something truly wrenching, I thought, about the news that Mario Machungo, the Frelimo prime minister, while traveling in the northern province of Nampula in September 1990, had been telling local activists, "There are still some people here who speak of Marxism-Leninism—we've given that up a long time ago." Machungo was "surprised" that the Nampulans hadn't heard about this change—which had happened, after all, "a long time ago." Meanwhile, a local official complained, "Mr. Prime Minister, the administrators here in the province of Nampula don't even have a bicycle, but we know that vehicles were distributed to administrators in the south, Maputo and Gaza."[9]

There is no escaping history. Colonialism shaped the first generation of postcolonial African leaders, who naturally respected their own points of entry to power—military, educational, bureaucratic—and then largely tried to reproduce those structures after independence. The modern nation-state has become the basic political unit, and all African countries seem condemned to the struggle to build such a thing, complete with flag, national anthem, and standardized language, just as the nations of Europe did, most of them in the late nineteenth century. And yet nation-building in a situation of gross dependence on wealthier, more powerful countries—and without benefit of an Industrial Revolution—is a very different proposition from what most European nations faced. Without some extraordinary natural resource, such as oil, it is not at all clear that a severely underdeveloped country, firmly on the periphery of the modern world system, has even a fighting chance of development. In Mozambique's case, moreover, its dependence is not only on the developed North. More directly and more profoundly, it is on South Africa.

A shiver of democratic change ran through Africa in 1990, reflecting events in Eastern Europe and the Soviet Union and forcing concessions to political pluralism from the leaders of a slew of countries, including Angola, Benin, Cameroon, the Cape Verde Islands, the Central African Republic, Chad, Congo, Gabon, Ghana, Ivory Coast, Madagascar, Mali, Niger, Nigeria, Rwanda, São Tomé and Principé, Sierra Leone, Togo, Zambia— even, for what it was worth, Zaire. The authoritarian governments of Ghana, Guinea, and Kenya were also under steady democratic pressure. In March 1991, Mathieu Kérékou, the military dictator of Benin for nearly two decades, became the first national leader in independent Africa to accept defeat in a free election. Others seemed likely to follow. And yet all this political ferment was taking place in an extremely stark context. For

Africa's poverty—a virtual guarantee of political instability and tyranny—was only getting worse. The overall economy of the forty-five countries in sub-Saharan Africa shrank by more than 20 percent in the 1980s, private outside investment fell by nearly 80 percent between 1982 and 1986, and commodity exports plummeted as Africa steadily lost world market share to competitors in South Asia, where operating costs were roughly half what they were in Africa and the rate of return on investment was estimated to be nine times higher.[10] Meanwhile, population growth was spiraling out of control, seemingly condemning Africa to generations of want. As David Ewing Duncan framed the dilemma, "In the United States the average woman will be a source of fourteen children, grandchildren, and great-grandchildren; the comparable figure for an African woman is 258."[11]

The problems of governance in such economic circumstances are obviously immense. Add an ultradestructive, country-wide bush war—and low-intensity conflict strategy specifically, according to its critics, "strikes at the very heart of the development process"[12]—and the problems can begin to seem insuperable. In Mozambique, Frelimo had been talking since independence about the need to "decentralize problem-solving in the countryside," and yet all its own instincts had been centralizing. The Portuguese administrative legacy included centuries of nominal, ineffectual rule and then a few decades of rigid, extractive, pervasive control. Frelimo's cadres had experienced the latter period, with all its abuses, but they also feared, with good reason, the stagnation of what Gunnar Myrdal has called the "soft state"—that style of government, too common in the Third World, characterized by, in Myrdal's words, "all the various types of social indiscipline which manifest themselves by: deficiencies in legislation and in particular law observance and enforcement, a widespread disobedience by public officials on various levels to rules and directives handed down to them, and often their collusion with powerful persons and groups of persons whose conduct they should regulate. Within the concept of the soft state belongs also corruption."[13]

This was, again, Frelimo's deepest political problem: how to reconcile local realpolitik with modern ideals. To administer Mozambique—to fight Renamo—Frelimo clearly needed to decentralize with a vengeance: to cut a thousand local deals with a thousand local honchos. Few of these arrangements would be exemplary. In Nampula, government officials in 1989 gave their blessing to a Portuguese firm's efforts to organize peasant cash-cropping, using traditional chiefs as overseers. The firm's operations dated from colonial times, and, according to one observer, "The degree to which peasants are free to refuse to participate in such schemes is unclear."[14] In some areas of the country, the opportunities for the emergence of warlordism—possibly on a scale not seen since the Afro-Portuguese *prazeros* of the Zambezi Valley defied Lisbon, as they routinely did from the seventeenth century to the early twentieth—seemed excellent. In remote rural areas, particularly those where Renamo was strong, Frelimo simply lacked the capacity to govern effectively, even if the war were to end. Thus, alliances with other structures had become indispensable. Frelimo's leadership—modern men all—undoubtedly found it hard to accept that a successful secular state was an impossibility at Mozambique's stage of development (and the idea was also quite unacceptable internationally). This was, nonetheless, the conclusion that the country's deterioration increasingly suggested. The pieces were too small, the structures of power too dense and personal, the people too soaked in the sacred.

The structures with which Frelimo needed to work included, of course, traditional authorities. The liberation movement had worked with traditional leaders during the *luta armada*, as noted, but with nearly as much cynicism, it seemed, as the colonialists had employed in the same enterprise. As Barry Munslow, a sympathetic historian, described Frelimo's strategy, "By harnessing the legitimacy of the traditional intellectuals of the pre-capitalist social formations, the nationalist movement was able to win the support of the peasants." (The terminology here is taken from the work of the Italian writer and revolutionary Antonio Gramsci—the "traditional intellectuals" meant are chiefs and *curandeiros*.) "Only later," Munslow continued, "were the organic intellectuals of the under-classes, in combination with a revolutionary fraction of the traditional intellectuals formed under colonial capitalism, able to establish the 'moral isolation' of both colonialism and the chiefs and spirit mediums."[15] The revolutionary goals of Frelimo—the end of exploitation and the creation of a classless society—may have seemed to require the destruction of traditional authority, with all its ancient injustices, but this strategy may also be seen in another light: as the urban-oriented mission elite, organized along political lines almost wholly imported from Europe, plotting to "harness the legitimacy" of rural African social structures in order to establish total hegemony over them. (The internal Frelimo clash between the revolutionary line and the Gwenjere faction in the late 1960s, while framed by the "revolutionary fraction of the traditional intellectuals" as a battle against the elitism of the conservative urban petite bourgeoisie, may also be seen as basically a dispute over *who* among the mission-educated elite would dominate the rural masses *how*.)

In a sense, this type of struggle transcends the distinction between socialist and capitalist development. The core issue is modernization, the breaking up of old polities, the replacement of rank hierarchies with a modern class system based on production.

But building a unified nation from a material base as underdeveloped as Mozambique's was a project without a blueprint. It had not been done before. Certainly, no European model existed. The true task of "mental decolonization" was, as Luís Bernardo Honwana put it, "to harmonize traditional beliefs with our political project." Among Mozambique's neighbors, Zimbabwe had fashioned some enviable compromises between modern and traditional political structures. And yet the Zimbabwean government had hardened its commitment to a one-party system, steadily reducing its own accountability in an atmosphere of corruption and political repression. In early 1991, Mozambique was groping in the opposite direction, toward a pluralist politics. Some of the crises shaking Africa clearly precluded compromise—the AIDS pandemic, for instance, which was only worsened by traditional practices such as ritual scarring with unsterilized blades. And yet, if political structures were to be viable over time, they simply had to reflect a country's diversity.

In Mozambique that meant, among other things, far greater sensitivity to ethnic passions and loyalties than Frelimo had shown in the past. President Chissano was, as noted, taking steps in this direction. At the Fifth Party Congress in July 1989, he reshuffled the Frelimo Political Bureau, expanding its membership from ten to twelve, and the members added were Makonde, Makua, and Ndau.[16] At the same time, however, Renamo was moving to expand *its* ethnic base. The rebels were reported to be cultivating tribal power blocs by promoting local chiefs to senior positions. Afonso Dhlakama was reported to carry with him on his travels a list of dozens of government officials, down to the third or fourth rank, with notes on the ideology, performance, *and ethnicity* of each. This attention to ethnicity (and if the story of Dhlakama's list was apocryphal, there was much other evidence of his preoccupation with the subject) could be interpreted as sincere concern for the representativeness of government—or as research for tribalist incitement. Either way, it underscored the importance for Frelimo of allaying the widespread feeling in Mozambique that the central government was dominated by southerners. But perhaps "central government" will seem a misnomer. For it remained to be seen how much popular response Renamo would find to its demand, made with increasing volume in 1990, that the national capital be moved from Maputo to Beira.

Renamo's ability to make coherent demands was itself enhanced in 1990 by a major breakthrough: the beginning of direct talks between Frelimo and Renamo. Frelimo, unwilling to give its opponents the political victory that negotiations represented, had long spurned any suggestion of talks with "the bandits." Indeed, in 1987, Mozambican church leaders who proposed official contacts with Renamo were denounced by President Chissano as "apostles of treason."[17] In 1988, however, with Renamo successfully isolated internationally, President Chissano quietly authorized some of the same Catholic and Anglican churchmen to contact Renamo in Nairobi. While the government kept its distance publicly—in December 1988, Chissano told the People's Assembly, "The people will not allow us to talk to the assassins"[18]—the churchmen acted as go-betweens, and in mid-1989 preliminary talks between the two sides began, with Zimbabwean president Robert Mugabe and Kenyan president Daniel Arap Moi acting as mediators. Kenya had, by this stage, emerged as an important backer of Renamo. President Moi, a conservative strongman with imperial ambitions, seemed to see the war in Mozambique (where Kenya had no direct interests) as an opportunity to establish himself as a statesman and power broker in southeast Africa. His permanent secretary for foreign affairs, Betwell Abdu Kiplagat, was widely considered to be Renamo's main diplomatic adviser.[19] But Moi and Mugabe were retired as mediators in 1990, after President Chissano proposed, and Renamo accepted, direct talks.

The first effort to meet, in Malawi in June, was aborted when Afonso Dhlakama and the rest of the Renamo delegation abruptly fled the country just as talks were about to begin. Renamo spokesmen later cited security concerns. The venue for talks was moved to Rome, where the Santo Egidio Community, a Catholic lay charity with long experience in Mozambique and close ties to the Vatican, agreed to provide facilities. Four observers were selected—two from Santo Egidio, one from the Italian government, and the Catholic Archbishop of Beira, a conservative Ndau-speaker named Jaime Gonçalves. The Frelimo delegation was led by Armando Guebuza (he of the squeaky-clean airports), the Renamo delegation by Raul Domingos, the rebels' secretary for external affairs. A first round of talks was finally held in July. A second was held in August. By early 1991, five rounds of talks had occurred, and a limited cease-fire had been signed, restricting Zimbabwean troops to the Beira and Limpopo Corridors. A Joint Verification Commission for the cease-fire had been established, with forty-six monitors from ten countries.[20] In December 1990, three Renamo monitors were granted diplomatic immunity to permit them to go to Maputo to join the commission.

Within two months, the commission had work. Renamo was reportedly attacking the Beira and Limpopo Corridors, in violation of the cease-fire, as well as the international highway through Tete, the suburbs of Maputo, and villages across the country. There was speculation that the Renamo leadership simply could not stop such attacks—except that the Nacala railway, linking Malawi to the coast, had not been hit since Renamo's leaders declared a moratorium on attacking it a year before.[21]

Renamo's leaders appeared to be at something of a loss. They had reaped, through the Rome negotiations, a great and sudden profit in international credibility, but they seemed unsure what to do with it. Their central demand, for a multiparty political system and elections in Mozambique, had been met. Some Renamo leaders claimed that their demands had *produced* the reforms, and yet it was clear that President Chissano had stayed well ahead of them, setting the reforms in motion before negotiations began. Renamo, moreover, rejected the reforms. Raul Domingos scorned the multiparty system in the same words Luís Serapião used, calling the new parties emerging in Mozambique "creations of Frelimo."[22] There were indications that Renamo was really interested only in a *two*-party system, in which spoils would be divided between itself and Frelimo and elections would be irrelevant. (And in a straight power-sharing scheme such as this, the independence of all parties *was* crucial; any governorships, say, parceled out to "creations of Frelimo" would, for Renamo's purposes, remain in Frelimo's hands.) There was also speculation that Renamo's leaders were being inhibited by the observers in Rome from talking turkey: the cash, farms, and government fiefdoms that they wanted in exchange for calling off the war.

But the most likely explanation for Renamo's apparent disorganization was that the group really was disorganized. Embezzlement by its overseas representatives had led to yet another shakeup in the external leadership, as well as a severe cash shortage.[23] Communications with Dhlakama were notoriously poor. Above all, Renamo almost certainly lacked the wherewithal to transform itself from a guerrilla army to a political party, and the leadership knew it. And so Renamo was buying time by "moving the goalposts" in Rome, violating the ceasefire, and repeatedly delaying the talks. At the time of writing— August 1991—the Rome talks seem to be at a standstill. Fierce fighting is being reported in northern Mozambique, where Renamo has apparently gained a foothold for the first time on the Mueda Plateau—the remote Makonde country where Frelimo began the *luta armada* nearly twenty-seven years ago, and where it was widely believed Renamo would never be able to operate. Meanwhile, a Renamo recruiting drive has reportedly been launched among the thousands of Mozambicans stranded in the former German Democratic Republic, and among the tens of thousands of Mozambicans working on the South African mines.

The United States was heavily involved in the Mozambican peace process. Government-to-government relations remained good: Mozambique was the largest recipient in sub-Saharan Africa of American aid in 1990, and Washington publicly endorsed the new constitution. In January 1990, President Bush removed Mozambique from a list of "Marxist-Leninist" countries whose access to U.S. trade credits was restricted, and in March President Chissano took the occasion of a meeting with Mr. Bush in Washington to announce his government's willingness to enter unconditional direct talks with Renamo. At the same time, the State Department had begun to cultivate a relationship with Renamo. Herman Cohen, the Bush nominee for assistant secretary of state for African affairs, told Senator Jesse Helms at his confirmation hearings, "I think the situation [in Mozambique] is so bad and the need for peace is so great, I will talk to anybody."[24] Contacts at various levels with Renamo began, and in November 1990 Assistant Secretary Cohen himself met with Afonso Dhlakama in Rome.

The declared object of U.S. policy was simply to stop the war as soon as possible. But while support for the new constitution and for elections seemed unanimous among American policymakers, splits were still being reported between pro-Renamo and pro-Frelimo analysts, with the main source of Renamo support still said to be in the Defense Intelligence Agency—military intelligence. There were also suggestions that, their official enthusiasm notwithstanding, the Americans were uneasy about a multiparty political system in Mozambique, where an abundance of accountability might create popular pressure on the government to abandon "structural adjustment"—the IMF-approved economic-recovery plan that squeezed ordinary people so pitilessly. Certainly, the United States, in its official contacts with Renamo, was taking the opportunity to begin the education of the rebel leadership in international diplomacy and political and economic reality. Meetings with Dhlakama revealed that he especially was in need of tutoring. He apparently had no idea, for instance, that a country such as Mozambique needed a foreign-investment code regulating the flow of profits out of the country to prevent it from becoming a pure labor colony for a regional power such as South Africa.

It seemed unlikely, in any case, that Dhlakama would soon be confronting the problems of civilian leadership, given Renamo's unpreparedness to enter electoral politics. (And for that reason, too, President Chissano was eager to have elections. Whatever

Frelimo's political problems, which would be revealed in parliamentary voting, Chissano was by far the strongest presidential candidate in sight. As this went to press, elections were scheduled for mid-1992.) Still, there were American strategists who were thinking aloud about "pulling a Nicaragua" in Mozambique. The Sandinistas had been finally toppled not by war but by war plus elections, and for those gringos who agreed with Renamo that Frelimo's leaders were Communists and that Communists never really changed, the prospect of making Renamo an American client, and of seeing the rebels come to power in internationally supervised elections, was enticing. In early 1991, a proposal for a high-level international commission to oversee a cease-fire and elections in Mozambique was being floated in Washington—with Nicaragua explicitly named as a successful precedent for such an initiative. Some of Frelimo's supporters in the United States were alarmed by this emerging "parallel,"[25] but there was little evidence that Frelimo's leaders themselves feared American manipulation of their democratization. The United States had, after all, few real interests at stake in Mozambique—far fewer than in Angola, say, where a total cease-fire was finally signed, after sixteen years of war, in May 1991 (and a multiparty system was also being developed under a government that had also abandoned Marxism-Leninism, and elections were also scheduled for the second half of 1992), and where the presence of oil and, until the cease-fire ended the war, of Cuban troops had long lent the American role some strategic urgency.

Besides, Mozambique had another capitalist power to worry about, one with all too many vital interests in the country: South Africa. Pretoria had relatively little experience with manipulating *elections* in neighboring countries; and its major efforts in this field, during the independence elections in Zimbabwe in 1980 and Namibia in 1990, had backfired in the first case, where Pretoria's favored candidate, Bishop Abel Muzorewa, was humiliated at the polls, and achieved only ambiguous results in the second. And yet the dreams of South Africa's regional strategists of creating a "Monroe Doctrine" for southern Africa were undimmed.

Military supremacy was being deemphasized; the massive buildup of "total strategy" was finally being reversed, in fact, with bases closing, military budgets and manpower reduced, and conscription relaxed. The "thump and talk" strategy which had produced the Nkomati Accord had entered, under President F. W. de Klerk, a prolonged "talk" phase. Regional diplomacy still had its awkward moments. Pretoria had, after all, for many years attempted to treat its neighbors and armed surrogates much as it treated its Bantustans—with contempt and racist condescension. (Captured Renamo documents displayed these attitudes *in flagrante*.) But the grand apartheid scheme that centered on the Bantustans was unraveling by 1991, and Pretoria seemed to be struggling to reform its approach to black leadership generally. In November 1990, Foreign Minister Roelof ("Pik") Botha held a "prayer breakfast" in Lusaka with President Kenneth Kaunda of Zambia (the leader of the antiapartheid Frontline States coalition), President Chissano, and President Yoweri Museveni of Uganda, at which Botha called his companions "my African brothers" and preached peace. (The idea for a "prayer breakfast" was Museveni's, who said he had once attended such a thing with some U.S. congressmen. According to the Associated Press, Museveni "wanted to organize something similar . . . but as he was not a good Christian he asked Kaunda to be host.")[26] In May 1991, Botha boasted to the South African parliament that his government would be establishing diplomatic relations with fifteen new countries by the end of the year—and among the countries mentioned were Togo, Ivory Coast, Morocco, and Madagascar.[27]

Mozambique–South African relations had never been warmer. To help improve security on the battered Cahora Bassa power lines, Pretoria began providing military equipment to Maputo, and in early 1989 the restrictions on the number of Mozambican mineworkers were lifted. The South African trade mission in Maputo was expanded, and its new housing complex, built "on the choicest stretch of Maputo beach," was gallantly named after Pik Botha's wife, Helen.[28] But the gesture that best captured the nature of the new bilateral relations, somehow, was the exchange of gifts between Presidents Chissano and Botha at their meeting in September 1988. Chissano gave Botha a superb example of Makonde sculpture. Botha gave Chissano a Krugerrand.

Official South African support for Renamo seemed to have ended. That left the question of free-lance support. As the novelist Nadine Gordimer wrote, "It is not enough to wash one's hands of South Africa's shameful past involvement in the destabilization of Mozambique by disclaiming any present involvement of the South African government. . . . If the South African government is not supporting Renamo, other forces in South Africa are. [President] De Klerk has the power and country-wide network [of] resources to seek out individuals or clandestine agencies who, evidence is clear, continue to arm and supply Renamo's brutal and senseless campaign of pillage and murder. Are such individuals and agencies above the law? Is it not—all considerations of humanity apart—a crime against the sovereignty of a neighbouring country to turn a blind eye while these people promote the devastation of that country? Is theirs not an act of sabotage against De Klerk's own policy of promoting peace in Southern Africa?"[29] Nelson Mandela, shortly after his release from prison, also called on de Klerk to make assisting Renamo a crime.[30]

Frelimo's relations with the ANC, which had suffered from the expulsions required by the Nkomati Accord, were again excellent. Mandela made Mozambique the final stop on his fourteen-country marathon 1990 tour, and a public holiday was declared in Maputo to welcome him. At public rallies in Maputo and Beira, Mandela praised Frelimo for its contributions to ending white-minority rule in southern Africa, and he promised to look into the possibility of a postapartheid government's paying reparations to Mozambique for the devastation wrought by Pretoria. It was a historic visit, with triumphalist overtones, but not, from all accounts, overly solemn. At the Maputo rally, Chissano surprised Mandela with a framed copy of a warrant for his arrest issued by the Portuguese colonial authorities in 1962; the warrant said Mandela had last been seen "wearing a long beard and a chauffeur's uniform, with a beret."[31] Of course, there was no saying when Mandela and the ANC might actually come to power in South Africa. And there was no saying just how Mozambique would be protected, either, after the war with Renamo ended, from the vast economic power of its mineral-rich neighbor. Maputo was already rife with rumors that South African corporations were buying up huge tracts of Mozambican farmland under the liberalized foreign-investment codes.

Multinational corporations were another of the structures

with which Frelimo was going to have to learn to share power in a pluralistic Mozambique. The fear among nationalists of every political hue was that the country, "opened up," would simply revert to a system resembling that of the early twentieth century, when foreign-owned chartered companies were, for a fee, given free rein to exploit the territory's people and resources. Because of the war, so little foreign investment had materialized that these fears were as yet untested. But in my brief jaunt with Gimo, the regional planner, around the Lonrho cotton farm in the Beira Corridor, I had been struck by the findings of his household survey. It seemed that Metuchira, the area around the Lonrho farm, had, largely because of the farm, more jobs than most areas in the Corridor, but at the same time it had one of the worst quality-of-life ratings of any area studied. Infant mortality was appallingly high, and an unusually high percentage of households had no possessions whatsoever. Gimo was at a loss to explain the findings—beyond observing that low-wage agricultural jobs seemed to do nothing to alleviate poverty. A Lonrho official in London later told me, referring to the company's investments in Mozambique, "We try to bring a bit of peace and tranquility and order to a country with very little of that." Metuchira, he said, was "a microcosm" of what a company like Lonrho could do for a country like Mozambique.[32]

Gimo's colleague, it may be recalled, had dismissed some of the attacks on settlements in the Corridor as "social banditry." "Among us," he had said. "Not Renamo." In the terrible equation of the war, this was the great unknown factor: How much of the violence was free-lance, possibly immune even to a permanent cease-fire? Profound social change has often been accompanied by widespread social banditry. The Soviet Union swarmed with rural bandits for years after the Bolshevik Revolution and the ensuing civil war, and so did southern Italy in the early twentieth century as industrial capitalism made its first incursions there. In modern Africa, many countries suffered waves of banditry after gaining independence. In Uganda, the phenomenon was known as *kondoism*, and its ravages helped create a general instability that contributed to the rise of Idi Amin. In Mozambique, the extension of Portuguese rule in the early twentieth century helped generate an eruption of banditry at its frontiers.[33] But just as there is a critical distinction to be made between a guerrilla army and bandits, historians distinguish between "social banditry" and ordinary robbery and violence.[34] Social bandits are peasants who oppose central authority and often enjoy a certain amount of local popularity. Idealized, they are Robin Hoods. They are ill organized, traditionalist, and rarely survive for long. In Mozambique, the *matsangas* themselves bore some of the markings of classical social bandits— their legendary invulnerability to bullets, for instance,[35] and their deep peasant's hatred of the state and all its works.[36]

Nobody could say with precision—certainly I couldn't—what percentage of the men living by the gun in the bush in Mozambique fell where on the spectrum that ran from politically motivated guerrillas through antiauthoritarian peasant social bandits to mere criminals. The spectrum itself had been badly twisted by the creation, under colonialism and since, of a deracinated class of African peasant-soldiers that Ali Mazrui, while writing about Uganda, has called the "lumpen militariat." Renamo's internal leadership was apparently made up largely of such men, men whose few skills loomed frighteningly large in Mozambique simply because, as Mazrui writes, "control over the means of destruction . . . was more decisive in a situation of technical underdevelopment than was the control over the means of production."[37] The central role of this lumpen militariat did not mean, however, that Renamo and the various types of bandits working in Mozambique were therefore a fundamentally military problem. Those who persisted in believing that South Africa was the satanic puppeteer who kept the war going were, in essence, clinging to this conception. But the evidence was everywhere that Renamo and the anarchy in Mozambique had long since become a fundamentally political problem—a painful reflection, that is, of profound internal conflicts.[38]

Periods of widespread hardship and upheaval also give rise, typically, to millenarian movements. In the early twentieth century, a series of antiwitchcraft movements swept through southeast Africa, often in response to the disruptions caused by the introduction of the migrant labor system. Men returning to their villages with their savings would find themselves plagued by thieves or importunate neighbors and relatives, overcharged by *curandeiros* or prospective in-laws, or despairing of their wives' fidelity. In a world where misfortune was routinely ascribed to witchcraft, these sorts of difficulties called for a spiritual solution. Hence the rise of the Murimi movement around 1915 in Inhambane, the Chaviari movement around Beira in 1931, the *muchape* movement throughout southeast Africa in 1934, and the Zionist movement, which began in the cities of South Africa in the 1920s and soon spread across the region.[39] Some of these movements had Christian elements, others did not, but all had prophets who promised to purify the world of sorcery, restore the balance of society and the vitality of the earth, banish misfortune, and otherwise usher in the millennium.[40] Frelimo tapped a vein of peasant millenarianism during the *luta armada*, when the dream of a world utterly transformed after colonialism merged more or less seamlessly with the modern revolutionary's hard-nosed military and political strategy.[41] Renamo, too, tapped this vein with its faith in "miracles" and with its display of at least some of what E. J. Hobsbawm has suggested are the leading characteristics of millenarian movements, including "a profound and total rejection of the present, evil world" and "a fundamental vagueness about the actual way in which the new society will be brought about."[42]

But the true millenarian movements to rise from the ashes of the war and famines that consumed Mozambique in the 1980s were not really associated with either side. In southern Gaza province in the late 1980s, a prophet named Mongoi brought peace to a small area that was completely surrounded by war. The spirit of a village headman who had died some thirty years before, Mongoi, speaking through the body of his niece, so impressed the local Renamo commanders with his powers that, as of 1990, there had been no attacks in the area since 1987. Provincial officials were said to oppose Mongoi, but local officials had refused to suppress him—they even participated in religious ceremonies conducted by the prophet—and President Chissano had ordered that Mongoi be left alone.[43] Meanwhile, in Zambézia, a major millenarian movement was developing under the leadership of a young, Makua-speaking *curandeiro* named Manuel António. Known as Naprama, Makua for "irresistible force," António claimed to have died of measles, been resurrected after six days in the grave, and gone to the mountains, where Jesus Christ showed him how to make an antibullet vaccine and commanded him to take back the land from Renamo, but without using violence. With a small force of vaccinated, spear-wielding followers known as Napramas, António chased Renamo out of several areas of Nampula and then, in 1990, traveled south to Zambézia, where he began his work in earnest.[44]

By early 1991, António and his followers had, according to reports, completely transformed large sections of eastern Zambézia. Their approach to ending the war was strikingly simple. If they proposed to liberate Murrua, they went to camps for *deslocados*, gathered everyone from Murrua, vaccinated the men by rubbing a magic plant into three cuts made in their chests, and marched to Murrua. Their uniform consisted of a red ribbon pinned to their clothes. They carried spears and machetes, rattled tin cans, and blew on cow horns—and the *matsangas*, terrified, fled at their approach. The Napramas believed António was Jesus, and he periodically reenacted his death and resurrection. He claimed to lead as many as 30,000 men. Whatever their number, the Napramas were not, blessedly, a full-time army. When they were needed, they marched. Otherwise, they stayed home and farmed. And by early 1991, the Napramas had resettled at least 100,000 peasants on the land. It was an infinitely more successful campaign than any Frelimo had launched in more than a decade of war. Best of all, the peasants in eastern Zambézia seemed to be enjoying one of those rare moments in Mozambique's recorded history: they were actually being left alone. Frelimo considered the Napramas allies, but had not hastened to reassert its authority in the newly liberated areas. The International Committee of the Red Cross, which had by now worked out its differences with Renamo, could not seem to work out anything with Manuel António. Free of war, famine, forced labor, forced villagization, and international aid, the peasants were even, it was said, starting to get decent prices for their crops.

I never heard what became of most of the Zambézians I met. I never heard whether the Namanyangas, the family wearing tree bark in Morrumbala, were resettled on their land; whether Augusto Mainyoa, who had been bayonetted by soldiers, became a Naprama; or whether Orlando Galave, the *mutilado* living across the border in Malawi, ever dared to return to Mozambique.

Geoff Mwanja, the kindly administrator in Nsanje, got letters from *deslocados;* passersby like me did not. The scraps of news that did find me were worrisome. "Little Annie" finally crashed, I heard, in 1989 in Caia. (A friend who saw the wreckage at the airstrip there said she had heard—but rather doubted—that nobody was hurt in the accident.) In mid-1989, the road from Quelimane to Ile, the home of Luísa Sábado and the other children who listened so raptly to Dividas's stories about the flying pig and the heartbroken crocodile, was finally reopened. It may have been too late. On April 10, 1989, a Reuters story had reported that "some 3,800 people, mainly children, died in a measles outbreak" in the districts of Gile and Ile in January and February.

The last letter I had from Dividas, in mid-1990, said that he was doing well—still working for CARE International, looking forward to a training course in England, "still living in that rough building without water." People in Maputo, he wrote, were "very eager to know the outcome of the conversation between Renamo and Frelimo. . . . You know, what we want now is PEACE. Then we will solve the rest." Dividas was enthusiastic about the recent reforms, writing, "Now I understand we have some freedom of speech—Chissano is a nice guy." He still traveled up-country as an interpreter, and on his last trip to Zambézia, he had heard some interesting news. It seemed that Renamo had attacked Ile early on the morning after we were there. "I am sure they thought we were still there because we had lost our flight back to town," Dividas wrote. I remembered his confidence that the plane would return. It had never occurred to me that our presence—my presence, really—could provoke an attack. Had it occurred to the people I met? If it had—and it must have, at least to some people—why hadn't they been more hostile? Dividas didn't say whether anyone was hurt in the attack. He just wrote, "Luck still with us."

Then there was Manhiça, where the attacks never seemed to stop. Less than two months after I was there, twenty-two people were killed at a secondary school outside the town. Two months after that, twenty-seven were killed and forty kidnapped at Maragra, the agro-industrial center where Lina Magaia once worked. The following month, another fifteen were killed at Maragra. The news of these attacks reached me in staccato situation reports from the United Nations, or as small items buried in a long list of similar items published in a "Destablisation Calendar" in the Mozambican news agency's monthly newsletter. I read them in my office in New York City, trying to picture some of the events they described—the terror, the grief—and failing utterly. Then, on a Monday morning in November 1990, I got a phone call from Lina. She was crying. She said that Zeca De Sousa had been killed in an attack on the highway the day before. "He was a good man!" she shouted. "He loved my country!" Lina's sobs shook the long phone line between us.

Notes

One

1. Africa Recovery Programme, United Nations Economic Commission for Africa, *South African Destabilization: The Economic Cost of Frontline Resistance to Apartheid* (New York, 1989), p. 6, Table 2, and p. 21. This figure is for deaths caused directly and indirectly by the war between 1980 and 1988. It includes nearly 500,000 infants and children under five. Deaths indirectly caused by the war include those of people who "perished through the disruption of food production, prevention of food distribution and the spread of disease as a result of the destruction of health facilities and interruption of vaccination campaigns" (p. 21).

2. The 3,000,000 figure is from an item in the *Washington Post*, November 26, 1990. The other figures are from a report prepared jointly by the United Nations and the Mozambican government and presented to a World Bank meeting in Paris in December 1990 (cited in Iain Christie, "Mozambique Needs a Million Tons of Food Aid to Avert Hunger," Reuters [Maputo], December 9, 1990; Jonathan Clayton, "Millions at Risk in Africa in One of Worst Famines Ever Known," Reuters [Nairobi], December 19, 1990).

3. Roy A. Stacy, deputy assistant secretary of state for African affairs, speaking in Maputo at an international conference sponsored by the United Nations (reported in *New York Times*, April 27, 1988).

4. One was a DC-3, carrying a group of French geophysicists, shot down in 1981. The other was a Malawian commercial airliner with ten people aboard, shot down in 1987.

5. *Washington Times*, December 15, 1986.

6. Paul Moorcraft, "Mozambique's Long Civil War," *International Defense Review* (Geneva), October 1987, p. 1314.

7. By 1988, the number of cattle in Mozambique was estimated to have declined by nearly two-thirds since independence—1,400,000 head had become 490,000. According to the National Livestock Directorate, most of the decline was attributable to the depredations of Renamo and of rustlers who sold meat illegally in the cities (Mozambique Embassy, "Update," Washington, D.C., April 6, 1990, citing Radio Mozambique). Leroy Vail points out, however, that in Zambézia in the late 1970s large numbers of cattle were dying from sleeping sickness (African trypanosomiasis). In regions affected by the tsetse fly, which carries the disease, cattle must be—but were not being—treated against it.

Big game and other wildlife in Mozambique were also under severe pressure from the war. The elephant population was estimated to have declined by 70 percent in less than a decade—from 54,800 in 1979 to 16,600 in 1988—mainly as a result of poaching by Renamo, the army, the popular militia, and the Zimbabwean troops stationed in central Mozambique. The white rhino had disappeared, and in early 1987 there were reported to be fewer than one hundred black rhino left. Leopard and zebra hides were being illegally exported, along with rhino horns and vast quantities of elephant tusks—illegal ivory trading was, according to many sources, a major source of income for Renamo. Mozambican ivory was reportedly being smuggled out through Swaziland and South Africa—where the army was also involved in a massive illegal ivory trade from Angola—and through Burundi. See Craig Van Note, "Statement on U.S. Enforcement of the Convention on International Trade in Endangered Species," testimony before the Subcommittee on Oversight and Investigations of the House Merchant Marine and Fisheries Committee, July 14, 1988 (Washington, D.C.) (Van Note was executive vice president of Monitor, a consortium of major conservation, environmental, and animal welfare organizations); Eddie Koch, "Did 100,000 Elephants Die to Pay for the War in Angola?" *Weekly Mail* (Johannesburg), September 2–8, 1988; Don Allan, "Conservation Activities Collapse in Mozambique," *World Wildlife Fund News* (Washington, D.C.), January–February 1987.

Two

1. August 17, 1988.
2. For a discussion of Renamo's relations with *régulos, majubas,* and *curandeiros,* and of the role of Ndau-speakers, see Chapter 9.
3. Such attire did not mean, as some readers might assume, that the family had returned to neolithic privations. The everyday use of bark clothing had not ceased in Zambézia until the mid-1950s (Leroy Vail and Landeg White, *Capitalism and Colonialism in Mozambique: A Study of Quelimane District* [Minneapolis, 1980], p. 376).
4. A European journalist who worked on a Frelimo magazine in Maputo shortly after independence told me that he was mystified at first by his editor's insistence that President Samora Machel's image be featured on the cover of virtually every issue. Was the editor, a Mozambican, trying to create a Machel cult? No, the editor explained to the European, he was just trying to create an awareness that Mozambique now *had* a president, and that this was what he looked like.
5. This goes for local chiefs and headmen such as Tandekia as well, of course. Vail and White (in *Capitalism and Colonialism,* p. 105) describe a Chief Mponda, who lived in the nineteenth century on the shores of what is today Lake Malawi and "was reported to keep two flags in a sack, British and Portuguese, for hoisting as diplomacy demanded."

Three

1. *Independent* (London), February 24, 1988.
2. *New York Times,* March 20, 1988.
3. Dr. Abdul Noormahomed and Dr. Julie Cliff, Mozambican Ministry of Health, *The Impact on Health in Mozambique of South African Destabilization,* 3rd ed. (Maputo, April 1990).
4. Dr. Abdul Noormahomed and Dr. Julie Cliff, Mozambican Ministry of Health, *The Impact on Health in Mozambique of South African Destabilization,* 2nd ed. (Maputo, December 1987).
5. *New York Times,* July 24, 1987; *Times* (London), December 16, 1987.
6. Report by the Coordinating Council of the Mozambican

Ministry of Education, cited in *Mozambiquefile* (Maputo), August 1990, p. 11.

7. "General Plan No. 1 of 24 February 1984," *Documentos da Gorongosa* (Maputo, 1985). These documents, which included the notebooks of the secretary to Renamo's commander-in-chief, were captured when the Renamo headquarters at Gorongosa, in central Mozambique, were overrun by Mozambican and Zimbabwean forces in August 1985, and excerpts were later published in English translation by the Mozambican Ministry of Information. The elements of this "General Plan" were (1) "Destroy the Mozambican economy in the rural zones"; (2) "Destroy the communications routes to prevent exports and imports to and from abroad, and the movement of domestic produce"; (3) "Prevent the activities of foreigners (cooperantes) because they are the most dangerous in the recovery of the economy."

8. Statement issued at a conference in Hammanskraal, South Africa, September 28, 1984, and cited in Joseph Hanlon, *Beggar Your Neighbours: Apartheid Power in Southern Africa* (London, 1986), p. 146.

9. August 24, 1987, p. 29.

10. September 18, 1987.

11. Robert Gersony, Bureau for Refugee Programs, U.S. Department of State, *Summary of Mozambican Refugee Accounts of Principally Conflict-Related Experience in Mozambique* (Washington, D.C., April 1988), p. 35.

12. This perceptual shift, simple as it sounds, was not smooth. One of the first former captives of Renamo I interviewed was an Italian priest who had been marched by the rebels from Luabo, near the mouth of the Zambezi, to Malawi over forty days. I found him in a monastery on the outskirts of Quelimane. In our interview, he subtly but firmly refused to demonize his captors, and I was surprised to find myself annoyed, even appalled, by his reticence, and by the "moral equivalence" between the two sides that I thought his sad, quiet, apolitical descriptions of the war implied. Subsequent interviews with other former Renamo captives and *deslocados* only added to my confusion, as I continued to get a vastly more nuanced, ambiguous description of the war than I had expected to find. I grew disoriented even in Maputo. When someone there told me about a ring of car thieves,

I somehow couldn't picture who its members might be. It was as if my idea of Mozambique did not include a category for simple car thieves. My informant, taking pity on a clueless foreigner, tried to reassure me by saying, "Don't worry. I'm sure it's just Renamo taking the cars." This strange and disabling aporia began to ease only after I left Mozambique for a fortnight's R & R in Zimbabwe. There I met an American correspondent who had done a great deal of reporting in rural Mozambique. I was intermittently delirious with a case of malaria contracted in Zambézia, but he listened to my fevered stories of chaos and paradox with great understanding, corroborating many of my impressions and saying simply, "It's a complicated war." I took this talismanic remark back with me to Mozambique, where it helped me keep my balance thereafter.

Four

1. The brief history of Mozambique which follows is drawn largely from the following sources: Allen Isaacman and Barbara Isaacman, *Mozambique: From Colonialism to Revolution, 1900–1982* (Boulder, Colo., 1983); Thomas H. Henriksen, *Mozambique: A History* (London, 1978); M. D. D. Newitt, *Portuguese Settlement on the Zambezi* (New York, 1973); Joseph Hanlon, *Mozambique: The Revolution Under Fire* (London, 1984), pp. 15–76. For a fuller history of Frelimo's development, see Chapters 13 and 14.

2. Isaacman and Isaacman, *Mozambique*, pp. 31–32.

3. This remained true into the modern era. Of Boror, a giant coconut company in Zambézia, Leroy Vail and Landeg White (in *Capitalism and Colonialism in Mozambique: A Study of Quelimane District* [Minneapolis, 1980], p. 374) write: "[I]t was not until 1966 that Boror first used artificial fertilizers, having previously kept many of its cattle under the coconut palms and relied on nature. To the company's surprise yields went up by 90 percent. In the same year Boror began to experiment with the dwarf *palmeira ana* from Malaysia in place of the 80-foot-high *grande moçambicana*. By 1976 it was clear that the attempt to produce a hybrid was phenomenally successful, the new trees producing more, larger and sweeter nuts only 10–15 feet from the ground and occupying 60 percent of the soil space. Yet similar dwarf trees had been grown for decades as close as Mada-

gascar and their use had been advocated as early as 1888 by Augusto de Castilho. The tea industry also showed similar sluggishness."

4. Leroy Vail points out that these figures may be misleading. Because of the system of shifting cultivation required by conditions in most of Mozambique, perhaps only one-third of the country's land should ever be under cultivation at one time. In Malawi, where similar agricultural conditions exist, population pressure prevents the necessary fallowing, with disastrous results for soil quality and productivity.

5. Figures are from Isaacman and Isaacman, *Mozambique,* p. 33.

6. Hanlon, *Mozambique,* p. 18.

7. Ibid., p. 21.

8. Ibid.

9. Ibid., p. 40.

10. Ibid., p. 22.

11. This is the figure most often given. See, for instance, Wilfred Burchett's interview with Alberto Joaquim Chipande, an eyewitness. Chipande was a founding member of Frelimo and, at the time of the interview, Mozambique's minister of defense. At the time of the Mueda massacre, he was a twenty-two-year-old schoolteacher. He concludes his account, "Over 600 people were killed" (Wilfred Burchett, *Southern Africa Stands Up: The Revolutions in Angola, Mozambique, Zimbabwe, Namibia and South Africa* [New York, 1978], pp. 130–31). Thomas Henriksen, however, endorses the estimate of a Portuguese eyewitness who told him that only between 60 and 80 people were killed (Thomas H. Henriksen, *Revolution and Counterrevolution: Mozambique's War of Independence, 1964–1974* [Westport, Conn., 1983], pp. 19, 220).

12. Iain Christie, *Machel of Mozambique* (Harare, Zimbabwe, 1988), p. 141.

13. The camp was at Nyazonia, in northern Manica province. Reports on the number of people killed varied. Hanlon (*Mozambique,* p. 51) gives a figure of 875, without citation. Barry Munslow (*Mozambique: The Revolution and Its Origins* [New York, 1983], p. 167) gives a figure of 600 killed. The New York magazine *Southern Africa* (10, no. 5 [June–July 1977]: 7) reported 640 dead.

14. Ken Flower, *Serving Secretly: An Intelligence Chief on Record, Rhodesia into Zimbabwe, 1964 to 1981* (London, 1987), p. 301. For another version of Renamo's origins and the Zimbabwe liberation war from the Rhodesian military perspective, see Barbara Cole, *The Elite: The Story of the Rhodesian Special Air Service* (Amanzimtoti, South Africa, 1984).

15. The brief history of Renamo which follows is drawn largely from the following sources: Hanlon, *Mozambique*, pp. 219–33; Isaacman and Isaacman, *Mozambique*, pp. 176–78; Phyllis Johnson and David Martin, "Mozambique: Victims of Apartheid," in *Frontline Southern Africa: Destructive Engagement*, ed. Phyllis Johnson and David Martin (New York, 1988); Andre E. A. M. Thomashausen, "The Mozambique National Resistance (Resistência Nacional Moçambicana—Renamo)," in *Weerstandsbewegings in Suider-Afrika*, ed. C. J. Maritz (Potchefstroom, 1987); Joseph Hanlon, *Beggar Your Neighbours: Apartheid Power in Southern Africa* (London, 1986), pp. 139–50; Paul Fauvet, "Roots of Counter-Revolution: The Mozambican National Resistance," *Review of African Political Economy* (Sheffield, England), July 1984, pp. 108–21; Colin Legum, "The MNR," *CSIS Africa Notes* (Georgetown University, Washington, D.C.), no. 16, July 15, 1983; Paul Fauvet and Alves Gomes, "The 'Mozambique National Resistance,'" *AIM Information Bulletin* (Maputo), no. 69, n.d.

16. Hanlon, *Beggar Your Neighbours*, pp. 133–35.

17. Flower, *Serving Secretly*, p. 262.

18. The Zimbabwe-Maputo, Malawi-Beira, and Malawi-Nacala lines had all been cut. The Zimbabwe-Beira line was still operating, despite frequent attacks.

19. In November 1984, "the MNR sent letters to large numbers of colonial-era residents living in Lisbon, urging them to return to Mozambique and promising that their former property would be returned when the MNR comes to power" (Gillian Gunn, "Post-Nkomati Mozambique," *CSIS Africa Notes* [Georgetown University, Washington, D.C.], no. 38, January 8, 1985, p. 3). Among the Portuguese-owned businesses reported to be channeling support to Renamo from South Africa were import-export companies, catering firms, air and ground freight services, and travel agencies. President Samora Machel, who usually insisted that Renamo was strictly a South African proxy

force, with no other political identity, nonetheless elaborated eloquently the Portuguese connection in a December 1982 speech to representatives of religious organizations: "Do you know who pays the armed bandits? It is your former bosses. The ones who lost private schools, clinics, hospitals and maternity homes. Who pays the armed bandits are the former owners of buildings throughout our country, who lost them to the benefit of the Mozambican people. They are the lawyers who lost their practices, the cattle farmers, the haulage contractors, the aircraft owners who transported troops. These are the bosses of the armed bandits" (*AIM Information Bulletin* [Maputo], no. 78, n.d., p. 28).

20. At, for example, the seventeenth annual conference of the World Anti-Communist League, held in San Diego in September 1984, Renamo representatives were reportedly looking for 500 surface-to-air missiles, AK-47 ammunition "for up to 30,000 people," 500 bazookas, 100 Jeeps with gun mounts, 5 coastal cutters, and Special Forces equipment and instructors ("enough for 30 teams") to carry out "special assignments" (Scott Anderson and John Lee Anderson, *Inside the League: The Shocking Exposé of How Terrorists, Nazis, and Latin American Death Squads Have Infiltrated the World Anti-Communist League* [New York, 1986], p. 259).

21. For a fuller treatment of United States policy toward Mozambique, see Chapter 18.

22. A sampling: In November 1988, according to the Mozambique Information Agency, General A. J. Liebenberg of the South African Army publicly acknowledged that forces inside South Africa were still supporting Renamo, and in April 1989, according to the same agency, a Renamo attack on the border town of Ressano Garcia, in which ten civilians were killed, featured direct South African military participation, including transport for Renamo fighters in a South African Army vehicle and searchlights directed into the town (*Mozambiquefile* [Maputo], December 1988, May 1989). In March 1990, the South African *Weekly Mail* reported an array of ongoing contacts between the South African military and Renamo inside South Africa, as well as support for Renamo being provided by two Portuguese civilians living near the border with Mozambique (Eddie Koch, "Renamo's Secret SA Bases," *Weekly Mail* [Johannesburg], March 16,

1990). On May 14, 1990, according to the Mozambique Information Agency, the Mozambican Army overran a large Renamo base at Ngungwe, in a mountainous area only a mile from the South African border, and found a supply road built from the base to the border, along which the rebel survivors fled (*Mozambiquefile* [Maputo], June 1990). Despite such incidents, President Chissano told the *Washington Post* (as reported in its October 17, 1990, issue), "I feel that the government of South Africa is not supporting Renamo." Chissano did add, however, that he felt "there are negative elements in South Africa," including perhaps "some elements" in the South African military, that might still be supporting the rebels.

23. *Independent* (London), November 4, 1987.

24. Fernandes' murder generated many charges and countercharges and at least one diplomatic scandal—resulting in the expulsion from Portugal of a Mozambican diplomat named as a suspect and the expulsion of a Portuguese diplomat from Mozambique in retaliation. In April 1989, Alexander Xavier Chagas, a Portuguese national, was convicted of the murder after telling a court in Cascais that he had killed Fernandes on instructions from South Africa (*Mozambiquefile* [Maputo], June 1989). Many observers believed that Chagas was actually working for the Serviço Nacional de Segurança Popular, the Mozambican secret service, and that Fernandes was killed in the course of a bungled operation after he had refused a Frelimo offer to defect. See Alex Vines, *Renamo: Terrorism in Mozambique* (London, 1991), pp. 37–38.

Five

1. This was the estimate of a French slave trader testifying before a British Commission of Enquiry at Mauritius (Edward A. Alpers, *Ivory and Slaves in East Central Africa* [London, 1975], p. 216).

2. *Financial Times* (London), August 15, 1988.

3. *Weekly Mail* (Johannesburg), March 4–10, 1988.

4. *Emergency Mozambique* (Maputo), October 1988.

5. *Newsweek*, August 8, 1988, p. 12.

6. "General Plan No. 1 of 24 February 1984," *Documentos da Gorongosa* (Maputo, 1985).

7. "From 1981 to March 1986, at least 34 foreign-contracted

workers . . . were murdered, 66 kidnapped, and five wounded by the MNR. They included nationals of Brazil, Britain, Bulgaria, China, France, the German Democratic Republic, Ireland, Italy, Portugal, Romania, the Soviet Union, Sri Lanka, and Sweden. At least 12 priests and nuns were among those murdered and kidnapped" (Phyllis Johnson and David Martin, "Mozambique: Victims of Apartheid," in *Frontline Southern Africa: Destructive Engagement,* ed. Phyllis Johnson and David Martin [New York, 1988], n. 45, p. 474).

8. *Independent* (London), June 11, 1990.

Seven

1. Then, in July 1989, I read that three Calamidades officials in Quelimane had been arrested for stealing 456 sheets of zinc roofing. The accused were the provincial head of logistics, the provincial head of merchandising, and a forwarding agent named Ismail Taibo—just possibly my former escort. In April 1990, it was reported that the three men had each been sentenced to twelve years in prison (*Mozambiquefile* [Maputo], July 1989, p. 11; April 1990, p. 11).

2. Of the 5,998 first-level primary schools in Mozambique in 1983, 3,096 (51.6 percent) had been, by 1989, destroyed or forced to close by Renamo. In Zambézia, 72.3 percent of first-level primary schools had been lost (Report by the Coordinating Council of the Ministry of Education, cited in *Mozambiquefile* [Maputo], August 1990, p. 11). Jan Overvest, the provincial director of education in Zambézia, also told me that so many children, their education disrupted by the war, had been forced to start school over again that a majority of students in Zambézia were, by 1988, in the first grade. More than half of the province's first-graders were, in addition, *deslocados*, who were often too hungry to attend school, preferring to spend the precious daylight hours searching for food. Teachers went hungry as well. According to Overvest, one of his teachers had gone three days without eating, then fainted dead away in front of his class. In Mopeia, he said, his teachers were spending their days in the forest, foraging and testing wild shrubs for toxicity. All schools were expected to develop food-production units: a garden, a fishery, chickens, rabbits. In Morrumbala, Overvest said, forty teachers—all male; female teachers were not sent to places consid-

ered highly vulnerable to attack—were living without their families. Many of his teachers, Overvest said, had been kidnapped or killed, and several had been mutilated. Some had lost all of their possessions three or four times, and were now psychologically traumatized. Over half of the children in Zambézia were similarly scarred, he estimated. Many thousands were orphans. His department had started offering a training course for teachers to help them work with troubled children.

Eight

1. In an effort to control military spending, the IMF-approved economic-recovery program had ordered a reduction in the size of the armed forces—from around 40,000 men. But defense still consumed more than 40 percent of the Mozambican national budget.

2. The British were offering a three-month course for approximately 350 Mozambican soldiers a year at Nyanga Camp in eastern Zimbabwe. The course was, as the director of training told the *Independent* (London) of October 4, 1987, "very basic training. Ironically, these guys will return to Mozambique and be considered specialists, after just 12 weeks." The Soviets were offering a somewhat longer course inside Mozambique, in the province of Nampula, and the "red berets" produced by the Soviet program were the army's most effective force, having spearheaded the crucial 1987 counteroffensive in Zambézia. The differences between the training provided by these programs (and other internationally funded programs) and what the Mozambican Army could afford to provide its own recruits were, from all accounts, profound. I was told, for example, that in six months of Mozambican military training, a recruit could expect to fire no more than thirty live bullets.

3. This figure was given by both the *New York Times* and the *Washington Post* on July 31, 1988. Other estimates were lower. Renamo's estimates were, naturally, higher.

4. The *New York Times* of February 21, 1988, suggested that it was costing Zimbabwe as much as a million dollars a day to keep soldiers in Mozambique. The Zimbabwean government would acknowledge spending only about one-tenth that amount.

5. Renamo "declared war on" Zimbabwe in October 1986, in retaliation for President Mugabe's decision to send Zimbab-

wean troops into Mozambique. Between June 15, 1987, and April 9, 1989, Zimbabwe reported 375 Renamo attacks, most of them on villages along the Mozambican border, with 335 civilians killed, 280 wounded, 667 kidnapped, and more than 400 unaccounted for (*Washington Post*, June 5, 1989).

6. Why President Machel avoided "the Angola option"—inviting Cuban troops to defend Mozambique—was the object of much speculation. Some of the explanations offered included Mozambique's inability to pay for help in hard currency (Angola's ability to do so flowed from its oil wealth), Frelimo's determination not to provide the Soviet Union (or any other foreign power) with military bases (Moscow had hoped to gain at least a naval base when Mozambique won its independence), Cuban and/or Soviet unwillingness to become more deeply involved in the war, and Mozambique's fear of endangering its supply of Western aid. The several hundred Cuban military advisers working in Mozambique throughout the 1980s stayed clear of combat and concentrated on militia training. See Gillian Gunn, "Mozambique after Machel," *CSIS Africa Notes* (Georgetown University, Washington, D.C.), no. 67, December 29, 1986; and "Cuba and Mozambique," *CSIS Africa Notes*, no. 80, December 28, 1987.

7. William Minter, "The Mozambican National Resistance (Renamo) as Described by Ex-Participants," research report submitted to the Ford Foundation and the Swedish International Development Agency, March 1989, p. 12, citing sources in Harare. Further details supplied by Minter in interview.

8. *Washington Post*, July 31, 1988; *Africa Confidential* (London) 29, no. 18 (September 9, 1988): 2.

9. Quoted in the *Times* (London), December 15, 1987. Kurt Vonnegut, after a brief trip to Mozambique, went Geldof one better when he described Renamo as "an incurable disease . . . no more to be discussed in terms of good and evil than cholera, say, or bubonic plague" (*Parade* magazine [New York], January 7, 1990).

10. *New York Times*, July 24, 1987. Renamo denied responsibility for the Homoine massacre, insisting it had been committed by disgruntled Frelimo troops, or by Frelimo troops seeking to discredit the rebels. Renamo supporters demanded to know why Western journalists and diplomats had been unable to reach

Homoine immediately after the massacre (see William Pascoe, "Massacre or Manipulation?" *Washington Times,* July 30, 1987). But in January 1991, a Renamo spokesman in the United States may have inadvertently revealed in an interview the rebels' real memory of Homoine. We were discussing the career of Raul Domingos, who had recently left the post of military chief of staff to become Renamo's secretary for external affairs. The spokesman couldn't tell me, when I asked, where Domingos had received his military training, but he did tell me, with a sigh, that Domingos had never actually had much training—that, in fact, and here the spokesman sighed heavily, "Domingos was commander of military activities in southern Mozambique at the time of Homoine." According to one of Renamo's American supporters, "General Domingos" was still Renamo's commander for southern Mozambique in 1988 (Jack Wheeler, "Mozambique," in *The New Insurgencies: Anticommunist Guerrillas in the Third World,* ed. Michael Radu [New Brunswick, N.J., 1990], p. 178).

11. See Christian Geffray and Mögens Pedersen, "Nampula en guerre," *Politique africaine* (Paris) 29 (March 1988): 28–40; and Christian Geffray, *La Cause des armes au Mozambique: Anthropologie d'une guerre civile* (Paris, 1990).

12. A Zimbabwean Army captain described the *deslocados* in another camp in Sofala as "the masses we have captured from the enemy" (*Independent* [London], April 27, 1988). Concerns about an "uncaptured" peasantry have plagued many African states, including peacetime Tanzania.

13. Two months after I was there, Chibabava *was* overrun by Renamo. Thirty-one people were reported killed, and fifty-three wounded. Frelimo soon regained the town, but as of October 1990 Chibabava was still accessible only by air, and food-supply flights had become irregular because of a lack of funds (United Nations, "Emergency Sitrep" [Maputo], mimeograph, October–December 1988; *Mozambiquefile* [Maputo], October 1990).

Nine

1. *Washington Post,* July 31, 1988.

2. The preponderance of published accounts favored the Frelimo view of Renamo as murderous thugs. For a pro-Renamo

account, see Holger Jensen, "Mozambique: Inside the Liberated Zone," a three-part series in the *Washington Times*, December 15–17, 1986. See also the following articles in *Soldier of Fortune* magazine (Boulder, Colo.): "Mission Mozambique" (January 1988); "Renamo: Freedom Fighters' Agenda for Victory" (May 1987); "Marxism Under Siege" (March 1987).

3. The following description of *curandeiros* draws on Carol Barker, "Bringing Health Care to the People," in *A Difficult Road: The Transition to Socialism in Mozambique*, ed. John Saul (New York, 1985), pp. 337–39. Because there is such a range of religious beliefs and practices in different areas of Mozambique, this description is highly synthetic.

4. The same thing happened in many other African countries. In the Dande district of colonial Rhodesia, "the people of Dande shifted their allegiance from the chiefs of the present to the chiefs of the past, the *mhondoro*, who could, of course, only be made available to them by their [spirit] mediums" (David Lan, *Guns and Rain: Guerrillas and Spirit Mediums in Zimbabwe* [Harare, Zimbabwe, 1985], p. 140). Traditional religious authorities also sometimes played an important role in *selecting* chiefs from among the claimants to a vacant post (see, for instance, M. F. C. Bourdillon, S.J., "Traditional Religion in Shona Society," in *Christianity South of the Zambezi*, ed. J. A. Dachs [Gwelo, Zimbabwe, 1973], 1 : 18). And while the balance of religious and political authority vested in chiefs varied from place to place, an overall effect of colonial rule in Africa was clearly to secularize the chiefly function, to push chiefs out of the rainmaking business and into tax collection.

5. African armies have very often relied on such methods. In fact, belief in the magic properties of an animal tail, known as a *nyumbe*, was a prominent feature of the Barue army's strategy in its war of resistance against the Portuguese in the Zambezi Valley in 1902. "By raising the *nyumbe* in battle, [the Barue chief] Makombe's general had the power to turn bullets into water" (Allen F. Isaacman, *The Tradition of Resistance in Mozambique: The Zambesi Valley 1850–1921* [Berkeley, 1976], p. 63).

6. Documents found December 5, 1981, at Garagua, Mozambique.

7. The Ndau are best understood not as a "tribe" but as a regional system of chieftaincies and totemic clans in which a dis-

tinctive dialect of Shona is spoken. This system was apparently part of the Mbire state, a province of the Muenemutapa empire, in the sixteenth century. (According to some historians, however, most of the modern Ndau dynasties were established in the seventeenth century, after the southeastward flight of groups of Shona-speakers known as Rozvi from the Portuguese and from civil wars in the Mutapa state; see D. N. Beach, *The Shona and Zimbabwe, 900–1850* [London, 1980], p. 254; and M. F. C. Bourdillon, *The Shona Peoples: An Ethnography of the Contemporary Shona, with Special Reference to Their Religion* [Gweru, Zimbabwe, 1982], p. 12.) Because its territory contained no gold, the region experienced almost no European penetration until the late nineteenth century. Though agriculturally rich, it conducted relatively little external trade, and the people apparently had no ethnic self-awareness beyond their chiefly group and patronymic clan—indeed, the term *Ndau* only came into use in the nineteenth century, as an expression of contempt by the Nguni overlords of the Gaza state for their Shona subjects. (The term described, according to J. K. Rennie, "their submissive salutation"; see "Christianity, Colonialism and the Origins of Nationalism among the Ndau of Southern Rhodesia 1890–1935" [Ph.D. diss., Northwestern University, 1973], p. 155.) According to Beach (p. 190), "the Ndau-speaking Shona called themselves 'Shangaans' after the Gaza ruler Soshangane." They began calling themselves "Ndau" only after the early European missionaries and linguists did so.

As with many other ethnic and linguistic designations made in Africa by Europeans, however, those that defined the Ndau were arbitrary and problematic. As Rennie (p. 43) writes, "If there is a language called 'Ndau' this is at least partly due to the historical accident of its having received missionary recognition and having been accorded the status-symbol of a dictionary and a mission vernacular literature." One of the main distinctions between Ndau and other forms of the Shona language is, in fact, the large number of Gaza words it came to include (Terence Ranger, "The Nineteenth Century in Southern Rhodesia," in *Aspects of Central African History*, ed. T. O. Ranger [London, 1968], p. 118). For a fascinating description of the interaction between European missionary linguists and some of the descendants of Soshangane's people, see Patrick Harries, "The Roots of Ethnicity: Discourse and the Politics of Language Construction in South-East Africa," *African Affairs* (Bristol, England) 87, no. 346 (1988): 25–52. For some of the projection of this story into modern South African politics, see Patrick Harries, "Exclusion, Classification and Internal Colonialism: The Emergence of Ethnicity among the Tsonga-Speakers of South Africa," in *The Creation of Tribalism in Southern Africa*, ed. Leroy Vail (Berkeley, 1988), pp. 82–117.

Ndau resistance to the imposition of Gaza Nguni rule was led, incidentally, by local religious practitioners, whose talents included the ever popular ability to turn the invaders' bullets to water (Rennie, "Christianity," p. 150). European missionaries and farmers settled in Ndau country primarily on the Rhodesian side of the imperial border—where perhaps a third of all Ndau-speakers lived. On the Portuguese side, where the chartered Companhia de Moçambique reigned, there were, at least before World War II, very few Europeans and no cash economy to mention except around Beira—and yet the Companhia did collect taxes, cotton, and rubber from the Ndau, and the colonial state did press-gang large numbers of Ndaus into forced labor on the roads and, near the coast, the white-owned salt works and coconut, sugar, and cotton plantations (ibid., pp. 41, 43, 169, 354–55).

8. This comparatively permeable color bar in the Portuguese colonies helped give rise to the theory of "lusotropicalism," popularized by Gilberto Freyre, a Brazilian anthropologist, who argued that the Portuguese colonialists and their darker-skinned subjects understood and sympathized with one another more fully than colonialists from northern Europe and *their* subjects did. This theory was happily adopted by the Salazar dictatorship as part of its justification for the Portuguese overseas empire, and it continued to inform the attitudes of many Portuguese officials even after the dissolution of the empire. In 1988, in an interview in Lisbon, José Manuel Durão Barroso, the Portuguese secretary of state for foreign affairs and cooperation—roughly equivalent to the American assistant secretary of state for African affairs—told me that he was confident about the future of Portuguese relations with Mozambique partly because Portuguese technicians could live in the tropics on low pay whereas northern Europeans demonstrably could not; that the

lingering affection for Portugal of former subjects in Angola and Mozambique could be seen in the eagerness with which those who owned radios listened to Portuguese football results; that, indeed, he himself had been told by lusophone African leaders, "We prefer to have been colonized by Portugal"; and that the Salazarist conception of the overseas possessions as provinces rather than colonies had been so sincere that, during his own childhood, Portuguese schoolchildren had been required to learn the names of the mountains and rivers in Mozambique and Angola. Of course, schoolchildren in those colonies had been obliged to learn a great deal about Portuguese geography in their turn— an aspect of the educational system which the Mozambican government, for its part, pointedly discarded after independence.

For a magisterial refutation of the thesis of lusotropicalism, see C. R. Boxer, *Race Relations in the Portuguese Colonial Empire 1415–1825* (London, 1963). As Boxer notes, "Modern Portuguese writers who claim that their compatriots never had any feeling of colour prejudice or of discrimination against the African Negro unaccountably ignore the obvious fact that one race cannot systematically enslave members of another on a large scale for over three centuries without acquiring a conscious or unconscious feeling of racial superiority" (p. 56). In Mozambique, Boxer points out, a seminary for training local black priests was ordered to be established by the eighteenth-century Portuguese dictator the Marquis of Pombal. Nearly two centuries later, not one black priest had yet been ordained in Mozambique (p. 57).

9. Andre E. A. M. Thomashausen, "The Mozambique National Resistance (Resistência Nacional Moçambicana—Renamo)," in *Weerstandsbewegins in Suider-Afrika*, ed. C. J. Maritz (Potchefstroom, 1987), p. 45.

10. Ibid., pp. 58–59 (quoting Department of Defense of Renamo).

11. Paul Fauvet and Alves Gomes, "The 'Mozambique National Resistance,'" *AIM Information Bulletin* (Maputo), no. 69, n.d., p. 5. For a somewhat different account of the betrayal of Matsangaíssa, see Mota Lopes, "The MNR: Opponents or Bandits?" *Africa Report* (New York), January–February 1986, p. 69.

12. The 25,000 figure was given by the *New York Times* of August 30, 1987. The 8,000 figure appeared in the *Washington Post* of July 31, 1988.

13. The psychologist Dr. Neil Boothby, who was working at the Lhanguene Center, described the turning point of this training as a terrible decision about whom to identify with in the midst of violence: the victims or the aggressors. Once a boy made the choice to identify with the powerful and not the powerless, he was a *matsanga*. Reinaldo Mucavele, the director of Lhanguene, told me that his charges reacted violently, however, when other children in the neighborhood called them *bandidos* or *matsangas*. They were now struggling mightily, he said, to shed that identification. The neighborhood children had learned their lesson, but on a field trip to a football match, an adult who recognized the Lhanguene boys made the same mistake, and the boys put him in the hospital.

14. See, for instance, Karl Maier, "The Battle for Zambezia," *Africa Report* (New York), March–April 1989, p. 15.

15. William Minter, "The Mozambican National Resistance (Renamo) as Described by Ex-Participants," research report submitted to the Ford Foundation and the Swedish International Development Agency, March 1989, p. 5.

16. *Mozambiquefile* (Maputo), November 1989, p. 6.

17. This sort of choice had been faced before, of course, by many Africans, especially young men, when invading armies swept through their homelands. In Ndau country, for instance, where no standing army had existed prior to the Gaza Nguni invasion, young men who adopted certain Nguni cultural practices, such as the invaders' language, were eligible to join the Gaza army. And, according to Rennie ("Christianity," pp. 147–50), "Membership in the army was membership in a new type of political community. The pre-Gaza chieftaincies were firmly rooted in a territorial basis. Individuals or communities coming under the protection of one of these chieftaincies would ask for a 'place.' . . . [There was a] conflict of political loyalties between the traditional territorial chieftaincies, and the new mobile military state. . . . The Gaza state tended to detach men from their land, and incorporate them into a political unit less closely tied to territory. In this it was similar not only to the other states of the Nguni dispersion, but also to the mobile military states in West Africa such as Samori's state or Sansanne Mango of northern Togo." In Renamo's case, units were often marched across large parts of Mozambique, operating far from the homelands of

many of their fighters, and rebel spokesmen sometimes countered suggestions that the Renamo leadership was narrowly and exclusively Ndau with an argument that many Renamo commanders were *mistaken* for Ndaus simply because they always spoke Ndau. In fact, the spokesmen said, all Renamo commanders had had to learn Ndau to communicate in the early days, when the movement was largely based in Ndau country, and thus the language had become the lingua franca of the leadership.

18. The London publication *Africa Confidential* (23, no. 15, July 21, 1982) describes such an occurrence in the province of Inhambane in 1978, as does Joseph Hanlon in *Mozambique: The Revolution Under Fire* (London, 1984), p. 228. Some of the *régulos* and other traditional authorities put forward by their constituencies for the 1977 local elections—and rejected out of hand by Frelimo—may also belong in this group of rebel supporters.

19. Christian Geffray and Mögens Pedersen found that, in the northern province of Nampula, Renamo had had its greatest success in those areas where villagization had been most extensive. Particularly susceptible to Renamo recruitment, according to Geffray and Pedersen, were youths who had found their own social and educational advancement blocked by the lineage elders who dominated the Frelimo power structure in the villages ("Nampula en guerre," *Politique africaine* [Paris] 29 [March 1988]: 28–40). Such generational conflict has been common throughout recorded African history. The European colonial powers, for instance, often empowered African elders at the expense of African youth, hoping thereby to increase their own social control—and characterizing such arrangements as "traditional" whether they bore any resemblance to preexisting arrangements or not. See Terence Ranger, "The Invention of Tradition in Colonial Africa," in *The Invention of Tradition*, ed. Eric Hobsbawm and Terence Ranger (Cambridge, England, 1983), pp. 254–57. Once again, the Ndau experience under the Gaza state may be relevant. Rennie ("Christianity," pp. 268–69) describes "a latent conflict between young and old, which found no institutional expression in Ndau traditional society. Under Gaza rule was introduced the age-based regimental system, emphasizing the valor and achievements of youth as well as the experience of age; a political system which gave young men considerable geographical mobility, broke kinship ties or weakened

them; and an economic system which allowed youths more independence than in traditional Ndau society. Gaza youths, for example, who went to the mines traditionally kept control of their earnings, turning over to their parents a part, in contrast to Shona youths, who handed over their earnings to their parents and received back sufficient for their needs."

Geffray, an anthropologist, and Pedersen, an agro-economist, conducted their research in Nampula between 1983 and 1985—Renamo arrived in force in the region in 1984. When Geffray returned to Nampula in September 1988, he found that Renamo had not only effectively identified and exploited the lines of conflict between local lineages, between state-favored groups and those who had lost power or property since independence, and between youth and elders, but had actually succeeded in rallying whole populations, "sociétés entières" (*La cause des armes au Mozambique: Anthropologie d'une guerre civile* [Paris, 1990], p. 39), to its side. "Là où nous imaginions des ralliements individuels et presque honteux, il y eut une sédition collective, effectuée en outre, selon tous les témoignages, dans l'enthousiasme et l'espoir: l'entrée en guerre a eu le caractère d'une reprise d'initiative politique des populations face au Frelimo et à son État villageois. Le simple fait d'avoir donné militairement aux populations les moyens de se placer hors de portée de l'État a permis à la Renamo d'ancrer son intervention dans la dynamique des conflits locaux. . . , sans que la formulation d'un projet politique fût requise pour la légitimer. La simple reconnaissance de l'existence sociale des populations rurales par une force armée, quelle qu'elle fût, suffisait à conférer aux yeux des habitants un sens politique à l'intervention de cette force" (ibid.). ("Where we had imagined individual and almost shameful rallyings, there had actually been a collective rebellion, carried out, according to all accounts, with enthusiasm and hope: joining the war had the character of a reassertion of political initiative by the people against Frelimo and its village state apparatus. The simple fact that the people had been given the military means to put themselves beyond the reach of the state permitted Renamo to plant itself firmly within the dynamic of local conflicts. . . , without having to formulate a political plan to legitimize itself. The simple recognition of the social existence of rural populations by an armed force, such as it was, sufficed to confer, in the eyes of the inhabitants, a political meaning to that force's intervention.")

But the fate of those populations who had followed their chiefs into Renamo's embrace was not, Geffray found, a happy one. "Ce faisant, les populations dissidentes sont tombées dans un piège dont elles parviennent rarement à se dégager aujourd'hui. Elles se sont trompées . . . sur la nature de la Renamo, dont elles furent finalement les dupes. La Renamo n'est certes pas une association de brigandage, contrairement à ce que laisse entendre la propagande du Frelimo et celle de toutes les nations—occidentales et 'de l'Est'—qui le soutiennent à bon droit dans la guerre. Mais elle n'est certainement pas non plus une organisation politique, elle ne nourrit aucun projet pour les populations du pays qu'elle saigne abondamment depuis près de quinze ans. . . . [G]uerre, qui est la condition de la reproduction de la Renamo comme institution armée, constitue par elle-même son véritable projet—et . . . la vie en guerre peut constituer un projet de vie pour certains, tel que toutes les populations civiles deviennent directement ou indirectement les otages soumis, exploités, assassinés, des hommes en armes" (ibid., p. 41). ("In so doing, the dissident populations fell into a trap from which they have rarely succeeded in escaping. They were wrong . . . about the nature of Renamo, and were ultimately the movement's dupes. Contrary to the propaganda of Frelimo, and of all the nations—West and 'East'—that legitimately support Frelimo in the war, Renamo is certainly not a group of bandits. But neither is Renamo a political organization; it has offered no program to the people of the country that it has bled abundantly now for fifteen years. . . . *War*, which is necessary for the continued existence of Renamo as an armed institution, constitutes in itself the group's true program—and . . . war can constitute a life program for some people, such that all civil populations become, directly or indirectly, the submissive, exploited, assassinated hostages of armed men.")

20. For young African men blocked from advancement but without the option of bandit life, rebellion and fun-seeking have sometimes combined in more picturesque, less murderous ways. Wyatt MacGaffey, writing about a colonial Bakongo village, describes "the Dikembe, a social club catering to the unmarried men. . . . Dikembe culture, an interesting caricature of the serious magico-religious beliefs and principles of the older generation which it defies, *contains the seeds of an anti-society.* . . . The doors of the bachelor huts bear such inscriptions as 'Palais

d'Amour' in Gothic lettering. . . . The culture of the Dikembe is that of *billisme,* whose heroes are the stars of romantic French and American movies [and] takes its name from Buffalo Bill, 'sheriff du quartier Santa Fe, metro d'amour'" (*Custom and Government in the Lower Congo* [Berkeley, 1970], pp. 223–24; quoted in Ranger, "The Invention of Tradition in Colonial Africa," pp. 255–56; emphasis added).

Geffray, in his assessment of life with Renamo, writes of the "life of a wild army" ("vie d'armée sauvage"—*La cause des armes,* p. 219) and its rewards: "la vie en guerre . . . peut être pour les soldats une source d'exaltation et de *promotion sociale*" (ibid.). ("A life of war can be for the soldiers a source of elation and *social advancement.*")

21. Zambézia saw very little of the armed struggle against Portuguese colonialism. After a few months of fighting in 1964–65, Frelimo withdrew from the province, not to return as a fighting force until an attack on Morrumbala on June 26, 1974. After independence, the new government had trouble collecting taxes in Zambézia, and agricultural productivity plummeted, with many villagers and plantation workers openly blaming Frelimo for the disruptions in employment and services caused by the departure of the Portuguese. In Errego in September 1977, "Frelimo's Vice-Minister of Defense, passing through, insisted his passage should be kept secret, for 'the Lomwe did not support Frelimo.' Thus the incorrigible Lomwe who to the Portuguese had been 'savages', to the companies 'weak and lazy', and to the Sena people 'dirty', were to their new Frelimo rulers 'not liberated'!" (Leroy Vail and Landeg White, *Capitalism and Colonialism in Mozambique: A Study of Quelimane District* [Minneapolis, 1980], pp. 371, 391–92).

22. Gilberto Magid, the Unamo spokesman I found in Lisbon (he was also known as Gilberto Fernandes), attributed Unamo's break with Renamo to disagreements between Gimo Phiri, Unamo's leader, and Afonso Dhlakama. Phiri, according to Magid, had argued that Renamo ought to acknowledge publicly the support it received from South Africa, and openly invite other foreign backers to supplant Pretoria. Dhlakama, who was closely controlled by Pretoria, was not authorized by his masters to make such an acknowledgment, according to Magid. Phiri was also unhappy in Renamo, Magid said, because he was

not Ndau—and Dhlakama had ordered that all non-Ndau Renamo commanders were to be killed! Phiri, who reportedly worked with the Portuguese against Frelimo in Zambézia during the anticolonial struggle, had been based in Malawi for many years, but it was in Zambézia that he wielded whatever power he had.

23. Reports of drug use among Renamo fighters came from all over Mozambique. I interviewed a man in Zambézia who said that the *matsangas* were smoking marijuana at the very time they captured him! He often saw the fighters take pills, he said, before they launched an attack. The boys at Lhanguene Center also reported that they were given pills when they were not sick and, though they did not smoke, were forced to smoke strange cigarettes—"for courage."

24. Although Renamo ostensibly recognized the International Committee of the Red Cross as a neutral, humanitarian organization, the rebels' leaders had put a halt to ICRC relief flights in Mozambique in December 1987, with a threat to shoot down its planes. Flights resumed after four months, but then Afonso Dhlakama, in a July 1988 interview, again threatened to shoot down Red Cross planes that had not asked for clearance (*New York Times*, July 31, 1988).

Ten

1. This description fit not only Renamo's military leaders, such as André Matsangaíssa and Afonso Dhlakama, but its "political" leaders as well. Orlando Cristina, the first Renamo secretary-general, was an agent for the colonial secret police, as was his successor, Evo Fernandes. Both had worked for Jorge Jardim, the owner of the Beira daily newspaper, *Notícias da Beira*, and one of the most powerful Portuguese settlers in Mozambique. During the war of independence, Jardim organized and paid elite military units, including paratroopers, who fought Frelimo and later provided a battle-hardened nucleus for Renamo.

Ali A. Mazrui (in *Soldiers and Kinsmen in Uganda: The Military Ethnocracy* [Beverly Hills, 1975]) has described the rise in independent Africa of a "lumpen militariat," which he defines as "that class of semi-organized, rugged, and semi-literate soldiery which has begun to claim a share of power and influence in what would otherwise have become a heavily privileged meritocracy of the educated" (p. 127). Mazrui traces the roots of the lumpen militariat in Uganda to precolonial military traditions and, through the career of Idi Amin, that premier overachiever among ill-educated African soldiers, demonstrates its modern formation—replete with deep cultural conflicts and complexes—under colonial rule. In Renamo, ex-soldiers from the colonial forces fight alongside ex-guerrillas from Frelimo, greatly complicating the ideological picture, and the army in question is, of course, not identified with state power but opposed to it. Nonetheless, there are elements of a warrior-class formation in opposition to an educated bureaucracy, elements that resonate throughout a continent plagued by uncontrollable armies.

2. Alexander Sloop of United Press International may have been the first foreign journalist to do so. His report appeared in the *International Herald Tribune* (Paris), September 14, 1983. Sharon Behn of the *Independent* spent four weeks with Renamo in 1987. Her rather favorable report appeared in the *Independent* (London) of March 26–27, 1987, and in *Africa Events* (London), May 1987, pp. 24–26.

3. Almerigo Grilz, killed in May 1987 while filming a Renamo attack on the town of Caia (*AIM Information Bulletin* [Maputo], no. 141, April 1988, p. 7).

4. There was ample precedent for such rivalry. Christian missionaries had been actively hostile to traditional African religious beliefs for centuries, putting traditional religious authorities on the defensive. In Rhodesia, where traditional healers were known as *ngangas,* a 1972 newsletter produced by the African Ngangas Association gave poignant expression to the healers' hopes of reconciliation with Christian teachings: "We fear God and we work with the Bible. Our work is blessed by God. . . . We practice proper medicine as shown in Jeremiah 46:11. We don't guess anyone's cause of illness. . . . We admit that illness is natural, but we believe it can be healed up. So we try to give what we consider is the true remedy, e.g. for boils 2 Kings 20:7; Fractures, Ezekiel 30:21; Stomach ache, 1 Timothy 5:24; Use of oil in curing ailments, Luke 10:34; James 5:14" (quoted in G. L. Chavunduka, "Traditional Medicine and Christian Beliefs," in *Christianity South of the Zambezi,* ed. M. F. C. Bourdillon, S.J. [Gwelo, Zimbabwe, 1977], 2:141).

5. Evo Fernandes, quoted in the *Independent* (London), February 24, 1988.

6. Also quoted in the *Independent*, February 24, 1988.

7. December 17, 1986.

8. The Catholic Church hierarchy was a main pillar of Portuguese colonial rule, and the crackdown on its operations in Mozambique after independence was much harsher than the mere neglect accorded *curandeiros*. Frelimo and the churches began to mend their relations in the 1980s, and by 1990 most of the churches' confiscated property had been returned. In July 1990, private schools, including church schools, were made legal again.

9. *Times* (London), September 11, 1987; *Wall Street Journal*, May 11, 1987.

10. Mozambique Solidarity Campaign leaflets, London, August 1988. Thomas Schaaf, a Renamo spokesman in the United States, demonstrated some of the same talent for sheer inversion in an interview in November 1988. Schaaf told me that it was *Frelimo* that had sent South Africa's deputy foreign minister, Louis Nel, to see Afonso Dhlakama in Gorongosa, as revealed in the Gorongosa documents (which Schaaf simultaneously denounced as forgeries), and that it was *Frelimo* killing teachers and health workers throughout Mozambique. Schaaf detected conspiracies—what he called "corrupt triangles"—everywhere. The main conspiracy seeking to obscure the true situation in Mozambique, he said, was a corrupt triangle between a dictator (President Chissano), "corrupt multinationals" (notably the London-based Lonhro), and "corrupt bureaucrats" (notably Chester Crocker, then United States assistant secretary of state for African affairs).

11. Professor Werner Kaltefleiter of the University of Kiel, a foreign-policy adviser to German chancellor Helmut Kohl, and Professor Andre Thomashausen of the University of South Africa, a former student and colleague of Kaltefleiter's, were perhaps the most prominent of these. In the United States, Professor Thomas H. Henriksen of the Hoover Institution on War, Revolution and Peace, at Stanford University, was probably the best known. In June 1987, Professor Henriksen, in a statement to the Senate Committee on Foreign Relations, argued that "America's best interests are served by a strong Congressional stand

that this country is on the side of RENAMO" (U.S. Senate, Committee on Foreign Relations, Subcommittee on African Affairs, *Mozambique and United States Policy,* Hearings, June 24, 1987 [Washington, D.C., 1987], p. 69).

12. August 8, 1988, p. 12.

13. *Washington Times,* December 17, 1986.

14. Orlando Cristina, the first Renamo secretary-general, was killed near Pretoria in April 1983. Two senior Renamo officials, Mateus Lopes and João da Silva Ataíde, were killed in Malawi in November 1987. Lopes and Ataíde were returning at the time from a meeting with Afonso Dhlakama inside Mozambique, a meeting at which, according to Oliveira, a decision had been reached to try to distance Renamo from South Africa. According to Chanjunja Chivaca João, another high-level Renamo defector, Dhlakama had appointed Ataíde, who was a former Mozambican ambassador to Portugal, the new Renamo secretary-general at the meeting. Lopes and Ataíde died on a highway in Malawi, where the authorities at first denied that there had been a car accident, then denied that it had involved Renamo leaders, then said that Lopes and Ataíde had died "when their car collided with a petrol tanker" (*Herald* [Harare, Zimbabwe], April 25, 1988). The two men were widely believed to have been murdered on orders from South Africa. Their bodies were never released to their families (Anders Nilsson, *Unmasking the Bandits: The True Face of the M.N.R.* [London, 1990], p. 55). Finally, Evo Fernandes, the former secretary-general whom Ataíde would have replaced, was killed, as noted, near Lisbon in April 1988.

15. *Washington Post,* July 31, 1988.

16. Andre E. A. M. Thomashausen, "The Mozambique National Resistance (Resistência Nacional Moçambicana—Renamo)," in *Weerstandsbewegins in Suider-Afrika,* ed. C. J. Maritz (Potchefstroom, 1987), p. 44.

17. Notes from a meeting in Zoabostad, South Africa, October 25, 1980, found at a Renamo base in Garagua, Mozambique, December 5, 1981.

18. Colin Legum, "The Counter Revolutionaries in Southern Africa: The Challenge of the Mozambique National Resistance," *Third World Reports* (West Sussex, England), March 1983, pp. 1–22; cited in Allen F. Isaacman, "Mozambique: Tugging at the Chains of Dependency," in *African Crisis Areas and U.S.*

Foreign Policy, ed. Gerald J. Bender, James S. Coleman, and Richard L. Sklar (Berkeley, 1985), p. 54.

19. Steve Askin, "South African Connections," *Africa News* (Durham, N.C.), December 21, 1987. Roland Hunter passed information about SADF support for Renamo to Derek and Patricia Hanekom, a white Zimbabwean couple, who in turn passed it on to the then-outlawed African National Congress, which in turn passed it on to the government of Mozambique (SADF documents concerning the destabilization of Zimbabwe were likewise passed to the Zimbabwean government). Hunter also described arms supply operations, Renamo's radio station, and the payment of top officials. He and the Hanekoms were arrested by the South African authorities in December 1983, and all three were sentenced to prison terms.

20. *Africa Confidential* (London) 29, no. 18 (September 9, 1988): 1.

21. Paulo Oliveira and Chanjunja Chivaca João each described Renamo's links with the Bonn government's secret service, the Bundesnachrichtendienst (BND). According to João, the BND provided personal security for Artur Janeiro da Fonseca, Renamo's secretary for external affairs, who lived in Germany. According to Oliveira, a senior agent named Wolfgang Richter gave Evo Fernandes one million Deutsche marks to buy antiaircraft missiles (Prexy Nesbit, "Terminators, Crusaders and Gladiators: [Private and Public] Western Support for Renamo and Unita," paper presented at the European Campaign Against South African Aggression on Mozambique and Angola Conference, Bonn, December 1988, pp. 24–25). Nilsson (in *Unmasking the Bandits,* pp. 47–48, citing *Der Spiegel,* no. 1, 1984) describes a visit to West Germany made by Frank Wisner, then United States deputy assistant secretary of state for African affairs, in late 1983. Wisner went to express to the Bonn government the concern of the United States about the pro-Renamo activities of the BND representative in Pretoria. Nilsson suggests that the BND was acting not at the instruction of Helmut Kohl's government but in response to signals from Franz Josef Strauss, the powerful right-wing leader of the Christian Socialist Union.

22. According to *Africa Confidential* (29, no. 18 [September 9, 1988]: 1; 29, no. 24 [December 2, 1988]: 1–2), Renamo supporters in the Defense Intelligence Agency—American military in-

telligence—worked through retired generals and civilian contacts. The newsletter's comment: "Some supporters do so out of genuine belief, most out of a calculation that it is in the U.S. interest to control such a body" (December 2, 1988, p. 2).

23. Robert Gersony, Bureau for Refugee Programs, U.S. Department of State, *Summary of Mozambican Refugee Accounts of Principally Conflict-Related Experience in Mozambique* (Washington, D.C., April 1988), p. 28.

Eleven

1. *Foreign Economic Trends and Their Implications for the United States,* report prepared for the U.S. Department of Commerce by the United States Embassy (Maputo, June 1988), p. 5.

Twelve

1. U.S. Department of State, *World Refugee Report* (Washington, D.C., September 1988), p. 2.

2. *Mozambiquefile* (Maputo), February 1989, p. 23. The usefulness of tanks in the defense of small settlements surrounded by bush seemed to me doubtful—at Nhamatanda, a small town in the Beira Corridor, we saw a whole *row* of Soviet-made tanks parked with their cannons trained across the fields to the south, an impressive image indeed of Frelimo's preparation to fight not Renamo but World War II in the Ukraine. All this inappropriate technology caused me to wonder if the usefulness of tanks was not in fact more symbolic than military. That is, tanks represent a level of technology available only to governments in Africa (and, it seems, to very large corporations). Their display—and they are constantly displayed in military parades throughout Africa, often in countries where they will surely never be needed— may actually be intended, above all, to impress upon the *povo* the might and grandeur of the state, compared to which any rebel or dissident force must look puny.

3. Kindra Bryan, the American captive, wrote about her ordeal for the *Washington Post,* August 23, 1987. Bob Jordan, an American mercenary who helped arrange the missionaries' release, wrote about it in "Mission Mozambique," an article published in *Soldier of Fortune* magazine (Boulder, Colo.), January 1988, pp. 82–86.

4. Even foreigners living in Beira came quickly to understand

that the police were dangerous. I was visiting an American couple at their home in a Beira seaside suburb when one of their servants reported the theft of a roll of chicken wire from the garage. The servant was terribly distraught, apparently, until he was assured that the theft would not be reported to the police. The police, it was explained to me, would have automatically picked up the Americans' servants, held them for a few days, possibly beaten them, certainly robbed them, and probably forced them to do some menial work—despite the fact that everyone, including the Americans, knew perfectly well that it was not their servants who had stolen the wire, but a neighborhood criminal ring that bought protection from the police.

5. Quoted in Iain Christie, *Machel of Mozambique* (Harare, Zimbabwe, 1988), p. 159.

6. Ibid., p. 160.

7. Ibid., p. 158.

Thirteen

1. The União Nacional Democrática de Moçambique (Udenamo), organized in what was then Rhodesia, drew its membership from southern and central Mozambique. The Mozambique African National Union (MANU), founded in Kenya, had its main base among the Makonde people of the northeastern province of Cabo Delgado. The União Africana de Moçambique Independente (Unami), organized in Malawi, was composed of Mozambicans from the northwestern province of Tete. The brief history of Frelimo which follows is drawn largely from the following sources: Eduardo Mondlane, *The Struggle for Mozambique* (Harmondsworth, England, 1969; London, 1983); Thomas H. Henriksen, *Revolution and Counterrevolution: Mozambique's War of Independence, 1964–1974* (Westport, Conn., 1983); Iain Christie, *Machel of Mozambique* (Harare, Zimbabwe, 1988); Barry Munslow, *Mozambique: The Revolution and Its Origins* (London, 1983), pp. 79–148; Thomas H. Henriksen, *Mozambique: A History* (London, 1978), pp. 154–232; Allen Isaacman and Barbara Isaacman, *Mozambique: From Colonialism to Revolution, 1900–1982* (Boulder, Colo., 1983), pp. 79–188; Joseph Hanlon, *Mozambique: The Revolution Under Fire* (London, 1984), pp. 23–51; *Mozambique: A Country Study*, ed. Harold D. Nelson (Washington, D.C., 1985), pp. 46–69; John S. Saul, "The Context: Colonialism and

Revolution," in *A Difficult Road: The Transition to Socialism in Mozambique*, ed. John S. Saul (New York, 1985), pp. 36–74.

2. Even the Ndau experience under the Gaza state (discussed in the notes to Chapter 9) had not, from all accounts, left widespread hatred in its wake. Some Ndaus resisted the invaders, but many simply switched cultural allegiances, adopting the Nguni language and Nguni fashions (pierced ears, wax head ring, skin apron) and even intermarrying, while letting Ndau customs (filing teeth, ritual scarring) fall into disuse. The same combination of resistance and accommodation and partial acculturation seems to have taken place in other groups overrun by the Gaza Nguni—whose march of conquest, which began in Natal, South Africa, in 1821 as a breakaway from the Zulu state of Shaka, took them all the way to Tete, in northwestern Mozambique. Although the Ndau had relatively little contact with Europeans, the exactions of Portuguese and British colonial rule, when they came to replace Gaza rule in the late nineteenth century, were notably more onerous for Ndau-speakers than those they had suffered at the hands of their fellow Africans. See J. K. Rennie, "Christianity, Colonialism and the Origins of Nationalism among the Ndau of Southern Rhodesia 1890–1935" (Ph.D. diss., Northwestern University, 1973), pp. 146, 135, 266–67.

This is not to say that intra-African ethnic resentments did not exist in Mozambique—just that they were not institutionalized on anything like the scale that hobbled many other African countries at independence. Differences existed, of course, and some of these surfaced only later. The Ndau leadership of Renamo, for instance, seemed quite aware that Frelimo's first three presidents were all descended from the same Nguni lineages that once conquered the Ndau. Separate experiences *under* colonialism often served to drive groups apart as well. In Ndau country, for instance, Protestant missions were scarce on the Portuguese side of the colonial border and were eventually suppressed (Rennie, "Christianity," pp. 359, 514–15) by the colonial state in favor of the more conservative Catholic missions, in whose schools Salazarist ideology was dispensed and nationalist ideas firmly squelched. (There were exceptions to this rule, such as the liberal Catholic order known as the White Fathers— who were probably the priests that Dividas described recruiting boys in the Beira area for Frelimo. The White Fathers left Mozambique in 1971 in protest against Portuguese repression. On the whole, however, the Catholic hierarchy was solidly allied with the colonial state.) Meanwhile, Protestant missions survived in the south, despite regular harassment by the authorities. They used vernacular languages in their schools and greatly contributed to the creation of an African intelligentsia altogether more worldly and independent than the graduates of Catholic institutions. Much of what later became the Frelimo leadership attended Protestant mission schools in Maputo and Gaza. Samora Machel, whose father was a Free Methodist minister, was prevented from going to secondary school because of his refusal to study for the Catholic priesthood. Eduardo Mondlane went to Swiss Mission and American Methodist schools in Maputo and the northern Transvaal. It would be easy to make too much of this distinction—but it does seem significant that much of the Renamo leadership, including Afonso Dhlakama, attended Roman Catholic mission schools.

3. Mondlane, *The Struggle for Mozambique* (1983 ed.), p. 130.

4. Ibid., pp. 123–24.

5. For the problematic origins of such traditions, see Terence Ranger, "The Invention of Tradition in Colonial Africa," in *The Invention of Tradition*, ed. Eric Hobsbawm and Terence Ranger (Cambridge, England, 1983), pp. 254–57.

6. Saul, "The Context," p. 54.

7. Christie, *Machel of Mozambique*, pp. 26–27.

8. Other Frelimo dissidents implicated in Mondlane's assassination included Silveiro Nungu, from Beira, who was reportedly executed by Frelimo in June 1969 (another version of Nungu's fate—provided, without documentation, by Alex Vines in *Renamo: Terrorism in Mozambique* [London, 1991], p. 13—has him dying in a hunger strike); and Uria Simango, a Protestant minister and Ndau-speaker, who was Frelimo vice president at the time. After failing to succeed Mondlane as president, Simango denounced the Frelimo leadership and left the movement. He was later active in Coremo in Zambia, and after the 1974 Lisbon coup returned to Beira, where he tried to create an alternative to Frelimo, working with Gwenjere and Nkavandame and, ultimately, a desperate group of white settlers who tried to seize power by force in September 1974. In early 1975, Simango, Gwenjere, and other dissidents were publicly paraded

at the Frelimo camp at Nachingwea, in southern Tanzania, where many "confessed" to having been Portuguese agents, and Simango "confessed" to having helped Nungu transport the bomb that killed Mondlane. (See Henriksen, *Mozambique,* pp. 169–70, 180–81, 223–24, 227; for Simango's "confession," Henriksen cites *The Times of Zambia,* March 18, 1975. For Simango's ethnicity, see Rennie, "Christianity," p. 562.) Later, Simango was believed to be imprisoned in Mozambique and, later still, to have been killed or to have died in custody (Amnesty International, *Mozambique: The Human Rights Record, 1975– 1989* [London, September 1989], p. 13).

9. The war with Renamo seemed only to deepen this commitment. When Joaquim Chissano assumed the presidency of Mozambique, he told the opening session of his Council of Ministers, held on November 13, 1986, "During this difficult period, more than ever before, there is a need to close our ranks, to make our government a monolithic, cohesive and unwavering block— a body impenetrable to enemy thought and action" (quoted in Gillian Gunn, "Mozambique After Machel," *CSIS Africa Notes* [Georgetown University, Washington, D.C.], no. 67, December 29, 1986, p. 11).

10. Isaacman and Isaacman, *Mozambique,* p. 112; citing *Review of African Political Economy* (Sheffield, England) 4 (1975): 23.

11. Robin Wright, of the *Christian Science Monitor,* who traveled with Machel throughout Mozambique in 1975; interview with author.

12. Quoted in George Houser and Herb Shore, *Mozambique: Dream the Size of Freedom* (New York, 1975), p. 11, and cited in Isaacman and Isaacman, *Mozambique,* p. 46.

13. November 14, 1977; cited in Isaacman and Isaacman, *Mozambique,* p. 120.

14. President Machel, speaking to the People's Assembly in 1979; quoted in Hanlon, *Mozambique,* p. 82. The summary of the ten-year development plan that follows is drawn from Hanlon, *Mozambique,* p. 84.

15. Hanlon, *Mozambique,* pp. 100–101.

16. Mozambique had only a tiny proletariat, and it had played a negligible role in the *luta armada,* especially when compared

to that of the peasantry. The ideological confusion created by this situation was exemplified by Xiconhoca, a cartoon villain who became ubiquitous in magazines, newspapers, and schoolbooks after independence. Xiconhoca was the "class enemy" but, as Marina and David Ottaway point out in their book *Afrocommunism* (New York, 1986, pp. 78–79), it was never quite clear what class he belonged to. In one depiction, he was a corrupt bureaucrat. In another, a lazy worker. In others, an urban dandy or a treacherous peasant nostalgic for colonialism. Frelimo's propagandists could never seem to decide just who the revolution's true enemy in Mozambican society was.

17. Unlike most very poor countries, Mozambique did not suffer from widespread landlessness among its peasants—one of the few benefits, perhaps, of the rigors of Portuguese colonialism, which were largely responsible for the country's underpopulation. There was significant land pressure in some river valleys, however, and the insatiable land appetites of large state farms definitely made the lives of nearby peasants more difficult.

18. Hanlon, *Mozambique*, p. 123.

19. Isaacman and Isaacman, *Mozambique*, p. 156.

20. See Christian Geffray and Mögens Pedersen, "Nampula en guerre," *Politique africaine* (Paris) 29 (March 1988): 28–40; and Christian Geffray, *La Cause des armes au Mozambique: Anthropologie d'une guerre civile* (Paris, 1990).

21. The availability of land may have had a great deal to do with the peasants' attitude toward cooperative farming. In Ethiopia, where a Marxist regime was also struggling to achieve "socialization of the countryside," a shortage of land made cooperative farming far more attractive to peasants (Ottaway and Ottaway, *Afrocommunism*, p. 243).

22. Gervase Clarence-Smith, "The Roots of the Mozambican Counter-Revolution," *Southern African Review of Books* (London), April–May 1989, p. 8.

23. Geffray (*La cause des armes*, p. 40, note 15) provides a startling example of administrative ignorance concerning local allegiances. In 1987, Frelimo divided a region along the Mecuburi River in Nampula province into two new districts: Namapa in the north, Erati in the south. It turned out that the Makuan people, whose homeland was the new Erati district, were fero-

cious traditional enemies of the real Erati people, who lived to the north, in the area long known as Erati, but now suddenly called Namapa.

24. President Machel, in a speech in December 1985, appeared to have come full circle from his own youthful hatred of the system of forced cotton cultivation: "The government, be it central, provincial or local level, must demand of each family that it cultivate a minimum number of hectares. . . . The production of cotton is imperative. If every family, every peasant, produces half a hectare of cotton, we shall obtain a minimum of 300,000 hectares throughout the country." In 1986, the governor of Nampula was even more specific, announcing, "From next agricultural season, each peasant family in Nampula Province must prepare four hectares, in which they must obligatorily sow cotton, cashew nuts, maize, manioc, groundnuts, beans and *mapira*. . . . To demarcate lands and control the work process, there are the *capatazes*, whose job it is to force people to work in their fields. . . . When the first cock crows, all the villagers must awake. When the second cock crows, they must all go to their fields. When the third cock crows, they must all be bent over their hoes. . . . At midday, nobody must return to the village. They must eat in the fields, and continue their labour after eating. They may only return to the village when the sun sets. . . . Producing cotton or cashew nuts is not a request but an order from the state. . . . The administrator must cease to be 'Comrade Administrator' and must become 'Mr. Administrator.' . . . Some people will react to these measures by saying that it is forced labour. Yes, it is forced labour, so that people can be decently clothed and fed." Both of these quotes appear in Michel Cahen, *Mozambique: La révolution implosée* (Paris, 1987), and are cited in Clarence-Smith, "Roots of Mozambican Counter-Revolution," p. 8.

The carryovers, from colonialism to independence, of unhappy relations between peasants and the state seemed endless. Leroy Vail and Landeg White offer this example from Zambézia: "The Administrator of Ile reported in 1970 that 'for superstitious reasons' the Lomwe people 'will not plant cashew trees or any other kind of fruit trees.' In 1977 the Secretary of the Frelimo administration for Ile told the same story . . . in respect of sumauma trees, the Lomwe's refusing to live near them because such trees 'caused family quarrels.' The first sumauma trees were planted by the Lugella Company and the Lomwe refusal to live near trees is a refusal to be associated with any kind of plantation crop with its labour demands and its destructive effect on the family" (*Capitalism and Colonialism in Mozambique: A Study of Quelimane District* [Minneapolis, 1980], p. 367).

In the Ukraine, according to Nestor Makhno, a village anarchist who fought with the Bolsheviks in the civil war there, the peasants' word for government is *durak* (fool)—a term that did not change when the government changed from czarist to Bolshevik (*La Révolution Russe en Ukraine, Mars 1917–Avril 1918* [Paris, 1927], pp. 166–67; quoted in E. J. Hobsbawm, *Primitive Rebels: Studies in Archaic Forms of Social Movement in the 19th and 20th Centuries* [New York, 1959], pp. 185–86).

25. Sergio Vieira, a Frelimo leader, summarized the party's view in a 1977 speech: "The traditional feudal society is a conservative, immobile society with a rigid hierarchy. . . . It is a society which excludes youth, excludes innovation, excludes women. The correct term is gerontocracy" ("The New Man Is a Process," speech to the Second Conference of the Ministry of Education, December 1977; quoted in Ottaway and Ottaway, *Afrocommunism*, p. 79). This is a colonial view of African society—or, at least, a view of African society only as it was during the colonial era, when a dramatic "freezing of political dynamics" occurred, replacing, for the purposes of smoother colonial administration, "the pre-colonial competitive, shifting, fluid imbalance of power and influence" (W. M. J. Van Binsbergen, reviewing S. J. Natara's *History of the Chewa* in *African Social Research* [Lusaka, Zambia], June 1976, pp. 73–75; quoted in Ranger, "The Invention of Tradition," p. 248). Frelimo's leaders had recognized the mistake made by the "African socialists" in Tanzania and Zambia when they romanticized precolonial society as a classless utopia, but Frelimo replaced this fairy tale with another, distinctly self-serving, myth. Vieira, on another occasion, described Frelimo's opposition to traditional society in populist terms: "How is it that any person becomes a chief? There was a customary feudal law, a customary political law, as venerable perhaps as the British Constitution. It was necessary to abolish this system of entitlement to power to modify the conception of customary law as the foundation of power, to affirm the principle that

sovereignty belonged to the masses as opposed to the ancestors, or the spirits or a lineage" ("O Direito nas Zonas Libertades," paper presented to the Faculty of Law, Maputo, July 4, 1977; quoted in Munslow, *Mozambique,* p. 106). When Vieira, an urban *mestiço,* talked about traditional rural culture, he was talking about a foreign country. As for "the masses" who would achieve sovereignty, the official Frelimo magazine was more specific about just who deserved to inherit the power of the chiefs: "Now an awareness had developed for the establishment of new institutions which put more stress on *political devotion* than on traditional legitimacy of power" (*Mozambique Revolution* 34 [Dar es Salaam, 1967–68]; quoted in Munslow, *Mozambique,* p. 106; emphasis added).

26. See Christian Geffray, "Fragments d'un discours du pouvoir (1975–85): du bon usage d'une méconnaissance scientifique," *Politique africaine* (Paris) 29 (March 1988): 71–85. In *La Cause des armes* (p. 28), Geffray writes of "*l'ideologie de la 'page blanche.'*"

27. Transcript of "Selected Aspects of Parliamentarianism in African Countries," second session, August 4, 1987. Seminar hosted by the Friedrich Ebert Foundation and the Botswana National Assembly. Remarks quoted by Christina J. Tembe, of Mozambique, and D. N. Magang, of Botswana. For a masterly study of the decline of a chiefdom in Botswana, see Diana Wylie, *A Little God: The Twilight of Patriarchy in a Southern African Chiefdom* (Hanover, N.H., 1990).

28. David Lan, *Guns and Rain: Guerrillas and Spirit Mediums in Zimbabwe* (Harare, Zimbabwe, 1985), p. 208. Frelimo guerrillas in the field were not, in fact, entirely averse to alliances with local religious figures. Among the northern Shona of the Zambezi Valley, for instance, "Spirit mediums inflamed . . . anticolonial sentiment among their followers and it was believed that they provided FRELIMO with special medicines to neutralize Portuguese weapons" (Allen F. Isaacman, *The Tradition of Resistance in Mozambique: The Zambesi Valley 1850–1921* [Berkeley, 1976], p. 199).

29. Lan, in *Guns and Rain,* provides a brilliant study of this relationship in one rural district. The Rhodesian government, aware of the importance of traditional religious authorities, made efforts to co-opt them and their language. The results

could be unintentionally amusing. In 1975, for instance, a district commissioner, concerned about security, addressed the people of Chief Diduku, in Makoni district, as follows: "In your tribe, you have decided no longer to follow custom and it is quite apparent that your spirits are not satisfied with things. . . . You have failed to put the spirits in appeasement. . . . If no rain comes I will not be surprised. You have got yourselves into a dreadful state" (quoted in Terence Ranger, *Peasant Consciousness and Guerrilla War in Zimbabwe* [Berkeley, 1985], p. 201). According to Henriksen (*Revolution and Counterrevolution*, p. 235), "The Ian Smith regime mounted a counterspirit campaign among the Shona people to convince them that their spirit, Mhondora, was against the Zimbabwe guerrillas and was for the government forces."

30. A problem with this close identification of national independence and the government with an indigenous religious tradition—in this case, the Shona tradition of *mhondoro* spirit mediums—is that it excludes other religious traditions. In Zimbabwe, where there are two major ethnic groups, the Shona and the Ndebele, and the Shona dominate the central government, the difficulty for Ndebeles of identifying with the modern state only grows when the state drapes itself in Shona religious symbolism. See Lan, *Guns and Rain*, p. 222.

31. Careful distinctions were even made among the registered healers. According to Lan (*Guns and Rain*, p. 219), "those whose healing techniques do not include possession may add the initials TMP (Traditional Medical Practitioner) after their name. Those who are proficient at possession may use the letters SM (Spirit Medium)."

32. Frelimo *did* face a truly feudal mentality on the former plantations, especially in Zambézia, where a tradition of paternalism and dependence on company wages had forged a powerful relationship between workers and *patrãos*.

33. Demotions had actually become administrative anathema in the course of Frelimo's long quest for unity. Face-saving lateral "transfers" were the party's preferred response to incompetence and failure.

34. All figures from the *Financial Times* (London), August 15, 1988, sec. 3, p. 4.

35. *Independent* (London), January 15, 1990.

36. *Los Angeles Times*, December 11, 1990; citing the World Bank, *World Development Report, 1990* (New York, 1990).

Fourteen

1. Among the exiles who personally discovered this dark truth about Frelimo were Vasco Kampira Momboya, an artist who returned from Kenya in late 1974 and was arrested in Maputo a short time later; and Abel Mwabunda, who returned from Kenya in early 1975 and was reportedly arrested on arrival at the Beira airport. According to Amnesty International, these two men were still being held without trial *nearly ten years later* (*Long-Term Detention Without Trial of Political Prisoners in the People's Republic of Mozambique* [London, August 1984]).

2. See Amnesty International, *Reports of the Use of Torture in the People's Republic of Mozambique* (London, April 1985).

3. See Amnesty International, *Long-Term Detention Without Trial.*

4. Renamo and its supporters have published extremely high, unsubstantiated figures for the reeducation camps. The Heritage Foundation, for instance, in 1985 claimed that 300,000 people *still* languished in Frelimo reeducation camps, where, it said, 75,000 had died since independence (*The White House's Confusing Signals on Mozambique* [Washington, D.C., September 19, 1985]). Nine months later, the Heritage Foundation without explanation dropped the figure for those in reeducation camps to "over 200,000" (*The Resistance Can Win in Mozambique* [Washington, D.C., June 1986]). The United States government's best estimate for detentions in the late 1970s, the high-water mark for the reeducation camps, was "as many as 10,000" (*Mozambique: A Country Study*, ed. Harold D. Nelson [Washington, D.C., 1985], p. 65).

5. Amnesty International, *The Use of the Death Penalty in the People's Republic of Mozambique* (London, July 1983), p. 5; *Mozambique: The Human Rights Record, 1975–1989* (London, September 1989), p. 9.

6. A high school teacher named Leonardo Mabunda, for example, who was accused of criticizing Frelimo policies in an examination essay, was sentenced in April 1983 by the Revolutionary Military Tribunal to eight years in prison and forty-five

lashes (Amnesty International, *1987 Annual Report* [London, 1987]). Even just "writing a letter to the government complaining about arbitrary arrests and other abuses committed by the security forces" had landed one trusting Mozambican in prison, according to Amnesty International. At the time that this case was noted by Amnesty, in 1984, the prisoner had already been held without trial for more than a year (Amnesty International, *Long-Term Detention Without Trial*, p. 12). Leonardo Mabunda was released, along with a number of other political prisoners, under a Law of Pardon passed in December 1987 (Amnesty International, *Mozambique: The Human Rights Record, 1975– 1989*, p. 8).

7. U.S. State Department, *1988 Human Rights Report on Mozambique* (Washington, D.C., 1988), p. 4.

8. Amnesty International, *Mozambique: The Human Rights Record, 1975–1989*, p. 9.

9. It is notoriously difficult to verify information about the re-education camps. One afternoon, in the western part of Nicuadala district, in Zambézia, I was riding in a truck on a dirt track south of the highway to Morrumbala. From across a field, I noticed a crowd of about fifty men in blue overalls standing in rows under a grove of trees near a group of farm buildings. I asked my companions (one of them was a guide from the district administrator's office) who the men were. "Prisoners," I was told. "That is a reeducation camp." Later, when I made inquiries in Quelimane, nobody could tell me anything about the camp. There was no camp, I kept hearing—I had been misinformed. Maybe I was; maybe not.

10. Salome Moiane, speaking to the People's Assembly in Maputo; quoted in *Mozambiquefile* (Maputo), January 1990, p. 5.

11. Rachel Waterhouse, "Mozambique: Education for All, a Thing of the Past," Inter Press Service, October 25, 1990.

12. Frelimo Central Committee's report to the Fifth Party Congress; quoted in *Mozambiquefile* (Maputo), August 1989, p. 11.

13. Quoted in Joseph Hanlon, *Mozambique: The Revolution Under Fire* (London, 1984), pp. 67–70.

14. Michel Cahen, "État et pouvoir politique dans le Mozambique indépendant," *Politique africaine* (Paris) 19 (September 1985).

15. *Washington Post*, June 3, 1989.

16. *Independent* (London), January 8, 1990.

17. Reuters, "Mozambican Rebels Reject New Constitution," November 3, 1990.

18. *Washington Post,* November 4, 1990; United Press International, "Mozambique Violence," November 4, 1990.

Fifteen

1. See Patricia McGowan, *O Bando de Argel* (Lisbon, 1979); cited in Luís Serapião, "Mozambican Foreign Policy and the West 1975–1984," *Munger Africana Library Notes* (Pasadena), no. 76, August 1985, p. 13.

Sixteen

1. *Africa Confidential* (London) 28, no. 6 (March 18, 1987): 6; Phyllis Johnson and David Martin, "Mozambique: Victims of Apartheid," in *Frontline Southern Africa: Destructive Engagement,* ed. Phyllis Johnson and David Martin (New York, 1988), p. 38.

2. The brief history of Malawi which follows is drawn largely from the following sources: Philip Short, *Banda* (London, 1974); Carolyn McMaster, *Malawi: Foreign Policy and Development* (London, 1974); and David Hedges, "Notes on Malawi-Mozambique Relations, 1961–1987," unpublished article, Department of History, Eduardo Mondlane University (Maputo), 1988.

3. See Jonathan Kydd and Robert Christiansen, "Structural Change in Malawi since Independence: Consequences of a Development Strategy Based on Large Scale Agriculture," *World Development* (Oxford) 10, no. 5 (1982): 355–95; cited in Hedges, "Notes," p. 7.

4. M. W. K. Chiume, *Kwacha: An Autobiography* (Nairobi, 1975), p. 167; cited in Hedges, "Notes," p. 5.

5. Johnson and Martin, "Mozambique," p. 37.

6. See Eduardo Mondlane, *The Struggle for Mozambique* (London, 1983), pp. 131–32.

7. Quoted in Borges Coelho, "A primeira frente de Tete e o Malawi" (Arquivo Histórico de Moçambique, Maputo, 1984, mimeographed), p. 15; cited in Hedges, "Notes," p. 5.

8. *Financial Mail* (Johannesburg), September 17, 1982; cited in Hedges, "Notes," p. 14.

9. *Notícias* (Maputo), November 19, 1986, and December 16,

1986; cited in Hedges "Notes," p. 16. Gillian Gunn mentions 10,000 guerrillas leaving Malawi ("Mozambique After Machel," *CSIS Africa Notes* [Georgetown University, Washington, D.C.], no. 67, December 29, 1986, p. 6).

10. One good reason for not allowing journalists into Malawi was that such contacts placed local officials in danger. In 1986, Brown Mpinganjira, the Malawian deputy chief of information, was jailed for providing information to foreign journalists. As of 1990, he was still in jail (*New York Times*, April 3, 1990). Shortly after I was in Malawi, Osborne Mkandawire, also of the Department of Information, was arrested on suspicion of having passed information to foreign journalists. According to Africa Watch, a division of Human Rights Watch, Mkandawire was tortured to death. A couple of months later, Fred Sikwese, a senior economist in the Ministry of External Affairs, was arrested on suspicion of having photocopied documents concerning Malawi's relations with South Africa. Sikwese died in prison less than three weeks later. He was reportedly starved. Frackson Zgambo, a businessman suspected of trying to pass documents copied by Sikwese to a publication in Britain, was also arrested. He was killed in prison eleven days after Sikwese's death (Africa Watch, "News from Malawi" [London], April 24, 1989, p. 1).

11. And yet, by mid-1991, the number of Mozambican refugees in Malawi had grown to more than one million ("Malawi Flooded by New Refugees," Washington *Times*, June 6, 1991).

12. When the Malawian government did later cooperate with a study by the United Nations Children's Fund, this United Nations worker was proved right. Under-five mortality was found to be 258 per 1,000 live births. Twenty-four percent of Malawian children under four were found to suffer from moderate or severe malnutrition, with 61 percent of all children between the ages of twenty-four and fifty months suffering from "stunting" due to nutritional deficiencies (United Nations Children Fund, *State of the World's Children, 1991* [Oxford, 1991], pp. 102, 104).

13. Joseph Hanlon, *Beggar Your Neighbours: Apartheid Power in Southern Africa* (London, 1986), p. 141, citing the Mozambique Information Agency (Maputo), May 28, 1985.

14. These were the conditions for Mozambican workers in 1988. Under the constitution that took effect November 30, 1990, the right to strike was guaranteed.

15. Short, *Banda*, pp. 257–58. In October 1967—after a wave

of violence against them, most of it committed by Banda's youth groups—the Jehovah's Witnesses were banned in Malawi as "dangerous to the good government of the State." They were accused of trying to persuade people not to pay their taxes and not to renew their memberships in Banda's Malawi Congress Party, and their banning unleashed a further wave of violence against them. After several weeks of this, President Banda finally called a halt to "trouble with the stooges."

16. And they were well advised to do so. More than a year later, Renamo again attacked Milange, chasing routed Frelimo troops as far as two miles into Malawi (Alex Vines, *Renamo: Terrorism in Mozambique* [London, 1991], p. 58; citing the BBC World Service, "Focus on Africa," November 15, 1989, 17.20 GMT).

17. Mateus Lopes and João da Silva Ataíde. See Chapter 10, note 14.

18. A Kololo chief, agreeing with Andsen, once explained why Nyaus were not subject to normal judicial procedure for offenses committed during their ritual dances: "You cannot arrest and punish an animal which has hurt you because what it did was pure accident. There is no case because there is no accused" (quoted in Matthew Schoffeleers and I. Linden, "The Resistance of the Nyau Societies to the Roman Catholic Missions in Colonial Malawi," in *The Historical Study of African Religion*, ed. T. O. Ranger and I. N. Kimambo [Berkeley, 1972], p. 259). As a traditional religious institution, Nyau societies were a focus of local resistance to the imposition of European culture in colonial Malawi. They were opposed to modern education, successfully emptying the mission schools in various campaigns, and survived all attempts at their suppression. After independence, Nyau societies reportedly flourished.

Seventeen

1. Power outages began to afflict Maputo again in 1989, when Renamo took to sabotaging the city's transmission lines. Repairing the toppled pylons and damaged lines was complicated by land mines strewn around the sabotage sites, which killed and injured repair workers. The capture of the Renamo base at Ngungwe, on the South African border, in May 1990 (see Chapter 4, note 22), seemed to put a stop to the sabotage, but the lines

between the capital and South Africa remained highly vulnerable (*Mozambiquefile* [Maputo], June 1990, pp. 4–5; July 1990, p. 3).

Eighteen

1. Published in Graham Hancock, *Lords of Poverty: The Free-Wheeling Lifestyles, Power, Prestige and Corruption of the Multibillion Dollar Aid Business* (London, 1989).

2. Cited in Hancock, *Lords of Poverty*, p. 14.

3. Hancock, *Lords of Poverty*, p. 15.

4. Joseph Hanlon, "The New Missionaries," *New Internationalist* (London), February 1989, p. 23. For an exhaustive indictment of the aid industry's performance in Mozambique, see Joseph Hanlon, *Mozambique: Who Calls the Shots?* (London, 1991).

5. In a notable example of encouraging local production, the British relief organization Oxfam was buying cloth from a factory in Chimoio, taking it first by road to Beira, then by ship to Quelimane, and there having a local clothing factory turn it into "calamidades" for distribution in Zambézia.

6. Joseph Hanlon, *Beggar Your Neighbours: Apartheid Power in Southern Africa* (London, 1986), p. 144; citing *New Statesman* (London), February 3, 1984.

7. In March 1989, the Frelimo finance minister, Abdul Magid Osman, admitted that a driver for the United Nations in Mozambique earned a higher salary than his ministry could pay its best economist (*Mozambiquefile* [Maputo], April 1989, p. 15).

8. Thomas H. Henriksen, *Mozambique: A History* (London, 1978), p. 225.

9. The brief history of U.S. policy toward Mozambique which follows is drawn largely from the following sources: J. Stephen Morrison, "The Battle for Mozambique," *Africa Report* (New York), September–October 1987, pp. 44–47; Philip Nash, "'Dangling Carrots before Marxists': U.S.–Mozambican Relations since 1981," *The Fletcher Forum* (Tufts University, Medford, Mass.), Summer 1987, pp. 331–45; U.S. Congress, Senate, Committee on Foreign Relations, Subcommittee on African Affairs, *Mozambique and United States Policy*, Hearings, June 24, 1987 (Washington, D.C., 1987), pp. 1–215; Salih Booker, "The Other Engagement," *Africa Report*, January–February 1986, pp. 50–

56; Sam Levy, "Broken Promises?" *Africa Report,* January–February 1986, pp. 77–80; Allen F. Isaacman, "Mozambique: Tugging at the Chains of Dependency," in *African Crisis Areas and U.S. Foreign Policy,* ed. Gerald J. Bender, James S. Coleman, and Richard L. Sklar (Berkeley, 1985); Michael Clough, "American Policy Options," *Africa Report,* November–December 1982, pp. 14–17.

10. Reprinted in the *International Herald Tribune* (Paris), September 23, 1985.

11. As reported in the *New York Times* (July 2, 1987), Sam Joseph Bamieh, a California businessman, testified under oath before the House Foreign Affairs Subcommittee on Africa that in the early 1980s William Casey, the CIA director, had persuaded the Saudi royal family to give, in addition to aid to other groups, fifteen million dollars to "anti-Communists in Angola" in exchange for administration support of the Saudis' efforts to buy American advanced reconnaisance aircraft. Zaire, Morocco, and South Africa were also reportedly involved in the American efforts to circumvent the Clark Amendment and supply arms to Unita.

12. According to Chester Crocker, United States assistant secretary of state for African affairs, this meeting and the photographs taken of it provided the ammunition for a Soviet "disinformation effort" claiming that the United States was secretly backing Renamo (Senate Hearings, *Mozambique and United States Policy,* pp. 168–69).

13. Senate Hearings, *Mozambique and United States Policy,* p. 9. At the same hearings, Senator Helms asked Professor Thomas H. Henriksen of the Hoover Institution on War, Revolution and Peace, at Stanford University, "Is your professional judgment consistent with what [Assistant Secretary] Crocker said, that Mozambique is moderating its Marxist-Leninist ideology?" Professor Henriksen's reply: "No, it is not. I think what it will do is gladly join the IMF, the World Bank, take aid from the West. *This is your traditional Communist trick*" (p. 40; emphasis added).

14. *New York Times,* May 23, 1987.

15. The scope of these attacks could be breathtaking. For example, in a purportedly scholarly collection edited by Michael Radu, *The New Insurgencies: Anticommunist Guerrillas in the*

Third World (New Brunswick, N.J., 1990), Jack Wheeler, contributing a chapter on Mozambique, finds the timing of the release of the State Department's 1988 report on Mozambican refugees—the report which estimated that Renamo had killed 100,000 civilians—"disturbing," and goes on to suggest that Chester Crocker, the assistant secretary of state for African affairs, may have been involved in the murder of Evo Fernandes, the former Renamo secretary-general. The State Department's report was released on the day after Fernandes' disappearance, and Wheeler strongly implies that the murder was related to Crocker's consternation about a planned visit by the Renamo leader Afonso Dhlakama to the United States and Europe (pp. 186–87). (Dhlakama never made the trip. Wheeler told me, in an interview, that Dhlakama received the news of Fernandes' disappearance while staying with Professor Andre Thomashausen in Pretoria, en route to Europe and America, and changed his plans. Wheeler ridiculed the testimony of Alexander Xavier Chagas, the Portuguese citizen who was eventually convicted of Fernandes' murder, that he had killed Fernandes on instructions from South Africa. Why would South Africa have had Fernandes killed, Wheeler asked, when Fernandes and the South Africans were working together at that very moment to arrange Dhlakama's trip? These events were taking place, of course, *four years* after the signing of the Nkomati Accord, the terms of which Renamo's American supporters, such as Wheeler, normally insisted that Renamo and Pretoria had strictly observed. Frelimo killed Fernandes, according to Wheeler, whose "surmise" about Chester Crocker's involvement was, he said, that the assistant secretary of state for African affairs may have "alerted" Frelimo to Dhlakama's impending trip and then let Frelimo put a halt to matters in its own way.)

16. The phrase "privatized intervention" is Prexy Nesbitt's. It appears in "Terminators, Crusaders and Gladiators: (Private and Public) Western Support for Renamo and Unita," paper presented at the European Campaign Against South African Aggression on Mozambique and Angola Conference, Bonn, December 1988, p. 18.

17. More chilling still was the enthusiasm displayed for Renamo's methods by the hairy-chested rabble who straggle from war to war, offering the benefit of their experience on the losing

sides in Vietnam and Rhodesia and in the South African Ban-tustans to any group that calls itself "anticommunist." *Soldier of Fortune* magazine (published in Boulder, Colorado), which specializes in applauding this crowd, unwittingly caught the intersection of its terminal blowhardism with the real-world horror of a war like Mozambique's when, in a March 1987 article celebrating Renamo's "freedom fighters," the magazine published a photograph of a small boy learning to handle a rifle in a Renamo camp. The boy in the picture is gripping the rifle's barrel awkwardly, with just three fingers—because his other two fingers are missing. To anyone familiar with Renamo's treatment of children, it seems more than likely that the *matsangas* have cut off the boy's fingers. *Soldier of Fortune*'s caption: "Guerrilla wars demand commitment from everyone—including children. This young Renamo trooper gets a drill lesson" (p. 49).

18. U.S. Congress, Senate Select Committee on Secret Military Assistance to Iran and the Nicaraguan Opposition, House Select Committee to Investigate Covert Arms Transactions with Iran, *Iran-Contra Investigation*, Joint Hearings, July 7–10, 1987 (Washington, D.C., 1987), vol. 100-7, part I, pp. 156–57.

Nineteen

1. Joseph Hanlon, *Mozambique: The Revolution Under Fire* (London, 1984), p. 48.

2. Ibid. Original source: Leroy Vail and Landeg White, *Capitalism and Colonialism in Mozambique: A Study of Quelimane District* (Minneapolis, 1980), p. 1.

3. William Minter, "The Mozambican National Resistance (Renamo) as Described by Ex-Participants," research report submitted to the Ford Foundation and the Swedish International Development Agency, March 1989, p. 14.

4. Iain Christie, "Man Killed as War-Wounded Clash with Police in Mozambique," Reuters (Maputo), December 11, 1990.

Twenty

1. Joseph Hanlon, *Mozambique: The Revolution Under Fire* (London, 1984), pp. 9–10.

2. Allen F. Isaacman, "Mozambique: Tugging at the Chains of Dependency," in *African Crisis Areas and U.S. Foreign Policy*, ed.

Gerald J. Bender, James S. Coleman, and Richard L. Sklar (Berkeley, 1985), p. 133.

3. Richard Leonard, *South Africa at War: White Power and the Crisis in Southern Africa* (Westport, Conn., 1983), p. 13; Joseph Hanlon, *Apartheid's Second Front: South Africa's War against Its Neighbours* (Harmondsworth, England, 1986), p. 37. Leonard cites an interview with former South African Information Department secretary Eschel Rhoodie, which appeared in *Elseviers* magazine (Amsterdam), August 1979.

4. Joseph Hanlon, *Beggar Your Neighbours: Apartheid Power in Southern Africa* (London, 1986), p. 136.

5. Ibid., p. 139.

6. International Institute for Strategic Studies, *The Military Balance, 1989–90* (London, 1989), pp. 134, 139. Other figures given for the total troops South Africa could mobilize ranged as high as 1,000,000. Mozambican military spending was dropping, moreover, during the second half of the 1980s—in 1989, it was half what it had been three years earlier. South African military spending meanwhile rose by 9 percent in real terms in 1988 and was projected to rise by 8 percent in 1989 (ibid., p. 120). After F. W. de Klerk replaced P. W. Botha as president in late 1989, however, Pretoria's military spending was reportedly reduced and conscription relaxed.

7. See Gillian Gunn, "Cuba and Mozambique," *CSIS Africa Notes* (Georgetown University, Washington, D.C.), no. 80, December 28, 1987.

8. As of early 1989, aerial surveys showed that some 1,400 of the approximately 4,000 pylons inside Mozambique had been sabotaged (*Mozambiquefile* [Maputo], February 1989, p. 7). Estimates of the cost of the damage to Mozambique ran as high as $560 million (Phyllis Johnson and David Martin, *Apartheid Terrorism: The Destablization Report* [London, 1989], p. 16).

9. This description of South African strategy had an ironic analogue in the "corridors of peace" that the United Nations sought to establish in, first, Angola and then Mozambique as part of its effort to feed those facing starvation in each country in areas isolated by the war (see Vanora Bennett, "U.N. Wants More 'Peace Corridors' to Relieve African Famine," Reuters [Harare, Zimbabwe], November 14, 1990). In the case of Cahora Bassa, some pro-Frelimo observers argued that South Africa ac-

tually profited from Renamo's sabotage of the dam's transmission lines, and that Pretoria's public commitments to help protect the lines were really just another way of obscuring its support for Renamo (see Johnson and Martin, *Apartheid Terrorism*, p. 16). For those inclined to see it, Pretoria's hand was indeed visible in Renamo's every rampage. Five horrendous massacres in southern Mozambique in 1987, writes Anders Nilsson, with mysterious certainty, "in fact were another example of a specific strategy which the South Africans had already used in the Angolan town of Kassinga in 1978 when they killed more than 600 defenceless people. . . . [T]he MNR massacres were intended as a signal to Mozambique and to the world that, whatever the diplomatic developments and tensions going on within the external wing in Europe and the US, the 'politicians' had no control over what was happenning within Mozambique" (*Unmasking the Bandits: The True Face of the M.N.R.* [London, 1990], p. 56).

10. See Hanlon, *Beggar Your Neighbours*, p. 147, and *Africa Confidential* (London) 28, no. 24 (December 2, 1987): 3.

11. But nothing fed the mill more voluminously than an incident which began while I was in Maputo and which continued to make news for many months. It seemed that a West German ship, the *Edda*, after carrying a shipment of arms from Southampton to Mombasa, had docked in Beira in mid-August and then had disappeared from shipping records for nearly a month. The *Edda* spent at least part of that time anchored off a remote section of the Inhambane coast in southern Mozambique. Claims by the ship's agents that it had been detained by propeller trouble turned out to be false. According to the captain, he had actually stopped there to drop off two stowaways from Mombasa. The captain said that he and three sailors had gone ashore with the stowaways and were captured by Renamo. The prior relationship between Renamo and the stowaways was unclear. The captain and sailors were held by Renamo for nearly two months, and then he and two of his men were flown by light plane to South Africa. The captain told his story to *Der Spiegel* upon his return to Germany. Meanwhile, according to its crew, who were interrogated by Mozambican authorities after the ship was detained in Quelimane in late September, the *Edda* had sailed on to Richards Bay, South Africa, running with its lights off. From

there, the ship returned to Mombasa, where it made its reappearance in the shipping records and then proceeded—foolishly—to Quelimane to load copra. The crew also reported that the *Edda* had secretly picked up a barge from another ship while in Mozambican waters. An unidentified person had been aboard the barge, they said, which had previously been transferred from yet another ship. All these mysterious doings provided a rich trove for speculation—for veritable Eddas of Maputo conspiracy-spinning. The speculation centered, naturally, on the questions of German and South African support for Renamo, and did not immediately disappear after the *Edda*, which had been the subject of intense diplomatic negotiation between West Germany and Mozambique, was finally released and set sail for Durban, on March 21, 1989 (*Mozambiquefile* [Maputo], December 1988, pp. 6–7; April 1989, p. 17).

12. John D. Battersby of the *New York Times*, William Claiborne of the *Washington Post*, Spencer Reiss of *Newsweek*, and Mark Peters, a photographer. I refer to them here as "American journalists" only because they were all working for American publications, not because they are all American citizens. It should probably be noted that some fraction of the criticism their trip generated among journalists in Maputo and elsewhere in southern Africa was conceivably born of professional jealousy. The trip was a solid reporting coup.

13. Their stories appeared in the *New York Times* of July 31, 1988; the *Washington Post* of the same date; and *Newsweek* of August 8.

14. Paulo Oliveira contributed to these rumors by telling journalists after his defection that Dhlakama had been in South Africa roughly half the time during the period that he, Oliveira, lived there (*AIM Information Bulletin* [Maputo], no. 141, April 1988, p. 2).

Twenty-One

1. This attack was widely reported in the international press. The government-supplied figure of 278 or more dead appeared in, among other papers, the *Times* (London) and the *Guardian* (London) on November 2, 1987. In April 1990, the *Independent* estimated that at least 500 people had been murdered on the na-

tional highway between Maputo and Xai-Xai, 150 miles north, in the previous three years (Karl Maier, "Mozambique's Rebels Rule 'Corridor of Death,'" *Independent* [London], April 11, 1990).

2. There were also more immediate security risks involved in a general distribution of weapons. A high percentage of the guns distributed by the government as part of a rural self-defense program in 1983 apparently fell into the hands of free-lance bandits. (The United States deputy chief of mission in Maputo estimated in 1988 that 30 to 35 percent of the attacks on civilians in Mozambique were being carried out by free-lancers [*Washington Post*, January 24, 1988].) Some of the same weapons no doubt found their way to Renamo as well. And the problem was not just rural. In Maputo, where by the early 1980s pilferage on the docks had reached disastrous levels, it was decided that a strong unit of popular militia was needed. Virtually every dockworker in Maputo volunteered for the unit and was duly trained and armed; and, according to a researcher at Eduardo Mondlane University whom I interviewed, simple robbery on the docks became, overnight, armed robbery.

Twenty-Two

1. Quoted in Deon Geldenhuys, "Some Strategic Implications of Regional Economic Relations for the Republic of South Africa," *ISSUP Strategic Review* (Pretoria), January 1981, p. 3, and cited in Steven Metz, "Pretoria's 'Total Strategy' and Low-Intensity Warfare in Southern Africa," *Comparative Strategy* (Arlington, Va.) 6, no. 4 (1987). Geldenhuys is the best-known South African destabilization theorist. See also his "Destabilisation Controversy in Southern Africa," S A Forum Position Paper (Johannesburg), September 1982; and *The Diplomacy of Isolation* (Johannesburg, 1984).

2. South African Broadcasting Corporation, February 18, 1981. Quoted in Thomas M. Callaghy, "Apartheid and Socialism: South Africa's Relations with Angola and Mozambique," in *South Africa in Southern Africa: The Intensifying Vortex of Violence,* ed. Thomas M. Callaghy (New York, 1983), p. 269. In another radio broadcast some months later (on September 11, 1981), Malan expanded this lurid vision of South Africa's neighbors: "It's clearer today than ever before that what is happening in southern Africa right now has nothing to do with so-called liberation, but has everything to do with Soviet enslavement of

the peoples of southern Africa" (quoted in Callaghy, "Apartheid and Socialism," p. 269). The convenience to Pretoria of such an analysis—the way it deflected attention from demands for democracy in South Africa and an end to apartheid, while making de facto allies of the capitalist democracies of the West—did not go unremarked by its critics.

3. Metz, "Pretoria's 'Total Strategy,'" p. 437.

4. Col. John D. Waghelstein, "Post-Vietnam Counterinsurgency Doctrine," *Military Review* (Fort Leavenworth, Kans.), May 1985, p. 42.

5. The Pentagon's official definition of low-intensity conflict, issued in 1985, described "a limited politico-military struggle to achieve political, social, economic, or psychological objectives. It is often protracted and ranges from diplomatic, economic, and psycho-social pressures through terrorism and insurgency. Low-intensity conflict is generally confined to a geographic area and is often characterized by constraints on the weaponry, tactics, and the level of violence" (U.S. Army Training and Doctrine Command, *US Army Operational Concept for Low Intensity Conflict*, TRADCOC Pamphlet no. 525-44 [Fort Monroe, Va., 1986], p. 2; quoted in Michael T. Klare, "The Interventionist Impulse: U.S. Military Doctrine for Low-Intensity Warfare," in *Low-Intensity Warfare: Counterinsurgency, Proinsurgency, and Antiterrorism in the Eighties*, ed. Michael T. Klare and Peter Kornbluh [New York, 1988], p. 53).

6. *CIA: The Pike Report* (Nottingham, England, 1977), p. 214.

7. South African Broadcasting Corporation, December 7, 1982. Quoted in Thomas M. Callaghy, "Introduction: The Intensifying Vortex of Violence," in Callaghy, *South Africa in Southern Africa*, pp. 3–4.

8. The Soviet Union's foreign-assistance budgets are difficult to calculate, but the U.S. budgets are not. As the *Washington Post* reported on January 8, 1991, "Since 1985, mirroring the democratizing reforms in the Soviet Union and Eastern Europe, U.S. military aid to sub-Saharan Africa has fallen from $280 million to less than $39 million annually. In the same five-year period, U.S. annual economic assistance to the region has dropped 50 percent, to $850 million last year. Out of a total foreign-aid budget of $14.4 billion, poverty-ravaged sub-Saharan Africa now accounts for just 6 percent."

9. *Mozambiquefile* (Maputo), October 1990, p. 16.

10. All figures from David Ewing Duncan, "The Long Goodbye," *The Atlantic* (Boston), July 1990, pp. 20–22.

11. Ibid., p. 22. This deadly combination of shrinking economies and growing populations meant that, in 1990, per capita income in Africa fell for the twelfth straight year (*New York Times*, February 3, 1991).

12. Richard J. Barnet, "The Costs and Perils of Intervention," in Klare and Kornbluh, *Low-Intensity Warfare*, p. 216.

13. Gunnar Myrdal, *The Challenge of World Poverty: A World Anti-Poverty Program in Outline* (New York, 1970), p. 208.

14. Otto Roesch, "Nampula: What's Left?" *Southern Africa Report* (Toronto) 5, no. 2 (November 1989): 13.

15. Barry Munslow, *Mozambique: The Revolution and Its Origins* (London, 1983), p. 140.

16. Rafael Maguni, a former ambassador to Zimbabwe and governor of Manica province, more recently the minister of information, is Makonde-speaking. Feliciano Gundana, a former governor of Nampula province, more recently the minister of state in the president's office, is Ndau-speaking. Major-General Silva Nihia, a deputy minister of defense, is Makua-speaking. All three are *antiguos combatentes*.

17. *Guardian* (London), October 15, 1987. Actually, a few months after the signing of the Nkomati Accord in 1984, direct talks between the two sides were held in Pretoria. Renamo's representatives, reportedly in response to a mysterious phone call, walked out just as a cease-fire agreement seemed in sight.

18. *Mozambiquefile*, January 1989.

19. Kenyan support for Renamo allegedly included a military training camp on Kenyan soil; the transshipment of Renamo-bound arms bought in Europe; the training of a presidential guard for Afonso Dhlakama; and visits by Kiplagat, the commander of the Kenyan Defence College, and other Kenyan officers to Renamo headquarters inside Mozambique. The Kenyan government denied all these stories but admitted that it had provided the Renamo negotiating team with travel documents— with the approval of the Mozambican government. See Karl Maier, "Kenya Gives Backing to Mozambique Guerrillas," *Independent* (London), August 28, 1990; *Africa Confidential* (London) 31, no. 21 (October 26, 1990): 7; G. H. O. Josiah, "No Kenyan Support for Guerrillas" (letter), *Independent*, August 31, 1990.

20. The United States, the Soviet Union, France, Britain, Portugal, Zimbabwe, Italy, Zambia, Kenya, and Congo. Most of the commission's members were diplomats or military officers.

21. The moratorium on Renamo attacks on the Nacala railway, declared by Afonso Dhlakama in August 1989, was widely thought to be the result of a deal cut between, on the one side, the rebels and, on the other side, the Malawian government, which desperately needed the line for its exports, and Lonrho, which had links to Defence Systems Limited, the British firm charged with protecting the railway. When the moratorium broke down briefly with a Renamo attack in January 1991, there was speculation that Malawi had neglected to pay Renamo the "protection money" it had pledged. According to Alex Vines (in *Renamo: Terrorism in Mozambique* [London, 1991], p. 130), "Secret talks between Renamo and the Malawian authorities are said to have taken place to resolve this crisis."

22. *Guardian* (London), December 12, 1990.

23. See Witney W. Schneidman, "Conflict Resolution in Mozambique: A Status Report," *CSIS Africa Notes* (Georgetown University, Washington, D.C.), no. 121, February 28, 1991, p. 4.

24. *Washington Post*, May 5, 1989; also quoted in Schneidman, "Conflict Resolution," pp. 4–5.

25. "The experience of Nicaragua clearly shows that elections were used by the U.S. as an effective tool in their low-intensity warfare," wrote Jim Eitel and Chris Benner in "The Nicaraguan Elections: Lessons for Mozambique," *Mozambique Support Network Newsletter* (Chicago), Spring–Summer 1990, p. 5.

26. Melinda Ham, "Over Breakfast with Black Leaders, Pik Botha Preaches Peace," Associated Press (Lusaka), November 7, 1990.

27. *Christian Science Monitor* (Boston), May 21, 1991.

28. *Economist* (London), December 8, 1990.

29. Letter to the *Weekly Mail* (Johannesburg), February 2–8, 1990, p. 12.

30. *Mozambiquefile*, March 1990, p. 7.

31. *Mozambiquefile*, August 1990, p. 8.

32. Speculation about Lonrho's arrangements with the Renamo leadership was not cooled by the news that Afonso Dhlakama had arrived in Blantyre in June 1990, aboard a Lonrho

executive jet, for the abortive first round of direct talks with Frelimo. Dhlakama was reportedly traveling with Betwell Kiplagat and Roland ("Tiny") Rowland, the Lonrho chief executive (*Mozambiquefile*, July 1990, p. 4). It is possible, of course, that Rowland and Lonrho were, like the United States government, simply interested in furthering Dhlakama's education in the ways of the political and economic world, hedging their bets against the off chance that he might one day come to power. By the end of 1990, Lonrho owned, besides its farms in Mozambique, "a smart hotel and a gold mine" (*Economist* [London], December 8, 1990).

33. See Allen Isaacman, "Social Banditry in Zimbabwe (Rhodesia) and Mozambique, 1894–1907: An Expression of Early Peasant Protest," *Journal of Southern African Studies* (London) 4, no. 1 (October 1977): 1–30.

34. See E. J. Hobsbawm, *Bandits* (New York, 1981).

35. According to Hobsbawm (in *Primitive Rebels: Studies in Archaic Forms of Social Movements in the 19th and 20th Centuries* [New York, 1959], p. 15), Angelo Duca, a great eighteenth-century Italian social bandit, "was supposed to possess a magic ring which turned away bullets." Nikola Shuhaj, a Czech bandit of the early twentieth century, "was invulnerable because— theories diverged—he had a green twig with which he waved aside bullets, or because a witch had made him drink a brew that made him resist them; that is why he had to be killed with an axe. Oleksa Dovbush, the legendary 18th-century Carpathian bandit-hero, could only be killed with a silver bullet that had been kept one year in a dish of spring wheat, blessed by a priest on the day of the twelve great saints and over which twelve priests had read twelve masses. . . . Obviously none of these practices or beliefs are derived from one another. They arise in different places and periods, because the societies and situations in which social banditry arises are very similar."

Hobsbawm later expanded the seminal chapter on social banditry in *Primitive Rebels*, which relied exclusively on European—especially southern European—material, into *Bandits* (Harmondsworth, England, 1972; 2nd ed., New York, 1981), which ranged far more widely, gathering material from Asia and Latin America, in its search for examples of social banditry. In the 1981 edition, he reproduced the story of Weldegabriel, an African Robin Hood figure and the eldest of the Mesazgi brothers, a famous group of Eritrean bandits who operated in Italian-ruled Ethiopia. The Mesazgi brothers, according to Hobsbawm's account, made the roads unsafe for Italian drivers, with the result that "Eritreans, who had previously not been allowed to drive by the Italian administration or the British, were authorised to do so. This was welcomed as a rise in status and for the jobs which now became available. Many people said: 'Long live the sons of Mesazgi. They enabled us to drive cars.' The brothers had entered politics" (p. 14).

Hobsbawm's concept of social banditry generated a great deal of academic debate, and the relevance of his model to African experience was among the questions raised (see Donald Crummey, ed., *Banditry, Rebellion and Social Protest in Africa* [London, 1986], especially Ralph A. Austen, "Social Bandits and Other Heroic Criminals: Western Models of Resistance and Their Relevance for Africa," pp. 89–108). The Ethiopian example has been extensively studied (see Donald Crummey, "Banditry and Resistance: Noble and Peasant in Nineteenth-Century Ethiopia," in *Banditry, Rebellion and Social Protest*, pp. 133–49, and Timothy Fernyhough, "Social Mobility and Dissident Elites in Northern Ethiopia: The Role of Bandits, 1900–69," in *Banditry, Rebellion and Social Protest*, pp. 151–72), with Fernyhough observing, in terms that may seem resonant for Mozambique, that "banditry in Ethiopia appeared as a form of rebellion at once more primitive and more sophisticated than that described by Eric Hobsbawm. More primitive, in that it rarely raised itself above feuding and political conflict; more sophisticated, in that . . . it reinforced the Abyssinian perception of their society as a mobile one. When peasants defied their rulers and the law to become leaders of *sheftā* bands, they too could gain official appointment and noble status. . . . However, these limited chances for social mobility were not without their drawbacks. By presenting an avenue for advancement, banditry may have obstructed peasant mobilisation, diminishing peasant solidarity and class conflict" (pp. 165–66).

Isaacman ("Social Banditry in Zimbabwe") also weighs the relevance of Hobsbawm's model of social banditry—and he finds its relevance extensive—as he tells the stories of Mapondera and Dambukashamba, two turn-of-the-century bandits who led small groups of Shona peasant outlaws operating in the frontier region between Zimbabwe and Mozambique while the British and Portuguese colonial empires were seeking to extend their rule into the region by undermining and subordinating local institutions. The bandits were fed by villagers and, according to Isaacman, "repeatedly attacked the symbols of oppression that the colonial regimes had imposed. Operating on both sides of the unmanned border they raided government posts, ambushed tax collectors, attacked labour recruiters and burned the rural shops which were exploiting the peasants" (p. 14). The harsh lives of Mapondera's and Dambukashamba's rebels; their reliance on Shona spirit mediums to help them turn bullets into water, or to make themselves invisible; their occasional robberies of peasants and migrant workers—all these find echoes, too, in contemporary reports of life with Renamo.

36. "But even when such rebels triumph, victory brings its own temptation to destroy, for primitive peasant insurgents have no positive programme, only the negative programme of getting rid of the superstructure which prevents men from living well and dealing fairly, as in the good old days. To kill, to slash, to burn away everything that is not necessary and useful to the man at the plough or with the herdsman's crook, is to abolish corruption and leave only what is good, pure and natural" (Hobsbawm, *Bandits*, p. 65).

37. Ali A. Mazrui, *Soldiers and Kinsmen in Uganda: The Military Ethnocracy* (Beverly Hills, 1975), p. 142.

38. Ironically, the *purveyors* of the doctrine of low-intensity warfare are prone to a similar militarization of political conflicts, labeling political violence "terrorism" and so on. As Richard Barnet ("Costs and Perils of Intervention," p. 209) writes: "The grievances that drive men and women to the variety of desperate political acts now labeled 'terrorism' grow out of specific political and religious struggles over particular pieces of real estate. Military establishments are peculiarly ineffective resources for dealing with such an 'army,' for armed forces are designed to fight nation-states, not to police them. The military establishment is a blunt instrument to persuade governments to capitulate by breaking the will of their people. For terrorism to become a military problem, rather than the essentially political problem it is, the enemy must be turned into a state. So the ter-

rorists are assumed to be 'state-supported.' While it is true that some states, such as Libya, Iran, and Syria, do employ terrorists, and that many movements get some outside support, that is not the critical dimension. *Rather, it is the breakdown of state power and state legitimacy that creates the soil of desperation and disorder in which terrorism flourishes"* (emphasis added).

39. See J. K. Rennie, "Christianity, Colonialism and the Origins of Nationalism among the Ndau of Southern Rhodesia 1890–1935" (Ph.D. diss., Northwestern University, 1973), pp. 460–90. Rennie prefers the term *revitalization movements* to *millenarian movements* to describe these African crusades, because the latter term is associated with the Judaeo-Christian conception of the millennium: "Millennial ideas may have been present in many of the African movements, but they seem neither to have been fundamental nor universally present" (p. 495). For the broad correspondences I am trying to suggest, however, millenarianism seems descriptive.

40. Millenarian movements also appeared in southern Africa, of course, before the twentieth century, often in direct response to colonial penetration. One of the best known resulted in the great Xhosa cattle killing of 1857. Desperate to stop the European settlement of what was then British Kaffraria in what is today the Eastern Cape region of South Africa, the indigenous Xhosas followed the prophecy of a young girl named Nongqawuse, and destroyed their cattle and crops, believing that their ancestral spirits would feed them and punish the whites. Tens of thousands of Africans starved to death, and the white settlement of British Kaffraria went ahead unimpeded.

41. Yoweri Museveni, later to become president of Uganda, watched this process in the liberated zones of Cabo Delgado, and observed, "The peasants of Northern Mozambique have undergone the cleansing effect of revolution. . . . The peasant . . . becomes more scientific and discards most of the superstitions . . . and the whole magical superstructure that characterizes a frustrated colonial society. . . . The transformation of the peasant into a rational anti-imperialist fighter becomes a must" (quoted in Stan Made, *Made in Zimbabwe* [Gwelo, Zimbabwe, 1980], p. 20, and cited in Terence Ranger, *Peasant Consciousness and Guerrilla War in Zimbabwe: A Comparative Study* [Berkeley, 1985], p. 184). This transformation, while it may have been "a must,"

was inevitably incomplete—and quite likely to be reversed as postcolonial war and impoverishment *increased* the isolation and insecurity of rural life.

42. Hobsbawm, *Primitive Rebels*, pp. 57–58.

43. Karl Maier, "Guarded by the Spirit of Mongoi," *Independent* (London), February 25, 1990; Jane Perlez, "Spared by Rebels? The Spirit Says That'll Be $2," *New York Times*, August 24, 1990.

44. This description of the Napramas is drawn largely from the following news stories: Karl Maier, "Renamo Flees at Sight of Rag-Tag Army," *Independent* (London), July 27, 1990; Karl Maier, "Healer in Mozambique Leads Attack on Rebels," *Washington Post*, August 4, 1990; Howard Witt, "Mystic Warriors Gaining Ground in Mozambique War," *Chicago Tribune*, December 9, 1990; Bill Schiller, "Heart of Darkness Men of Myth Believe They're Bullet-Proof," *Toronto Star*, December 16, 1990; Karl Maier, "Triumph of Spears Over Guns Brings Refugees Home," *Independent*, February 23, 1991; Karl Maier, "War in Mozambique Leaves Town in Peace," *Washington Post*, May 1, 1991. The Mozambican media seemed to be ignoring Manuel António and the Napramas, reporting their string of victories over Renamo as Frelimo victories.

Index

Compositor:	G & S Typesetters, Inc.
Text:	10/13 Aster
Display:	Helvetica Condensed and Aster
Printer:	Princeton University Press
Binder:	Princeton University Press